HAKOAH HEROES

For future generations

David Goldberg

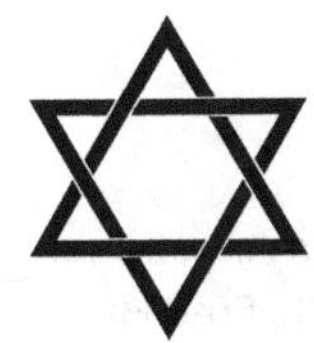

ISBN: 978 0 6481 3636 1 (pbk)
978 0 6481 3637 8 (mobi)

Front Cover left to right:

Manny Poulakakis, Hugh Murney, Jim Armstrong, Alan Stenhouse, David Baker, Keith Fry, Dick Van Alphen, Ted Smith, Fred Hutchison.

Holding the Dockerty Cup; Captain, John O'Neill

For future generations

Contents

Foreword

This book is dedicated to a man who took the world before him, and in the process created an empire within an empire.

The former statement could have been written for Caesar, or perhaps Alexander the Great, or indeed Churchill himself.

Yet the sheer power, dynamism and fortitude of those historical giants of the past is forever similarly epitomized by a simple man, one of our own, a Jew, who was so humble in nature, who lived a virtual hermit existence with his adorable wife Steffi and their enchanting daughter Lorraine, in his adopted country of Australia.

Kurt Defris lived his entire life for the betterment of others, and was a shining beacon of light and hope for all who came into his domain.

Kurt Defris gave his life to Jewish sport, with the 'Star of David' his emblem of pride and justification that gave heart to many Jews and non Jews alike, who represented a myriad of different Jewish sporting codes from the early 1920s through to 1981.

Association Football, Ice Hockey, Table Tennis, to mention but a few, were all co-ordinated, organized and monitored by Kurt Defris.

The story of Kurt Defris is a story that would and should grace any Steven Spielberg Hollywood movie.

This book aptly titled *Hakoah Heroes* is written for all, and especially to those who knew and remembered with reverence, the great Kurt Defris.

Just as importantly, this book is written for all following generations of young Jewish girls and boys, men and women, both in Israel and in the wider Diaspora, who will have an opportunity to read, learn and enjoy from the *Hakoah Heroes* article and photo gallery segments of this book all that this wonderful man created and worked for throughout his productive life.

A final message then, to Kurt Defris, from all who knew and loved him.

'Kurt, you were the very best of the very best of Jewish mankind, and you will never ever be forgotten, be sure of that!'

Hakoah Heroes is not a book simply written about Hakoah Melbourne Football Club that existed from 1927 to 1981, and all those who played and fought in its ranks for the honour of the Star of David.

Hakoah Heroes is rather, Kurt Defris and Kurt Defris is, and always will be known by all, as Hakoah Melbourne Football Club's number one Hakoah Hero!

Mr Kurt Defris AM
Order Of Australia

A Tribute To Mr Kurt Defris AM
Hakoah Melbourne Football Club

Kurt Defris was born into a prosperous middle class family in Vienna in 1909.

His father was an officer in the Austrian army and was highly decorated in the First World War. He was also an electrical engineer of great repute. Kurts's interests however lay elsewhere.

Although he completed an electrical engineering qualification he acquired a dedicated passion for sport. In Vienna he played Association Football, including a few games for Hakoah Vienna, a first division club which on many occasions won the Austrian football championship. Kurt also played table tennis and became an accomplished player. In Vienna he met Steffi who was to become his wife. She too was an accomplished table tennis player, and also played Hockey.

In 1938 Kurt and Steffi left Austria and settled in Shanghai, China. During the war Kurt became a successful sports administrator, organising football and table tennis competitions. Many thousands of Ex-Patriots attended the football matches each week.

After the war Kurt was visited by an important dignitary who offered him honorary Chinese nationality and wished to make him a vice minister of sports. She had heard of his sporting administrative talents and sought to utilise them in the new China. Because of the deference shown to this person, Kurt came to realise that this woman was someone of great importance. He was later told that she was

Madam Chiang Kai-shek. However, Kurt decided to leave China and join his parents and sister in Melbourne, Australia.

Kurt travelled from Shanghai to Melbourne by ship. He boarded the ship with only a few pounds, but left the ship in Melbourne with close to 30 pounds! Kurt made the money on board the ship, defeating fellow passengers at table tennis. Kurt took up residence in St Kilda, Melbourne.

Kurt initially went into his father's business manufacturing electric light fittings and then established his own business wholesaling buttons and buckles. However, his heart always lay in sport. Kurt's whole life revolved around the Hakoah Football Club, with Kurt its inaugural secretary/manager from 1947 through to its dissolution in 1982. Kurt also ran the Hakoah table tennis club. In addition to all of this, he held senior positions in the Victorian Soccer Federation and also became Vice President of the Victorian Table Tennis Association.

In later years he acquired an interest in ice hockey and became president of the Victorian Ice Hockey Association. In 1956 Kurt was appointed an official for the Olympic Games in Melbourne and participated in the organisation of the Association Football competition at the Olympics.

Kurt's total self was devoted to sport. Every night Kurt would attend a committee meeting, watch a sporting event or simply watch one of his teams in training.

Kurt maintained his devoted enthusiasm for sport and his busy schedule to the end of his life.

He became a member of the Albert Park Trust and was responsible in helping several Jewish sporting clubs secure playing fields in the Albert Park area.

In 1979 Kurt Defris was made a member of the Order of Australia for his services to sport. The award, made in 1979, was richly deserved for a man who devoted his entire life to Maccabi sport and to the many Jewish organisations that would be of assistance to the wider community.

Kurt Defris died in 1982 and was succeeded by his wonderful wife and his daughter. Unfortunately both died soon after and with those deaths the name of Defris passed into history.

Several sporting clubs chose to honour Mr Kurt Defris with annual trophies awarded in his name. These include:

- Maccabi Hockey Club
- Ice Hockey Victoria
- Maccabi Ajax Cricket Club
- Ajax Football Club
- Ajax Junior Football Club

Kurt was also awarded Life Membership with:

- Football Federation of Victoria
- Ice Hockey Victoria
- Table Tennis Centre of Victoria

Roll of Honour

Every man whose name that follows on this Roll of Honour brought great distinction and pride to the Jewish nation of Israel and to all those Jewish innocents who were fortunate to have escaped the rabid hate and prejudice of evil, to build a new life in a new country. These names that follow bear testimony to the faith, tenacity and dedication of those people, and to one man in particular, one of them.

A most humble kind man, Kurt Defris was a pocket size nuclear powered gentleman who unselfishly gave his life for his dream of creating a proud Jewish football club.

And but for Kurt Defris, Hakoah Football Club would not have given tens of thousands of good men and women for 54 years great joy in the Jewish cause of freedom, democracy and good will to all.

All the men named below were either Kurt Defris administrative generals or his multitude of warriors in the field of battle, and every one of them to the man, were justly proud to serve a club and a man who gave most of his soldiers a new life in a new land.

Each and every man named below past or present say as one
We thank you Kurt
Thank you for the honour
Mr Kurt Defris AM (Order of Australia)

'To wear the sky blue star of David shirt of Hakoah Football Club, whether it was worn only once or worn one thousand times was irrelevant, for to wear the Hakoah star of David shirt at all was the greatest honour any human being could achieve.'

Mike O'Hara

ABRAHAMS, Ryan 2002
AGUILLERA 1933
ACKERS, Jim 1974
ADAMGIKIS, Steve 1972
ADAMS, Bobby 1961
ALEXANDER, John 1960
ALLISON, Bill 1980
ALLISON, Colin 1980
AMICI, Albert 1977
ANDERSON, John 1959
ANDERSON, John 1970
ANTAL, Sandor 1999
ARBER 1941
ARMSTRONG 1933
ARMSTRONG, Jim 1966
ARONI, Nathi 1989
ARTNER, Walter 1959
AXELROD 1946
BADER, Harry 1950
BAILISON, Gary 1995
BAKER, David 1966
BALANTYS, Artur 1995
BALBERER, A 1947
BANNON, Ged 1980
BARDAS 1941
BARBOUR, Doug 1973
BARKER, Don 1959
BARRET, Clive 1980
BARRON 1933
BASSI, Serge 1954
BAYTCH, Henry 1965
BELKAN, Morrie 1928
BENAHARON, Rami
BENAHARON, Guy
BENZIL
BERKMAN 1941
BELA BIRO 1964
BETH-HALEVY, Abraham 1940
BEWICK 1964
BINER 1941
BINGHAM 1934
BLACK, Nat 1974
BLACKIE 1946
BLACKLEY 1959
BLAIR, Stewart 1973
BLEIBERG, Miron 1991
BLOCH, Stephen 1980
BLUZER, Henry 1989
BOGATIN 1941
BOLAND, Dennis 1971
BOLTON 1938
BOWMAN, J 1933
BOWMAN, Phil 1931
BOZINOVSKI, Branko 1973
BRAUDE, Steven 2002
BRECKER 1938
BRIDGE 1933
BRIDGEMAN, Nigel 1975
BRIGGS
BROSS 1965
BUNCE, Fred 1980
BURIANEK 1950

CALDAREVIC, Vlado 1954
CAMERON, Gordon 1978
CAMPBELL 1933
CANOLIDO 1941
CARMICHAEL, Duncan 1962
CARPENTER, Steve 1976
CARRICK, David 1980
CECIL, Jim 1962
CHALDI, Gerri 1964
CHAMARAVI, Yakov 1987
CHASKIEL, Johnny 1965
CLAREY, Mike 1977
CLARKE, Pat 1953
COHEN, Alon 1986
COHEN, David 1939
COHEN, Ted 1928
COLES, Jim 1978
COLLINS 1961
COMMON 1960
CONDIVITO 1938
CONDON 1933
CONLEY 1978
COOK, Billy 1963
COPELAND, Bill 1953
CRAIG, George 1978
DAPERIS, John 1973
DAVIDSON, Danny 1980
DAVIS, Meyer 1946
DAVIS, Gordon 1954
DEFRIS, Kurt 1947
(played and scored two goals for Hakoah in 1947)
DEMETRIE 1941
DE PLACIDO 1975
DIAMOND, Michael
DJURA 1950
DODD 1940
DONATO, Pocho 1976
DONATO, Roberto 1974
DOSEN, Anton 1978
DOUGLAS, Gordon 1974
DRACUP 1936
DREYFUS 1946
DREZNER, M 1965
DURAND, Jean 1973
DURANT, John 1974
DZIURA 1950
EAGER, Tom 1961
EDELSTEIN 1933
EDMONDSON, Gerry 1980
EFRON, David 1978
EHRENREICH, Steven 1980
EIZENBERG 1946
ELB AZ, Yehud Ah 1990
ELGART, Zhenya 2001
ELLINGHOUSE 1960
ELSE 1940
ERLICH, Shaye 1965
ESSEX 1950
ESTERMAN, Bruce 1983
ESTERMAN, Ross 1983
EVANS, Peter 1960
FARAONE, Andrea 2000
FEIGENBAUM, Shaya 1979
FENN 1937
FETTER, Bob 1928
FINKELSTEIN 1950
FITZGERALD 1939
FLETCHER, Barry 1972
FISHER, S 1933
FOLDIS, George 1975
FORREST 1946
FORREST, Alex 1940
FRASER, John 1975
FRANCK, Joseph
FRENCH, Graham 1977
FREUND, Andrew 1985
FREUND, Steven 1982

FRIDMAN, Danny 1965
FROMER, Henry 1975
FROMER, Martin 1975
FRYSZER, Michael 1978
FURMAN, Serge 1997
GADSBY, Steven 1970
GESOS, Michael 1980
GIBSON, Ian 1978
GINTER 1940
GODDARD, Alan 1954
GOLD 1950
GOLDBERG, Henry 1928
GOLDFINE, Sam 1928
GOLDMAN, Larry
GOLDSTEIN, Jerome 1996
GOTTESMAN, Joe 1954
GOTTLEIB, Jack 1980
GOW, Ian 1966
GRANT, Jack 1931
GREENFIELD, Henry
GREER 1941
GREGOR 1941
GRENFELL 1933
GREWSHKA 1941
GROENWALD, Gary 1979
GROSS, Victor 1965
GROSSBERG, Egon 1965
GULKO, Fima 1990
GURFINKEL 1966
GURFINKEL, Michael 1965
HAARBERGER 1950
HALPRIN 1941
HAMMOND, Phil 1973
HANDELSMAN, Stan 1965
HANNAH, George 1980
HARBURGER 1946
HARBURN, Bill 1955
HARBURN, Steve 1976
HAREL, Oran 1996
HARELFORD, 1946
HARRISON 1934
HARTLEY, Terry 1959
HARVEY, Brian 1973
HAWES, Bill 1959
HAWKES, George 1941
HAYDEN, Paddy 1931
HAYNES, Eric 1931
HENDERSON, Sandy 1968
HIRD, Ian 2001
HUCK 1933
HUCKER 1961
HUGHES, Gary 2007
HUGHES, Tony 1966
HUTCHISON, Fred 1966
INNARD 1955
JACK, Tom 1946
JACOBS, Jack 1966
JACOBS, M 1965
JACOBS, Stan
JOHNSTON 1946
JOHNSTONE 1933
JORDANOU, Bill 1978
JUDENBERG 1946
KALB, Zvi 1985
KALKOPF, Morrie 1980
KAMSNER, Lance
KAPSTEIN 1950
KATZ, Jeff 1983
KATZ, Joe 1970
KATS, Michael 2000
KAUFMAN, B 1965
KEDDIE, Steve
KEENAN, JOE 1964
KEITH, 'Dick' George 1966
KENT, Chris 1978
KEYZER 1954
KLAJNMANN, Henry 1931
KLAYMANN, Chaim 1928

KLINMAN 1936
KNOPP, Josef 1954
KORNHAUSER, E 1939
KORNHAUSER, J 1939
KLASSIC 1954
KLIEMAN, K 1936
KLUG, Rudi 1980
KLUGER 1950
KNOBS, Josef 1953
KODAK, M 1954
KOMESAROFF, Norman 1946
KOPSTEIN 1950
KORNHAUSER, Jack 1946
KRASNOSTEIN, Geoffrey 1965
KRAUS, David 1980
KRAUS, Michael
KRONGOLD, Dennis 1977
KULIK, Nick 1950
KURTA, Peter 1973
KURZWELL, Johnny 1950
LANE, Terry 1978
LANG, D
LAPIN 1941
LAPISH, J 1973
LASHANSKY, Ariel 2005
LATTO, Bill 1964
LAURENCE 1963
LECKIE 1934
LEGGARI 1941
LESTER, Fred 1946
LEVINE, Robert 1965
LEWIS, P 1936
LICHTENBAUM, Max 1975
LIU, Hanson 1999
LOCK, Daniel 2003
LOH, Michael 1979
LORENZONI, F 1954
LUKIC, Slobodan 1978
LUSTIG, Danny
LYUBIC, Igor 1999
MACKIE 1936
MACKEY, A 1941
MACLEAN, Jim 2001
MADDICK, Bill 1950
MAERISHEL 1954
MAIER, Hubert 1959
MAJMAN 1966
MAKRIGIANNIS, Louie 2003
MAKEY, A 1938
MALLAGHAN, Gary 1980
MALLIN, Leon 1996
MANDALIS, Michael 1973
MANNERING, Del 1959
MANSELL 1937
MARINO 1941
MARTIN, David 1963
MAZIN, Clive 1994
McDONALD 1936
McDONALD, Ian 1974
McINROY, Johnny 1960
McINTOSH, D 1955
McIVOR, Billy 1964
McIVOR, Frank 1941
McIVOR, Nat 1964
McLEAN 1963
McLEOD, I 1973
McLUNIE, Richie 1980
McCLUSKEY, John 2004
McCLUSKEY, Tom 1936
McMULLEN, Garry 2001
McNEIL, Ian 1977
McQUILLAN, Ben 1962
MARSHALL 1975
MELEK, Eli 1980
MELEK, Moshe 1980
MELEK, Simon 1980
MERKIN, Vova 1985
MEYER, Sam 1972

MEYERS, Albert 1946
MICEVSKI, Mike 1973
MICIC, Frank 1980
MIGDALEK, Charlie
MILLER, Laurence 2001
MILLER, Daniel 2003
MOUCHA, Frank 1954
MYERS 1947
MOLINSKY 1941
MONAN, Ian 1966
MONTEITH, Ian 1974
MORRIS, Martin 1961
MOSES, Jack 1946
MOSHE, Avi 1986
MOSS 1941
MOUCKA 1950
MUNZ, Jonathan 1980
MUR, Peter 1976
MURNEY, Hugh 1964
MUSAPHIA, Grant 1998
MUSMAN, Alex 1986
MYRON, Greg 1974
NADELMAN, Jeff 1987
NAGY, Les 1989
NAGY, Sandor 1980
NAHOOM, Robbi
NECHVOGLOD, Nick 1977
NEUHOLD, Johann 1959
REUVEN 2003
NISSEN, M 1946
NORRIS, Ollie 1965
O'HARA, Mike 1966
O'NEIL, Jim 1965
O'NEILL, John 1966
ORLOFF, Alec 1928
ORR, J 1938
OUGHTON, Graham 1960
OWENS, Les 1978
PALUCH, Doron 1990
PANETH, Ronnie 1980
PANTHER, Dennis 1976
PAVLIS 1941
PEJOVIC, Marko 1966
PERCZIKOW
PETERS, Issie 1947
PETERSEN, Hans 1959
PETERSON, Hans
PIERCEY, Ralph 1955
PINCH 1933
POLITZER 1948
POLLACK, Simeonne
PORTER 1946
PORTWOOD, Cliff 1976
POULAKAKIS, Manny 1966
(most successful Hakoah coach)
POWER, C 1941
POWERS 1933
POZNANSKI, Z 1974
PRYLES, Michael 1965
PRYLES, Peter 1965
PUGH, Steven 1985
PURDIE, Alex 1965
RABINOWITZ, Greig 1994
RAE, Billy 1971
RAINEY, Mike 1977
RAKOVALIS, Nick 1975
RAZ, Yoram 1997
REILLY, Jack 1970
RENO 1941
RESCH, Carl 1931
RESSLER 1954
RICE, Harry 1954
RICHTER, Nathan
RISCHIN, Adam 2004
RIGBY, Dave 1974
ROBERTS, Bruce 1977
ROBERTS, Ian 1973
ROBERTSON, Bobby 1975

ROESSLER, Isodor 1954
ROESSLER, Jack 1966
ROESSLER, Peter 1965
ROGERS, Doug 1962
ROGERS, Eric 1928
ROGERS, Kalman 1928
ROONEY, Sean 1980
ROSENBERG, Stan 1928
ROSENBERGER, Victor 1980
ROSENFELD, Joe 1946
ROSS, Yuri 1996
ROTELL 1941
ROTH, Aku 1930
ROTH, H 1938
ROTH, Johnny 1980
ROTH, Robert 1980
ROTHFIELD 1933
ROTHFIELD, Nathan 1953
ROTHMAN, Norman 1946
ROUBEL, Karel 1954
ROWLEY, Bill 1964
ROZANSKI, Chaim 1985
ROZNIC, Abraham 1941
RUDDOCK 1941
RUSIK 1950
SAMAROFF 1975
SANSON, Barry 1974
SAS, Paul 1961
SAUNDERS, Bob 1973
SCROBOGNA, Justin 1994
SEENAN, Albert 1962
SEREMITIS, A 1973
SEROSHTAN, Boris 1993
SERRY, Phil 1980
SHAPIRO, Leon
SHATIN, Joe 1928
SHATIN, Norman 1928
SHAW, Mark
SHENKER, Greg
SHEPPARD 1938
SHEPHERD 1941
SHER, Michael 1984
SHER, Ron 1984
SHIVAKOWSKY, Harry 1928
SILVER 1933
SILVER, Harvey 1980
SILVER, M 1928
SIMON, Norman 1964
SKOLNICK, Jack 1928
SKOLNIK, Yehudah 1928
SLACK, David 1981
SLONIM, Morrie 1931
SMITH, David 1965
SMITH, Mike 1973
SMITH, Ray 1975
SMITH, Ted 1965
SNELL, Victor
SPAREY 1938
SPEIGEL, Dudi 1981
SPEIGEL, Isaac
SPICER 1940
SPICER, Nat 1928
SPIERS, F 1933
SPIERS, W 1933
SPIZER, A 1933
STACKLE, F 1946
STENHOUSE, Alan 1966
STERN 1933
STERN, Max
STEWART, Willie 1964
STEWART, David 1978
STRAUBINGER 1973
SUDAKOV, Sasha
SUTHERLAND, Harry 1955
SZAJER 1947
TALIADOROS, Kimon 2003
TARASCIO, Sam 1964
TARQUINIO 1976

TEMKIN, Anatoly
THOMAS, John 1972
THOMAS, Syd 1954
THOMPSON 1937
THOMPSON 1974
THOMSON 1940
THOMSON, Les 1980
TOPOLANSKI, Shraga 1979
TUGAND 1933
VALLI, Chris 1977
VAMVAKAS 1961
VAN ALPHEN, Dick 1966
VAN WERKHOEVEN, Wim 1966
VERCHININ, Kosta 2002
VESOVIC, Milan 1954
VILLIERS, Alan 1961
WAALDYK, A 1973
WALKER, C 1965
WALKER, John 1965
WARBURTON 1933
WAUGH, KEN 1962
WALK, DAN 2002
WALLACE, JOHN 1978
WALLACE, NEIL 2005
WARBURTON 1938
WEBSTER, Stan 1980
WEIN, Bradley 1980
WEINBERG, George 1965
WEINGER, Peter 1965
WEINIGER, Peter 1970
WEINSTEIN, Michael
WEIR, George 1935
WEISS, Bernie 1966
WERTHER, Frank 1946
WEST, Bob 1954
WESTER, John 1966
WEXLER, Joe
WHEELER, Ken 1972
WHITE 1941
WHITESIDE, Bill 1978
WILLIS, A 1937
WILLIS, J 1937
WILSON 1940
WILSON, Jimmy 1980
WINNIKOF, George 1928
WISE, H 1941
WOLSSDORP 1935
WOODWARD, D 1960
WYNDHAM 1965
YAFFE, Charlie 1941
YAFFE, Sam 1928
YAFFE, W 1940
ZABLOCKI 1950
ZAITMAN, Harry 1976
ZELMAN, Henry 1965
ZEMEL, Ben 1964
ZOLOTAREV, Eddie 985
ZWIER, Alex 1980
ZYLBERSTEIN 1966

The Complete History of Hakoah Melbourne Association Football Club

1927–1981

CHAPTER ONE

The Beginning: The History of Vienna Hakoah Football Club

The family Weinberger lived at Rembrandstrasse 19, in the second district of Vienna. Their sons, David, Fritz and Solomon were all keen soccer players. Together with some other young friends from the neighbourhood they decided to form a Jewish football team. The young men met in the Weinberger apartment and when it became too dark, they had to finish their meetings under the street lamps outside.

The year was 1909 and football in Austria was still in its infancy. Boys used to play with tennis balls in the street or in the nearby park, Augarten. Often they were chased away by the over zealous local police, only to return when the police had gone. The Jewish football team, named Hakoah, which in Hebrew is a word meaning strength, conceived in the Rembrandstrasse, was one of a number of non registered teams (those not affiliated with the Austrian Football Association) who advertised in the local press to arrange friendly games with other non-registered teams.

Sports Club Hakoah (SCH) was officially founded on the 26 September, 1909, with the first football match taking place soon after against a team called Florisdorf. At the end of the match, which Hakoah lost, the opposing team captain proposed a merger of the two teams. He said he liked the uniform of SCH and thought that some of the better players would be useful in his side!

SCH created its first home ground on an uneven field, a part of the flood plain of the Danube. There each Sunday morning the goal lines had to be chalked in and the goal posts carried from a fisherman's hut some distance away. The players used the same hut to change and after their matches they cooled off and washed in the Danube.

In 1910, there were approximately 175,000 Jewish men, women and children in Vienna representing 8.6 percent of the population. Many of these were recent immigrants from the eastern regions of the Austrian empire. Most had severed their ties with the ghetto and were actively pursuing their integration into the predominantly German culture. However, the community was still sharply divided along religious, political and national lines. Apart from internal polarisation, Vienna Jewry constantly experienced virulent and overt anti-Semitism – a seemingly endemic disease that permeated across all classes of Austrian society.

This dangerous and widespread anti-Semitism in Austria created the trigger for the rise of political Zionism, mainly through the efforts and voice of Theodor Herzl. Other nationally orientated Jewish groups began to spring up in Austria. Among them were a number of small sporting organisations. The idealistic founders of Sports Club Hakoah wanted all Jewish youth in Austria to participate freely in physical activity, and so football became a natural medium by which this could be attained. Jewish youth had previously been restricted in non-Jewish clubs. The forward thinking SCH committee recognised the physical regeneration of Jewish youth and their membership of SCH could only improve Jewish youth's self-esteem. The SCH committee knew that sport was a big attraction for Jewish youth, not only for the participants, but also for the fans, and that success in open competition would serve to improve Jewish morale and simultaneously gain the respect of the non-Jewish population.

In 1910 Sports Club Hakoah, together with a number of other new clubs, sought affiliation with the Austrian Football Association. Whereas for most clubs this was a mere formality, SCH's application generated lively debate. Fears were expressed concerning the precedent of allowing a 'national' club (and specifically a Jewish national club) to become affiliated.

Strangely, it was the representative of Vienna Rapid (later a tough on field adversary of SCH) who supported the club's application. Vienna Rapid senior officials could not have foreseen that this small club, commencing its inauguration in the lowest division, in only a few short years would challenge Vienna Rapid for the championship of Austria and in the process draw tens of thousands of new fans to the sport.

These early years required a superhuman effort from the founders of SCH, principally Dr. I. H. Korners, a Viennese dentist, and Arthur Baar, an engineer. These two great forward thinking men encountered many difficulties in establishing the organisation of SCH and encountered strong opposition from the Jewish establishment who feared the 'separatism' of this movement through SCH would threaten the economic and cultural integration of Jews into Austrian society.

On the soccer field the team competed on unprotected grounds, opposition supporters often encroached onto the playing area and sometimes physically attacked Jewish players. Changing facilities were primitive and caused further embarrassment to the players. The primary aim of the SCH administration became the establishment of a permanent home for the club.

To this end a fund was created and the search for an appropriate ground began. The First World War intervened, and although a number of members of SCH were killed or wounded during the dark days of WWI, overall, the movement was greatly strengthened. By the end of the war, a further nine sections had been added to the original Sports Club Hakoah, including swimming, wrestling, athletics, fencing, hockey, table tennis, tennis, winter sports and an orchestra. Many Jewish members of non-Jewish clubs began to transfer to SCH. Among these sportsmen were a number of players in the top league football clubs.

By the end of 1919, in front of a crowd of 15,000 people, the former Sports Club Hakoah football team, now known throughout Europe as Vienna Hakoah Football Club, defeated Germania 2–1 to gain a place in the First Division of the Austrian Football League. Because of this extraordinary success, thousands of new fans joined Hakoah overnight. The Viennese Jewish community were justifiably proud of 'their' Hakoah. In their first year in the top grade, Hakoah finished a creditable fourth in a league comprising of thirteen clubs.

After this golden transitional period in the clubs history, Hakoah were constantly in demand for tournaments in Europe, and toured extensively in Germany, Poland, Czechoslovakia and Yugoslavia. Wherever Hakoah appeared they inspired the creation of new Jewish sports organisations and became ambassadors not only for the Jewish people but also for Austrian sport.

In the spring of 1923, when the top English Premier League side West Ham United was touring Europe, the English Football Association accepted Hakoah's invitation for the club to play a match in Vienna. Austria had not yet lived down its defeat in the Great War and the further humiliations of the Treaty of Versailles. The slogan 'Gott strafe England' (God punish England) was still in Austrian hearts, and no other club would have dared to host such an encounter. Yet despite the controversy surrounding the match, the game proved to be a sensation and the May 19th 1923 marked a milestone in Austrian football.

On this day nearly 50,000 people turned up to watch Vienna Hakoah hold the great English side to a 1–1 draw. A magnificent result in any language!

However, it was the Hakoah return match against West Ham United, on their home ground at Upton Park in London, on September 3rd 1923, that became its most memorable triumph. Hakoah was the first European team to play in England, the country where football is said to have had its origins. Hakoah started out as the 'underdogs' but after the first half had already managed to score three goals and at the end of the match had recorded an unprecedented 5–0 victory. In England, the usually reserved British press praised '"Hakoah", the Jewish team from Vienna.'

In Vienna the *Wiener Morgenzeitung* brought out a special edition which was sold out ten minutes after it hit the streets. People on street corners, in the cafés and on the trams hailed this win as a great Austrian victory. 'Hakoah' had become a household word and the youngsters playing football on the streets adopted the names of their favourite Hakoah idols.

In his welcome address to the team on their return home, Viennese town councillor, Dr. Leopold Plaschkes, put another perspective on the result.

> 'Let us rejoice that you have represented the Republic in such a splendid way and that through our Jewish colours you have honoured Austrian sport. But let us get this straight: it is and remains a Jewish success. A success of the Jewish body, the Jewish soul, and will, and the Jewish deed.'

By 1923 the dream of a ground and facilities of their own for the football section of SCH had become a reality. An area had been found on the edge of the 'Prater,' the expansive Viennese sport, fun and recreation park. Between the Krieau and the Handelskai, Hakoah laid out a football field surrounded by an athletic track, a further ground for hockey (reputedly the best in Vienna), six tennis courts, two sets of changing facilities, two caretaker's houses, stands seating 5000 people and standing room for a further 20,000 people. Soon hundreds of young sports minded people began to actively participate in sporting competition and thousands more came to watch. The single tramline servicing the route to the ground had to be duplicated. On match days, direct trams to the Hakoah ground were provided from every district in Vienna and extra carriages were put on to take the fans home after matches – a facility which to this day is still utilised for the stadium erected years later.

In the winter of 1923–24, Hakoah became the first European club to play in the Middle East with matches in Egypt and Palestine. They won seven of their eight encounters against the British army and local teams. However, team member and sportswriter, Egon Pollack, also recognised the significant public relations value of the tour. In *Sport-Tagblatt* he wrote: 'interestingly the Arabs, who normally are not too pleased with the Zionistic idea, were particularly friendly. I have the feeling that an era of understanding between Arabs and Jews in Palestine is beginning.' Sculptor, Karl Duldig, goalkeeper of the Hakoah team, shared this opinion. Interviewed in Israel in 1968, he recalled how the team was received with regal pomp in Egypt: 'They drove us in luxury cars through the streets of Cairo and after the match the King of Egypt presented each team member with a specially inscribed gold medallion.' For many members of the hundred strong entourage accompanying the team, the impressions of this journey were to lay the foundation for their future Aliyah.

During the 1924–25 season the fairy tale progress of the team continued. In Vienna they defeated Austrian premiership favourites Rapid Vienna 3–0 and in Prague defeated the Czechoslovakian premiers Slavia Prague, the first time this team had lost on their home ground for ten years. Hakoah then went on a tour to Germany, playing in Berlin, Leipzig and Munich. *Munchen Fussball* reported: 'Hakoah has destroyed the myth of the physical inferiority of the Jew. Through their play they could only win admirers. The players are on average tall, strong figures, absolutely fair and especially noteworthy, absolutely quiet on the field.'

The ultimate goal of winning the Austrian premiership seemed in sight. Austrian football was at an all time high and record crowds were attending all matches, especially those in which Hakoah was participating. After home and away matches at the end of the 1924–25 season, Hakoah finally headed the premiership ladder.

Paradoxically, it was to be the two ambitious and triumphant tours to America in 1926 and 1927 that signalled the impending downfall of this remarkable Jewish football team. The lure of the dollar was irresistible to the young football professionals from Vienna, and by the end of the second tour, ten Hakoah players had signed up with American teams. The depth of talent in the club could not overcome this setback and the achievements of the 1924–25 team was never equalled.

The mass appeal of the football team sometimes tended to overshadow the equally prestigious performances of other sections of the club. Yet the amateur sports continued to flourish long after the intrusion of professionalism had deprived Hakoah of its football superiority.

Large numbers of young people participated in athletics and swimming and under the guidance of the best available foreign coaches, high standards were achieved. Hakoah also excelled in waterpolo, winning the Austrian title for three consecutive years (1926–28).

Perhaps Hakoah's most renowned individual sportsman was the wrestler Nikolaus (Micky) Hirschl. He held the Austrian title over a number of years and was also champion of Czechoslovakia, Hungary, Poland, Italy and France. He won the Austrian pentathlon title in six successive years and in the 1932 Olympics in Los Angeles crowned his achievements by winning two bronze medals in wrestling. Largely due to his achievements, wrestling was probably the most consistently successful section of Hakoah. In the competition *Wien derstarken Manner* (Vienna of the Strong Men), Hakoah men proved to be the strongest and thus once again validated the club's name – Hakoah or 'strength' in Hebrew.

For ten years from the mid twenties this section had a veritable monopoly on the Austrian titles and Hakoah wrestlers travelled successfully throughout Europe. In fact their usefulness to the Sports Club Hakoah organisation often extended beyond the ring. Their mere presence at sports meetings often averted the possibility of otherwise nasty clashes with anti-Semitic hooligans!

Although not always in the limelight, the first Hakoah hockey team managed to win the Austrian title four times, 1925–26, 1927–28, 1934–35, and 1936–37. The section had so many players that a splinter group called the *Blau-Wiess* (Blue-Whites) was formed. Players from both these groups and from the women's section participated in Austrian teams, and at the Amsterdam Olympics in 1928 the Hakoah player, Erwin Nossig, had the honour of captaining the Austrian side.

The provision of tennis courts at the Hakoah centre opened this previously elitist sport to the masses. Hakoah's leading players competed successfully in open competition and in international tournaments. Club No.1, Willi Ehrenreich, later became the regular partner of King Gustav of Sweden, whilst Lisl Herbst was a winner of the Austrian Women's Singles Championships.

Table tennis was initially considered the social and recreational outlet for the club. However, it soon became as competitive as the other sections. The first men's team always competed in the top grade, and finally in the 1936–37 season managed to win the flag.

Richard Bergman, who for many years was World Champion in professional table tennis, was a product of Hakoah.

The fencing section also concentrated its efforts on promoting the sport to the young and handball also became very popular with both women and men.

S.C. Hakoah will also be remembered for winter sports. In 1934, 1500 Jews were involved in various winter sport activities which included walking tours in the summer months which other sections of Hakoah also participated in. Whilst commencing as a social organisation in 1913, the winter sports division started to produce competitive young skiers in slalom and downhill races in open Austrian competition.

In the cultural sphere, The Hakoah orchestra was formed in 1919, and under conductor Professor Braslavsky, it soon became the best amateur orchestra in Vienna. Its official appearances at Zionist Congresses in Vienna and on other official occasions were well received.

The social value of Hakoah to the Jews of Vienna cannot be over estimated. Uninhibited by religious or political affiliations the various club centres became convivial meeting places for Jewish youth. Nearly every week small social gatherings or dance evenings were arranged, as well as interesting and educational lectures. In this way the fellowship of the members and their friends was fostered and Hakoah members were like one big happy family.

On a different level Hakoah was influential in unifying the splintered organisations in Viennese Jewry. The Hakoah Centre was the neutral meeting place for the leaders of Viennese Jewry when they met to prepare a unified platform prior to the 1923 Austrian parliamentary elections.

At the beginning of 1938 Hakoah was firmly established as the largest and most successful all-round Sports club in Austria. Thousands of members and fans recognised its proud ideals and it had gained the respect of countless non-Jewish citizens. It was a real focal point for Vienna's Jewry and the source of community leaders in many other spheres. The physical presence of unofficial Hakoah vigilante groups ensured the ordinary Viennese Jew was no longer molested on the streets, in the Jewish precincts, or on the Jewish Holy days. The future looked incredibly bright and the Club had plans underway to extend its already outstanding facilities at Krieau by the addition of a swimming pool. But this was not to be.

On March 11th 1938, the Austrian Chancellor Schussnig capitulated under Hitler's pressure at Berchtesgaden and independent Austria ceased to exist. Two days later Hitler marched triumphantly into Vienna to be greeted by jubilant masses waving Swastika flags.

Like every other Jewish institution in Vienna, the assets of S.C. Hakoah were appropriated by the Nazi authorities. More than three decades of painstaking work was destroyed in a matter of days. Jewish teams and individuals were barred from open competition and their results removed from the records. Jews were refused admittance to their own fine facilities at Kirieau. During the Second World War, the concrete bunkers were built over the whole area and never re-established. Today, visitors to the nearby stadium alight at the one time Hakoah station and walk down the ramp past a weed covered hill, completely oblivious to the legend of S.C. Hakoah which lies buried underneath. Only on the Semmering the Hakoah Ski hut remains as an ongoing memorial to its intrepid founders.

Although physically destroyed, the spirit of the great organisation, and the feeling of fellowship and achievement was resurrected by the regular editions of the newsletter, *Brith Hakoah 1909,* founded in 1962, and local community come-togethers. Therein the bonds of the organisation were kept alive. In 1969, at a festive Jubilee reunion of original members in Israel, Karl Duldig's monument to Hakoah victims of the Holocaust was unveiled in the Maccabiah Village. In Australia Hakoah personalities, Hans Klimit, Nikolaus (Micky)

Hirschl and Kurt Defris were instrumental in perpetuating the name in a number of sporting and recreational institutions in Sydney and Melbourne. However, with unrestricted membership most of these clubs lost their Jewish identity.

By 1987, the number of original members had been reduced to 450 and today their numbers have dwindled even further. However, the archive trophies and other memorabilia of the club have been preserved in the Hakoah Room of Pierre Gildesgame Maccabi Museum in the Maccabiah Village in Ramat Gan, Israel. Dedicated curator of this museum and editor of the Newsletter, Arthur Hanak, has also undertaken the mammoth task of updating the Hakoah files into newly computerised records.

A further publication, titled *Hoppauf Hakoah* by John Bunzl, was published in Vienna in 1987. It covers the history of Jewish sport in Austria from its origins to the present day. Many of the famous achievements of S.C. Hakoah and its members are highlighted in this book which also examines the politics of anti-semitism, the Waldheim affair and the difficulties facing the regenerated S.C. Hakoah in the small Jewish community of post-war Vienna.

CHAPTER TWO

The Creation of Hakoah Melbourne Football Club

While the Hakoah Vienna story is truly amazingly inspirational, the Hakoah Melbourne foundation years also reveals monumental commitment from those tenacious and persevering Jews who made Hakoah Melbourne Football Club a part of the sporting fabric of Melbourne, Australia.

This then is the moving story of the conception, birth and growth of the Hakoah Melbourne Association Football Club, which developed into the most widely respected club in the Victorian football community. In its infancy, the Hakoah club in Melbourne formed as a football club with visions to emulate the sports club created in Vienna.

The club formed in late 1927 when an initiative to form a Jewish football club out of the local Jewish community predominantly residing in Carlton, Victoria occurred.

The Victorian Soccer Federation (VSF) today known as Football Federation Victoria (FFV) was established in 1884 and is one of the oldest sporting associations in Victoria. Football Federation Victoria is an affiliate of the governing body, Football Federation Australia (FFA).

The Football Association (FA) in England was formed in 1863, with Australia among the first countries to introduce the game. The first recorded game of football was played in Australia in 1880. By 1881 Sydney had five clubs competing and the following year the State's first Association was formed. 1884 saw the Anglo-Australian

Association in Melbourne as the first administrative football body operating within Australia. In 1885 the first State-wide Cup was held and won by Granville. 1904 saw the first International tour when New South Wales visited New Zealand and the following year, New Zealand reciprocated the visit.

The NSW British Football Association began in 1898 and through affiliation with the English Football Association (EFA) development grants to promote the game in Australia, were given. Football Association (Australia) was formed in 1923, with clubs from around Australia becoming affiliated. Many breakaway organisations were formed over the next forty years, with the last eventually becoming the Australian Soccer Federation (ASF) now known as previously stated, Football Federation Australia, which gained Australia-wide support and was officially established in 1961.

The Hakoah Melbourne Football Club was the first major 'ethnic' football club in Australia, as its predecessor had been in Austria, and was the fore runner to many post-war clubs in Australia predominated by eastern and southern European groups.

A common theme which led to the formation of this famous Hakoah sporting club was that it gave both Jewish and non Jewish migrants alike, a focal point of interest in a sport which they could relate too. Association Football was the game familiar to many of the young European migrants who had emigrated to Australia during the 1920s. Sports like cricket, Australian Rules Football and horse racing held little interest to an enthusiastic group of young Jewish men who enjoyed soccer first and foremost.

The Hakoah club's history relates back to a meeting in 1927, in a Carlton garage where the creators of the 'Hakoah' club, as it went on to be known, met to form the Hakoah Soccer Club.

A group of Jewish migrants, mostly from Poland, inspired by the tremendous success of Vienna Hakoah, decided to form a Jewish Soccer Club in Melbourne, so that the name 'Hakoah' would be kept alive in Australia.

Several meetings were held by a very enthusiastic group of Jewish football players at the Polish club in Neil Street, Carlton, that eventually led to the formation of the club.

The first official meeting took place outside Carlton Australian Rules Football Oval (Optus Oval), where about fifty young Jewish sportsmen responded to a small advertisement in the Jewish Herald newspaper. After a short meeting on that historic day, it was decided to form and register a Jewish Football Club and to name it after the famous 'Vienna' Hakoah. Those present at the meeting included legendary names like, Joe Shatin, Stan Rosenberg, Jack Skolnik, Kalman Rogers, Harry Spivakovsky and Sam Yaffe, now all deceased. Others later joined the club including Lou Miller, Alec Orloff, Sam Goldfine, M. Hirsch, H. Goldberg, M. Belkan and Bob Fetter.

The club was officially formed, with the name 'Hakoah' unanimously adopted, after which the club became affiliated with the VASF, which is now the equivalent of the Football Federation Victoria (FFV).

The Jewish community embraced the establishment of the new club, but some quarters of the community opposed the necessity of Hakoah to play in a Saturday competition due to religious beliefs.

Training and practice matches took place outside Optus Oval at North Carlton.

After training, the players and committee members would meet at the garage of one of their most enthusiastic supporters, Mr. Jack Lederman. Jack's garage also served as a storeroom.

The first election for a President of the Hakoah Association Football Club (known as Hakoah Soccer Club in those days) took place in January 1928. Mr. Sam Yaffe became the first president and proved to be an inspiring leader admired by all. He was observed as a fatherly figure, known to be kind by demeanour, but stern if the occasion warranted it. He was highly respected by everyone within the club and in the world of sport outside the club according to one of the club's legendary players, Mr. Aku Roth.

The player's collectively used to meet all the clubs operating expenses in those early days. To equip the team, the players relied on the generosity of several players and supporters.

In the clubs first full season in 1928, Hakoah was assigned by the VASFA (Victorian Soccer Federation) to the lowest grade, the Third Division. Original players in 1928 included Aku Roth, Willie Yaffe, Charlie Yaffe, Jack Skolnik, Yehudi Skolnik, Nat Spicer, Ted Cohen, Mendel Slonim, H. Silver, J. Orloff, L. Olbaum, N. Kleinman, G. Winikoff, S. Kaplan and K. Pesch.

The team manager was Joe Wexler and the club secretary was Harry Spivakovsky. Joe Wexler was considered an excellent sportsman and a man of high moral qualities, while Spivakovsky strengths included being an outstanding secretary who stimulated the club with his enthusiasm and visionary enterprise.

Hakoah's first game was played in 1928 at the North Carlton Oval against Fawkner Soccer Club with Hakoah victorious 1–0. The win was loudly applauded and well received by the large number of parochial Hakoah supporters who attended the match.

Another early game for Hakoah was against North Carlton at Fawkner Park and Hakoah again won the game 1–0. Hakoah by this time was officially affiliated with The Victorian Amateur Soccer [Football] Association.

Hakoah quickly gained a reputation for being an ambitious club by way of its emphasis on endeavouring to play an attractive brand of soccer at a level higher than anything previously seen in Victoria.

In a game against Springvale played at the North Carlton Oval in July 1928, Hakoah gave a splendid exhibition of soccer which incorporated a quick passing game and excellent cover in defence. Hakoah won the game 4–0. In the second half, thousands of fans coming out of the Carlton Australian Rules football match stopped to watch Hakoah and cheered the side on as they scored two splendid second half goals. This was often the case when the Carlton Australian Rules club and Hakoah matches coincided. There were often several thousand people watching Hakoah's home games after the Australian Rules football matches had concluded, while Hakoah was playing at North Carlton.

Other notable results in 1928 included a 5–2 victory over Alphington and a 3–0 win over later arch rival South Yarra.

On July 12th 1928, it was reported in the The Australian Jewish Herald newspaper that the activities of the Jewish Sports Club 'Hakoah' were progressing remarkably well.

The team was playing its home game at Princes Park, North Carlton and getting large and enthusiastic crowds.

The team was regarded as playing a quick passing and entertaining game and the supporters were proud of the clubs Jewish pedigree. As was commonly the case at the time, Hakoah took advantage of a large Carlton Australian Rules Football Club crowd cheering enthusiastically for Hakoah at the end of the football games which were played next door.

In May 1929, Hakoah played their first Dockerty Cup game against Wonthaggi Magpies. Hakoah later went on to become the most successful club in the prestigious Dockerty Cup competition winning it seven times.

In 1930, Hakoah played in Grade Three of an eight-team league, which included Albert Park, Richmond, Sunshine, Alphington, South Yarra, Camberwell and Heidelberg.

The South Yarra team was the best in the league in 1930, however Hakoah scored twice against them that season before being defeated 2–5. The scorer was Yaffe with two goals. (*The Sun* 12/5/30).

In other results in 1930, Hakoah was defeated by Alphington 1–4 and Albert Park 0–8 (14/6/30 & 21/6/30).

The teams in the top league at that time were, Grade One: Footscray Thistle, St Kilda Caledonians, South Melbourne, Brunswick, Australian Navy, Prahran and Melbourne Thistle.

As already stated the Hakoah club was named after the famous Vienna Hakoah club, which had achieved outstanding success in Austria.

The late and great Kurt Defris, who had been the illustrious secretary of Hakoah Melbourne Football Club since 1947, was a former player of the famous Vienna Hakoah. Hans Strohs and Vice President Fred Halpern were also involved with the legendary Austrian club.

CHAPTER THREE

Legends of The Pre-War Era

From humble beginnings, Hakoah Melbourne Association Football Club started to get into its stride in 1932 when it was promoted to League Two. At the end of Season 1932, Hakoah and Preston were the two teams promoted to League One.

From this point in time, Hakoah began to set the pace and became a benchmark club for others to try and emulate.

This was a time in Australia when the sport of soccer as it was commonly known then, was in its infancy and strongly opposed by the hierarchy of Australian Rules Football in the state of Victoria. This Australian Rules game, played nowhere else in the world except Melbourne, was supported feverishly by tens of thousands of patriotic fans every Saturday, come rain hail or shine.

The Australian Rules game in fact, at that time in history totally dominated all other sporting codes in the state of Victoria. Nevertheless competitive and well managed and supported soccer clubs like Hakoah Melbourne pioneered on, bringing gradual and inevitable change to the dominance of Australian Rules Football and a grand alternative for all Australian youth. The reality was that at that time multiculturalism was an unknown in Melbourne and it was quite common to hear racially biased Australians call the great world game, 'wogball' in reference to all European immigrants who loved and played the game in Victoria and indeed around the country with zeal and enthusiasm.

In 1933, the teams competing in League One were: South Yarra, Footscray Thistle, Hakoah, Preston, Brunswick, Box Hill, Caledonians, Brighton, Melbourne Thistle and Collingwood.

In 1933, Hakoah was the team to beat in League One. On Saturday, May 20th 1930, Hakoah defeated Caledonians 2–0 at the Exhibition Oval in front of a crowd of 4000 people, with the goals coming from Johnstone and Forrest (*Melbourne Sun* 22/5/33).

Hakoah was considered the supreme team of 1933, playing the kind of football that the crowds loved to see. The Hakoah defence in the game against Caledonians was considered 'impregnable'.

Hakoah went through most of season 1933 undefeated and thus began the successful history of a club that was to go on and succeed like no other club in the state had done before.

On May 27th 1933, Hakoah played Preston at the Exhibition Oval in what was a grudge match because the two teams were so competitive in getting promotion the previous year. Preston was fast becoming Hakoah's greatest rival with their ambition for success matched only by the Hakoah club.

In this game, several of the Hakoah players were reportedly unwell. However, they were still keen to play and retain their formidable record. Hawkes was unfit, Lang played outside left and Yaffe played outside right. Johnstone scored the only goal of the first half and Forrest scored a second half hat-trick for Hakoah to defeat Preston 4–0.

Johnstone was the 'shining light' in attack for Hakoah. Hakoah's goal difference after this game was 8–1.

The following week the team played against Footscray Thistle. The team was: Aguilera, P. Bowman, Hayden, J. Bowman, Roth, Huck, Hawkes, Mackey, Forrest, Johnstone, W. Yaffe. Subs: Lang, Fisher, Campbell.

State representation in 1933 followed for Hakoah players Aguilera, Hawkes, Forrest and Hayden. Hakoah always had a reputation for providing fine players for state and international teams, with these four players the first to represent Hakoah at the highest level.

On June 17th 1933, with the four state representatives back in the team, the leadership of League One was at stake in a match between Hakoah and South Yarra at Fawkner Park. Hakoah had a two point lead over South Yarra going into the game and was also undefeated in two seasons.

The team on this occasion was the familiar line-up with: Aguilera, Hayden, P. Bowman, J. Bowman, Roth, Huck, Hawkes, Mackey, Forrest, Johnstone, W. Yaffe. Sub: Lang.

The reserve team consisted of Rothfield, Campbell, Grenfell, Orloff, S. Fisher, Warburton, Arbor, A. Fisher, Bridge, F. Spiers and W. Spiers.

Hakoah lost the game against South Yarra 2–1 but retained top position on the ladder on goal difference. The game was controversial however, with Hakoah lodging a protest after the game about spectators encroaching onto the playing arena. The Hakoah players considered this protest justified in accordance with a breach of the rules by the home team in failing to control a crowd estimated at 4000 spectators.

The Association was then pressured to introduce a law forcing all important games in future, to be played on enclosed grounds.

In this game, Aku Roth was considered to be the most outstanding player on the ground. Some dubious refereeing decisions in both the first and second half, prevented Hakoah from getting two penalties after two deliberate and blatant hand balls. Forrest scored with fifteen minutes remaining and Johnstone almost scored an equaliser before the final whistle. It was reported in the daily newspapers as a shot which failed to score because 'The spin on the ball prevented him from connecting properly when he had an open goal.'

The loss against South Yarra was followed by a shock draw with lowly Collingwood the following week on June 24th 1933. Hakoah was struggling on the wings and Collingwood scored an early goal at the Exhibition Oval.

Before half time Collingwood made it 2–0, but in typical spirited fashion, Hakoah came back strongly in the second half. First Mackey scored and then Hayden scored the equaliser with a free kick taken from 50 yards!

During the last ten minutes, both sides contested strongly for a winning goal without result. Again, Aku Roth was considered to be the outstanding player of the match and Hawkes was effective as a forward.

On July 1st 1933, Hakoah surprisingly lost a Dockerty Cup semi-final to Melbourne Thistle. At this stage of the season, Hakoah had a number of players injured including Johnstone, who was considered one of the finest players of his era.

A further impediment for Hakoah was that J. Bowman was playing with injury, Melbourne took full advantage of this factor and duly scored first after seventeen minutes, but Hawkes equalised on the half hour. In the second half, Melbourne Thistle scored two more goals to make the result 3–1. South Yarra were also surprisingly beaten by St Kilda in a weekend of surprising upsets!

Hakoah then went on to play Footscray Thistle at Exhibition Oval on July 8th 1933. The Hakoah team was: Aguilera, P. Bowman, Campbell, Mackey, Roth, Huck, Hawkes, W. Yaffe, Forrest, Johnstone, Lang. The Hakoah Reserve team was: Rothfield, Bolton, Armstrong, Rogers, S. Fisher, Warburton, Bridge, Barron, S. Spiers, F. Spiers, Orloff.

Hakoah fell to third place after this game losing 3–2 to Footscray Thistle. The scorers were Lang and W. Yaffe.

On July 15th 1933, Hakoah played Melbourne Thistle for the third time that season at Exhibition Oval, after having beaten them in the Dockerty Cup semi-final. At this stage Melbourne Thistle were struggling to avoid relegation to League Two. Much to the supporters delight Hakoah won 2–1 with Forrest scoring both goals for Hakoah. Some over zealous refereeing saw three sending offs including Hawkes and P. Bowman for Hakoah, which spoilt the game.

Forrest scored a header from a free kick taken by Hawkes and a second from a Mackey through ball. Hawkes was sent off for wrestling.

On July 29th 1933, Hakoah played against Brighton at Exhibition Oval. Team: Aguillera, Campbell, P. Bowman, Mackey, Roth, Huck, C. Yaffe, Hayden, Forrest, W. Yaffe, J. Bowman, Lang. Reserves: Rothfield, Baron, F. Spiers, S. Spiers, A. Fisher, S. Fisher, Bolton, J. Orloff, A. Orloff, Warburton, Condon.

Hakoah defeated Brighton 4–2. The scorers were Mackey and Forrest with two each. Forrest scored both his winning goals in the last fifteen minutes.

On August 5th 1933, Hakoah lost to Box Hill which effectively cost the team the championship. Hayden was missing in defence, having gone to New Caledonia to play with the Australian national team.

The regular keeper, Aguilerra, was missing through injury and Bingham played in goal. Hakoah was 2–0 down at half-time after a 17th minute goal and a penalty to Brighton. Johnstone scored in the second half, but Hakoah could not force an equaliser.

With a group of players committed to success and a committee and team management providing excellent leadership, it did not take long for the Hakoah team to reach the Second Division. The team quickly won promotion from the Third Division, led by the brilliant Aku Roth, and then it began to collect the major honours of the sport. It was these triumphs that later gave the club its legendary status and respect amongst all clubs throughout Australia.

In 1934, the club started to become extremely ambitious and successful. Buses for away games used to leave from the corner of Faraday and Lygon Streets, Carlton on a regular basis.

On April 14th 1934, Hakoah defeated Preston 2–1 to record their third successive win for the season.

A Grand Hakoah Ball was held at New Kadimah Hall on May 5th 1934. These festivities were always eagerly anticipated and well attended by supporters and friends of the Hakoah Soccer Club. They also proved to be excellent fundraising activities for the club and also help generate interest in the team.

In 1934, Olympic Park was the clubs home ground and the club commenced an innovative initiative on April 20th 1934, when they commenced allowing cars to park inside the stadium at a cost of 6 pence per car.

Supporters were advised to let their friends off at the front gate and then drive their cars to the back gate to gain entry to the car park and thereby have a spectators view from their cars.

Mr. Jack Skolnik was the Vice-President of the club in 1934.

The club made Olympic Park their home ground in 1934. Their first home game at Olympic Park was against Box Hill in April 1934, which they won 5–2.

In May 1934, Hakoah defeated Melbourne Thistle 6–1 and St Kilda 5–1.

Hakoah also defeated South Yarra 5–0 at Olympic Park on 19th May 1934. At this point in time Hakoah Soccer Club was the most successful club in Victoria.

In a game against Brighton in 1934, Hakoah won 4–1 in the most amusing of circumstances. The journalists reports of the game described it as follows:

> 'The Brighton team was forced to concede three goals in the second half due to the intense pressure applied by the Hakoah team. While Brighton massed their defence in front of goal, they were still *compelled on account of the pressure to either allow the ball to go through goal or put it through themselves.*'

When the Hakoah team went to Adelaide in 1934 to play against Kingswood in the Champions of Australia game, the team received a rousing send off at Spencer Street railway station, Melbourne.

A farewell ball was held before the team departed and was attended by the players, committee and hundreds of the clubs supporters. The club balls were a focal fundraising activity for the club and attendances were often overwhelming at the New Kadimah Hall in Carlton. Such was the popularity of the Hakoah Soccer Club amongst the Melbourne Jewish population.

To commemorate Hakoah's historical visit to Adelaide to participate in the first interstate soccer match, a medal was struck and presented to all the players at the ball by two prominent supporters in RC Cleland and JA Karsten. At the Hakoah Ball, the two fanatical supporters promised to later donate a gold cup if the club were to return and win both the championship and Dockerty Cup.

In Adelaide, 6th July, 1934, the game was reported as follows:

> 'On July 5th 1934, Hakoah players and committee members arrived in Adelaide and were enthusiastically welcomed by South Australian Federation officials and the Jewish Community of Adelaide. An official reception was held by the Kingswood Club.'

The game was played on July 7th 1934 at Hindmarsh and 'Experienced followers of the game from Europe said that the play of the Hakoah boys could not be excelled'.

Hakoah won the Championship of Australia by defeating the strong Kingswood club 7–2.

Aku Roth was acknowledged as a brilliant leader (captain) of the Hakoah team. Several functions and presentations were held in Adelaide including one attended by the Lord Mayor, Mr. M. Cain. The event was recorded in all Adelaide newspapers!

On August 11th 1934, the club held a victory ball in Melbourne, to celebrate the triumphant Australia Cup win. In attendance was Secretary: S. Risckin, Manager: Joe Wexler, President: S. Yaffe, Vice-President: Lou Miller, and Committee: JW Fineberg, T. Orloff.

The players returned successfully from their conquest in Adelaide but disappointed in finishing only runners up in the Dockerty Cup, but made amends by winning the League Championship to add to their Australian Championship victory in what became a most successful year for the club.

Hakoah won the First Division Championship in 1934, winning every one of its games except for the final game, a 2–1 loss. The defeat cost the side the chance of creating a unique record, of going through an entire season unbeaten in a 10-team league.

In 1934, the club was coached by Johnny Orr who was the player-coach. He fractured his collarbone against Footscray Thistle on June 2nd 1934.

Hakoah defeated Box Hill 2–1 on 30th June,1934.

On Saturday June 15th 1935, Hakoah defeated Melbourne Thistle 17–1 with Melbourne Thistle scoring their goal from a penalty.

On Saturday June 29th 1935, Hakoah played Shepparton in the third round of the Dockerty Cup at Olympic Park. Hakoah won 9–1

On Saturday July 6th 1935, Hakoah played South Yarra at Olympic Park.

In 1936, Hakoah finished runners up in the league. Moreland took the championship.

In 1937, the team was considerably strengthened in order to replace a number of older players who had started with the club in the early days, but were now too old to compete at the highest level.

On June 11th 1937, Hakoah played against Prahran at Como Park near Chapel Street. Prior to this game, Hakoah had won three games in a row.

Sydney's Jewish community also created a Hakoah club in 1939, which also later folded in 1987, due to heavy financial burdens.

Things only got better for Hakoah in 1935, when the club was able to win the glorious 'double' including the prestigious Dockerty Cup and League Championship.

Aku Roth was a legendary player who represented Victoria and Australia over many years. The Hakoah squad in the mid 1930s, included legendary names like strikers, Frank Mclver, Alex Forrest and Charlie Yaffe, goal keeper Sol Aguilera, the Bowman brothers, Alf Mackay, Nat Spicer, Johnny Orr, Benny Molinski, Paddy Hayden, Sol Halperin, Tom Harrison, Fred Pollock, George Hawks, Jock Lurton, Andy Lang, Johnny Johnstone, Clarrie Power, Walter Huck and other well known names at the time like Lewis, Wise, McCluskey, Armstrong and Bardas.

These were times when soccer pitches were rough and players used to strip in sheds or out in the open. Showers and dressing rooms were practically unheard of. Hakoah however, was a very innovative club and often set the standards for other clubs to follow. Hakoah were in fact one of the first clubs to obtain an enclosed ground – the Exhibition Oval (near the Exhibition Buildings), which no longer exists.

The club then moved on to Princes Park, the old Motordome which was the original site of Olympic Park, St. Kevin's Oval, then finally to the purpose built soccer stadium at Middle Park.

A succession of club presidents then followed. Sam Yaffe was the first President followed by Michael Pitt, Harry Lapin, Nat Spicer, Tony Rubinstein, Jack Skolnik, Edward Zola, Dr. Henry Baytch, George Weinberg, Henry Krongold and in the final years Kurt Defris.

The club was always enterprising and innovative, with Hakoah the first club to organise and participate in an interstate game in 1933, when it brought Kingswood, the South Australian champions to Melbourne for a challenge match. Hakoah lost that game but then went on a return visit to South Australia the following year to defeat Kingswood 7–2.

In 1933, Hakoah played a game against Wally Hammond's English Test Cricket XI at the Motordome. Although the English cricketers included several soccer professionals, Hakoah won the game 3–1.

During the war years, when enlistments made it practically impossible to field a team, Hakoah combined with Moreland for the duration of the global conflict. The team won the First Division Championship in 1943 and the Dockerty Cup in 1945.

Amazingly, Aku Roth was still playing at this time – probably a record for length of playing service with a senior club in Australia.

In the late 1940s the club was boosted by the arrival of several Jewish refugees from Shanghai, China. These included Kurt Defris, the clubs long serving secretary, Erwin Eisfelder and Paul Eichler.

If there was ever a person who lived and breathed Hakoah Football Club it was Mr Kurt Defris. It is simply impossible to pay a sufficiently fitting tribute to this magnificent human being for his total commitment and devoted self-sacrifice over considerable time in the interests of sport and 'his' Hakoah club.

From the time Kurt Defris came to Australia as a refugee in the late 1940s until his and the clubs final days in 1981, the man was comprehensively committed and focused on the success of Hakoah Soccer Club every minute of every day of his life.

His generosity and commitment was unparalleled by anyone in the history of the club. He continually worked on enticing interest in the club when so many people of the Jewish community showed only a passing interest.

Kurt Defris always aimed and succeeded in keeping the Hakoah name at the forefront of the community. He recruited players to the club and attracted major sponsorship and supporters to the club. Coincidently, his untimely death came at the exact same time that 'his' Hakoah club died, with the merger of Hakoah and the powerful South Melbourne Hellas Club. Both the club and the man had done as much as they could in maintaining the name Hakoah. Accordingly Mr Kurt Defris and all those Jewish financial backers of the proud Hakoah club over many years are collectively assigned to history and legend!

Mr Kurt Defris and his magnificent contribution to sport in Australia did not go unnoticed, with this truly great man deservedly honoured by his adopted country with the award of Australian Member (AM) in 1976. A most fitting and just tribute to a magnificent human being.

The continuation of Hakoah superiority in the Victorian League continued and on April 14th 1938, Hakoah defeated arch rivals Moreland 5–1. Hakoah then played Heidelberg seven days later on April 21st 1938 at Olympic Park and proceeded to thrash the opposition.

Hakoah scored its first goal on the stroke of half time and then added another four in the second half. Outstanding players for Hakoah were C. Power, H. Roth, Forrest, Spicer and Warburton.

On Saturday May 28th 1938, Hakoah played against South Yarra at South Yarra Park. Both teams were undefeated at this point of the season, going into this game. Hakoah defeated its old rival, South Yarra 2–0.

It was described in the press as the most thrilling game witnessed in soccer for many years. Clarrie Power was outstanding in goal for Hakoah. Aku Roth, A. Spizer, C. Yaffe and A. Makey were other stalwarts for Hakoah.

Of all the great legendary players that pulled on the Hakoah sky blue shirt from 1927 to 1981, none was better than centre half Aku Roth who came from German club FC Nuremberg and became a regular member of the Victorian team.

On Saturday June 4th 1938, Hakoah played Yallourn (Gippsland) in the Dockerty Cup.

The *Australian Jewish News* reported the drive to get supporters to the game as follows:

> 'We appeal to our supporters with cars to go there and to take some of our players with them, it will be a very pleasant outing and at the same time, they will be able to see a good game. Get in touch with Mr. S. Yaffe (Central 1465). Yallourn is 80 miles from Melbourne on a very good road. We have to leave Melbourne not later than 12 Noon, so that we can be there at 2:30 pm.'

The first round of cars left for the ground from the corner of Faraday and Lygon Street at 12:00 noon. It is told that a large crowd attended the game, spurred on by this appeal. Details after this report are sketchy, with the result of the match unknown.

On June 11th 1938, Hakoah defeated South Melbourne 5–1. On Saturday July 18th 1938, Hakoah played Brighton at Olympic Park. Hakoah were undefeated in the 1938 season up to this point.

On July 2nd 1938, Hakoah replayed Prahran in the third round of the Dockerty Cup and won 3–0. Hakoah's best players were C. Power, A. Forrest and J. Orr.

On July 9th 1938, Hakoah played lowly placed Heidelberg away, and lost 6–4 in a surprise defeat. Hakoah were simply not at their best on the day.

On July 16th 1938, Hakoah played Moreland at Olympic Park and won 5–2.

On July 23rd 1938, Hakoah played Prahran at Como Park with the result unknown.

On Saturday August 1st 1938, Hakoah played Footscray Thistle with buses leaving the corner of Faraday & Lygon Street at 1:45pm to take supporters to the game in Footscray.

Hakoah at this time was very well supported despite the fact that 'soccer' as it was incorrectly labelled by the ill informed Australian

Rules Football fraternity in Melbourne, was still in its infancy.

On Saturday August 13th 1938, Hakoah played at Olympic Park against South Yarra. These games were now eagerly contested affairs between two teams who had now formed a great rivalry since being promoted together to League One from League Two at the end of the 1932 season.

Games against South Yarra were always well attended by everyone interested in the game.

From 1934 to 1938, for example, Hakoah won three Victorian First Division championships and a Dockerty Cup.

Plans were being made at this stage for a Palestinian representative team to tour and play against 'various Commonwealth soccer organizations'.

On June 3rd 1938, The *Australian Jewish News* reported that 'The Jewish population can now be informed with all certainty that a Jewish team from Palestine is coming over to play a representative team from Australia by the end of July. It will be a pleasure for the Jewish citizens to see they have not to be ashamed of their athletes.'

CHAPTER FOUR

The Tom Jack Era

Hakoah always tried to stay one step ahead of the other teams who often enjoyed larger spectator support and greater financial strength than Hakoah.

On April 22nd 1950, Hakoah defeated Park Rangers 3–0 in front of a crowd of about 1500 at Middle Park.

On June 12th 1950, Hakoah's All Jewish team played an annual inter club match against the Sydney Hakoah All Jewish team. A Cabaret ball was held at Samuel Myer Hall. On June 12th 1950, Hakoah played Sydney Hakoah for the AN Roth and J. Newton trophies.

This happening was the first time that annual inter club matches were played since the war ended in 1945.

> 'The Hakoah Sydney team work was too good for the local side on Monday (King's birthday holiday) at Olympic Park with the final score 5–2 in Sydney's favour.'

Ten minutes after play commenced, Lester, (Melbourne's captain) scored off a pass by Meyer. Constructive and controlled play by Sydney's midfield enabled Kohn to equalise 15 minutes later. After this setback Sydney compounded the misery for Melbourne fans when Selinger completely beat Essex (Melbourne keeper) with a first time shot to put the visitors ahead five minutes before half-time.

Melbourne Hakoah worked relentlessly and pressed hard after half-time, but all attempts to score were turned back by the solid Sydney defence. The visitors went further ahead when Kohn scored after 15 minutes and again 10 minutes later, after a scramble in front of goal.

Haarberger (Melbourne) brought the score to 4–2 ten minutes before time by converting a penalty. The Melbourne keeper left an empty goal for Sydney to make the score 5–2 shortly before the final whistle. Sydney Hakoah thus won the AN Roth and S. Newton trophy (K. Pollitzer). This Sydney victory marked the superiority held for years to come by Sydney Hakoah over it's Melbourne namesake.

Hakoah perhaps reached its greatest heights in the middle of the fifties, a period fondly remembered as the 'Tom Jack' era. Tom Jack led Hakoah to no less than four Dockerty Cup wins in a row, from 1953 to 1956. An incredible feat, never matched before or after. The club had assembled an array of talent which was the envy of clubs throughout Australia.

The first team squad included names like Harry Sutherland, Syd Thomas, David McIntosh, Milia Vesovic, Joe Gottesman, Harry Rice, Ralph Piercy, Issy Roessler, Bill Harburn and Aldo Vitti.

Harry Sutherland played in England for Leeds United, Exeter City and AFC Bournemouth, and was player-manager of Western League club Bedford Town before he came to Australia in 1953 at the age of 38. Harry's first job was with Brighton, where as player-coach, he led his new team into the Dockerty Cup final.

The following year Harry Sutherland joined Hakoah, which had beaten Brighton in the 1953 Cup final, and played there in '54, '55, '56 and '57. He stayed on as coach of Hakoah but later switched to Altona City which he coached from 1967 to 1972. Harry Sutherland finally returned to Hakoah as team manager. Harry Sutherland's 31 goals in 1954 still stands as the highest single season total by any Hakoah first team player.

The Hakoah team that won the Dockerty Cup four consecutive times between 1953 and 1956 featured the oldest forward line in Victorian top-league history. Inside forward Henry Rice from Scotland, winger Jackie Ressler and Czechoslovakian ball artist Joe were well into their thirties. Ressler was one of the great Hakoah stalwarts. His name became synonymous with Hakoah. John Slade was only 16 when he played in the 1954 Dockerty Cup final.

The reason for the demotion of the regular goalkeeper is unknown, but Slade is recorded to have acquitted himself well. However, Hakoah later got Aldo Vitti from Juventus, and Slade had to play second fiddle again. Dave McIntosh, a left back, was an accomplished Scottish player who later coached Hakoah and Milan. Vesovic was a strong, robust wing half from Yugoslavia.

Former Hakoah greats who have since died were full back Bill Harburn and Tom Jack, the latter of whom was capped many times for Australia and was also Hakoah's player-coach at one period of time. Bill Harburn, who played for Bishop Auckland in England and whose son Steve played in goal for Hakoah and Sandringham, was tragically killed in the West Gate Bridge disaster.

Hakoah had three more distinguished Australian internationals – Ralph Piercy, Syd Thomas and Angus Drennan. Piercy, a brilliant outside left, played for Chester in England and guested for many of the top English clubs during WWII. Sydney Thomas, from Scotland, played on the wing or at half back. Sydney Thomas played with Harry Sutherland before both switched to Hakoah and he played for Victoria as well as Australia. Angus Drennan won the Victorian Argus Medal while with Box Hill in 1959. He also played with ICI Deer Park and was remembered as a fine half back for Hakoah. Another great player of that era was Czechoslovakian full back Frank Moucha. Going further back into the late forties, we remember Alby Meier and Issi Petes as fine servants of Hakoah.

At this time the strength of the first team squad carried over to the Reserve team which also won a number of championships including the league in 1958, 1959 and 1960 and the Harry Armstrong Reserve Cup in 1956, 1958 and then later in 1964. From 1953 to 1956 inclusive, the Hakoah senior team won the Dockerty Cup four years running. In fact, Hakoah has won the Dockerty Cup eight times.

A record which still stands today.

CHAPTER FIVE

The Golden Days of the '60s

On June 13th 1964, Hakoah played Juventus in front of a crowd of about 2000 people. Fred Hutchison was the team manager at the time and before this game the two teams lined up for a minute's silence in memory of his son Lindsay Hutchison, who had died tragically at only five years of age.

Gerry Chaldi was in the Hakoah team before he took up a stint as coach of Hakoah in Sydney. He played in the midfield for Melbourne Hakoah for two years in the sixties.

The defence was Sam Tarascio in goal with Rogers, Stenhouse, Villiers, Latto as the back four. The midfield consisted of Murney, Biro and Chaldi with Rowley, Mclvor and McQuillan playing up front. Hakoah lost this game in a thriller 2–3 with Mclvor and Rowley scoring for Hakoah. (*Sporting Globe* 13/6/64).

On June 27th 1964, Hakoah lost 2–3 to hosts George Cross. This left the club with only 9 points from 12 games with the sky blues precariously placed at third last on the ladder. Slavia was on top of the table at this stage with Juventus, J.U.S.T. and South Melbourne Hellas in close pursuit.

An important 4–1 win against mid-table Wilhelmina the following week, lifted Hakoah into mid-table. On July 11th 1964, Hakoah played against hosts Triestina with McQuinlan, Chaldi, Stenhouse and Mclvor in good form and responsible for the clubs improvement.

Hakoah played in a block buster home game against South Melbourne Hellas on Sunday July 19th 1964 at Olympic Park, in what was its only Sunday game for the season. At this stage Hakoah was in eighth place and South Melbourne Hellas third, with seven points dividing the two teams. Hakoah lost this game 2–4, but defeated Melbourne Hungaria 2–0 the following week, to continue their excellent turnaround in season 1964. After 16 rounds the club was in seventh place 8 points from the top.

The following week the sky blues defeated title contenders Slavia 1–0. They then defeated bottom team Heidelberg Alexander, before facing Lions with Rowley and Mclvor in great form.

At the end of the 1964 season however, Hakoah finished a disappointing seventh and again in 1965, the club replicated its position in the table.

It is true to say that the middle sixties brought together Hakoah players who were not only world class in their ability to play football, but more importantly were brought from every corner of the world by a committee who at this time had great vision and who simply wanted the best players to make the best team, and that is exactly what ensued. At this time club President Dr Henry Baytch was a prime mover in this new age for Hakoah Melbourne Football Club.

The Golden days of the sixties began slowly, with Hakoah Melbourne Football Club finishing the season in fourth place. In 1963, Hakoah slumped to finish the season in tenth place.

Then in 1966 the Hakoah Genie escaped from the bottle and Hakoah Melbourne Football Club became a veritable all conquering powerhouse on the football field.

Much of this modern day success on the field from 1966 was created by a Yorkshireman named Fred Hutchison, a talented schoolteacher, who, together with the great Kurt Defris co-jointly developed a splendid international recruiting programme of players to Hakoah.

Some of the greatest players ever to wear a Hakoah shirt were recruited during this middle sixties period, two of whom, namely

David Baker and Mike O'Hara went on to create all time appearance records with Hakoah Melbourne.

The greatest player of the '60s was defender John O'Neill, a tough, rugged Irishman and Republic of Ireland international who joined the club in 1965. Before joining Hakoah, John O'Neill spent six years with Preston North End in the English First Division, playing alongside immortal English international legend Tom Finney, and was also with Barrow in the English Football League when a broken leg almost ended his career. John O'Neill won the Victorian Soccer Federation, Argus Medal, in 1969. John O'Neill's partner in defence was wing half Alan Stenhouse, who played in Scotland for Motherwell and Cowdenbeath before joining Hakoah in 1963.

Hakoah also had in its ranks Dutch international Dick van Alphen who had been a top player in Holland prior to coming to Australia, and was with Ringwood Wilhelmina before he came to Hakoah and was capped for Australia. He was one of the Socceroos who returned to Australia after a 10-match tour of Asia in 1967. George 'Dick' Keith, a brilliant full back from Scotland, also went on to represent Australia and to play in the 1969 World Cup elimination matches. George 'Dick' Keith was later transferred from Hakoah to APIA Sydney where he also starred and coached.

Dublin born Irish goalkeeper Mike O'Hara arrived at Hakoah in February 1966 aged 19 years of age from England where he had already made his debut for Luton Town in the Second Division of the English Football League when only 16 years old. This exceptionally talented and colourful player was also in the Swindon Town squad that won promotion to the Second Division of the Football League in 1962–63. The arrival of Mike O'Hara in goal for Hakoah welded the final bolt of solidarity to what then became a veritable juggernaut Hakoah defence.

Such was the impact that the teenage Irishman had on the Victorian soccer scene in 1966, that within months of his arrival he was selected to represent Victoria at Olympic Park against the Italian touring giants A. S. Roma. An all time official record attendance of 35,856 people, mostly Italians, watched the match.

The 1966 season also saw Hakoah finish an outstanding third in the State Premier League Championship and win the coveted Dockerty Cup, defeating a very powerful Port Melbourne Slavia 4–2 in the final. Hakoah's goals against record in 1966, was remarkable, conceding only 24 goals in 22 matches. A record that stood unbroken until 1977, when the Hakoah defence then set a new all time, goals against in a season record, conceding only 20 goals in 22 matches. Again, much credit for this all time Hakoah record must go to Irish goalkeeper Mike O'Hara, who had a brilliant season.

Such was the strength of the 1966 Hakoah team that all time Hakoah great David Baker could not get a place in the team upon his arrival from England in 1966.

1967 saw Hakoah continue to break all previous Victorian State League records for goals against from the start of any season, when Hakoah played its first seven and a half league matches in 1967 without conceding one single goal during 677 minutes of match play. This record remains unbroken and is accepted by Football Federation Victoria as a current State League record to this day. This incredible defensive display finally ended, when Mike Jurecki of Port Melbourne Slavia, scored in the 48th minutes of the eighth round of the 1967 State league season.

The abrasive, abusive but brilliant goalkeeper, Mike O'Hara, left Hakoah over a pay dispute with club Chairman Johnny Chaskiel, following the 1968 pre-season Ampol Cup semi final defeat to Port Melbourne Slavia 1–0.

O'Hara left for Europe and was not seen again in Australia until 1969, after which, he was promptly signed by fellow State League club Port Melbourne Slavia, where O'Hara replaced the Czechoslovakian world cup final goalkeeper Willi Schroif. Hakoah regained the services of O'Hara a few years later.

Mike O'Hara's replacement in goal for Hakoah in 1968 was yet another experienced Scot, named Sandy Henderson, who proved to be a competent custodian and assisted Hakoah Melbourne to the last Australia Cup two leg final in 1968, where Hakoah Melbourne were convincingly beaten by Hakoah Sydney 3–1 and 3–0 in the two leg grand Final.

In 1978 following his return to Hakoah, O'Hara was again enticed away from the sky blues to join Footscray J.U.S.T. in the brand new Philips National Football League, but after only one season with the Yugoslavian club O'Hara was back in goal for his self stated 'Beloved Hakoah.' Mike O'Hara had played off and on with Hakoah Melbourne from March 1966 to the end of the 1980 season, and stands today only behind the great Steve Gadsby, David Baker, the late and great Alan Stenhouse, and Hugh 'Shug' Murney for most matches played for the Sky Blues. Mike O'Hara played a total of 126 matches for Hakoah and conceded 142 goals, finishing with a goal against average of 1.13 % per game.

Incredibly, in his last season with Hakoah in 1980, Mike O'Hara did it again, conceding only 24 goals in 22 league matches in a strong Hakoah team that finished an excellent 4th under the outstanding leadership of English coach Freddie Bunce. In its final season of 1981 as a sole entity, with Mike O'Hara gone to George Cross, Hakoah conceded an alarming 41 goals!

Hugh Murney was a brilliant teenage talent in Scotland for Queen of the South and Morton before joining Hakoah in 1964. Hugh Murney still remains the youngest captain in Scottish football history. Hugh Murney had eight memorable seasons with Hakoah and then coached Albion Rovers, Fitzroy-Alexander reserves, Heidelberg and was an outstanding coach of Park Rangers.

Hugh Murney also gave many years of his retirement as a player to the Hakoah Ajax and the Hakoah Maccabi Football clubs, where the 'character of characters' Hugh Murney gave his brilliant football knowledge to all who would listen, and through his dynamic personality a myriad of young players improved their game.

All past pundits and correspondents over considerable time in Australian football still cannot fathom the enigmatic mystery of why Hugh Murney, one of the best mid-fielders ever to play in the Victorian Football League and indeed Australia, was never selected either for his state or for his country.

Hakoah's Irish goalkeeper Mike O'Hara rated Hugh Murney as the fastest, most tenacious and skilful midfielder he ever played with.

During the golden sixties at Hakoah many world class players came and went from its ranks. This included a diminutive and quietly spoken Australian known to his team mates as Teddy Smith. Teddy, still alive and well in his eightieth year as this book goes to press, in fact was one of the select few who can boast of having represented Australia at football in the Olympic Games. It was in Melbourne in 1956, the only time Australia has contested an Olympic soccer tournament.

Hakoah is also the club that gave the great Jim Armstrong his start in Australian soccer. Jim Armstrong had three and a half great seasons with the sky blues before transferring to South Melbourne Hellas for a hefty $5000 dollar fee. Armstrong then went on to star for Juventus. Jim Armstrong who was capped for Australia, retired after scoring a State League record 152 goals. This record is still unbroken! Jim Armstrong remains a legend in Hakoah club history.

The likeable Scot Jim Armstrong was greatly admired by Hakoah keeper Mike O'Hara, who always ribbed Jim Armstrong for not being able to score a goal against him. Jim Armstrong of course being the Victorian State League's highest ever goalscorer! Even today, Armstrong, Murney and O'Hara, all in their seventies, come together for a drink and a meal whenever Mike O'Hara is in old Melbourne town.

After 35 years in the wilderness of muddy paddocks and primitive playing conditions, Hakoah at last found a permanent home at Middle Park, which was regarded as one of the finest soccer stadiums in Australia in 1966.

The ground was built after a grant was negotiated between the club administration and the local government of the time. From a dream, the club was able to build a ground accommodating 25,000 spectators on a playing surface that stayed in perfect condition no matter what the weather.

A grandstand was also built to seat 5,000 spectators under cover with plans to extend into the concrete terraces at a later time.

A clubhouse was also built for social functions, and excellent facilities were also provided for visiting clubs, referees and the press.

In addition a spacious car-park was provided and South Melbourne Hellas were later invited to share the facilities because Hakoah felt it could benefit in many ways, from a share ground arrangement.

The integral people involved in establishing the ground were the club's Board of Trustees led by the visionary Kurt Defris and senator P. J. Kennelly, who was made a Patron of the club and who was at the time the Chairman of the Albert Park Committee of Management. His generosity and involvement in seeing Hakoah succeed was seen as a defining moment for the club.

The club continually had a history of people who made sacrifices for the club in the most amazing ways. They worked for it and fought for it, both on and off the field with their hearts and their souls and their pockets.

In the annual report presented by Kurt Defris at the end of Season 1966, Mr. Defris described the year as one of promise and a year in which the club came close to recapturing all of its former glories.

In that same year of 1966, Hakoah's Victorian State League goals against record of only 24 goals conceded in 22 matches was and remains to this day the third best Hakoah defence record in the history of the club from 1927 to 1981.

Ironically the best ever defensive record ever achieved by any Hakoah team in the clubs entire history was in 1977, the same season evergreen club captain David Baker won his second Best and Fairest Victorian State League medal.

In that same season of 1977 Hakoah finished a lowly ninth of twelve teams in the Victorian State League, winning only 4 games all season and struggled to find the net regularly, scoring only 16 goals in the process!

Nevertheless the 'padlock' Hakoah defence with Irish keeper Mike O'Hara and David Baker outstanding, conceded only 20 goals in 22 matches. O'Hara for his brilliance in the Hakoah goal all season was selected to represent Victoria State against the English First Division giants Middlesbrough at seasons close, and was named best Victorian goalkeeper of the season in 1977 by the late and great Scot, Les Shorrock, the Soccer News Chief Sports reporter. David Baker was also selected for the Victorian State team against Middlesbrough in 1977.

Reverting back to the creation of the fabulous 66–67–68 Hakoah Juggernaut, Hakoah missed reaching the pre-season Ampol Cup semi-finals on goal difference and then after a disappointing start to the season, changes were brought about which led to the run of success in 66–67 and 68.

Hakoah's past coaches have included some of the foremost names in soccer – Asa Robbins, John Kursweil, Dave McIntosh, Tom Jack, Manny Poulakakis, Jim Adam, Mike Mandelis, Milenko Rusmir, Sam Meyer and Frank Micic.

Mr Manny Poulakakis was appointed coach of the senior team for 1966. New players including Dick Van Alphen, Jimmy Armstrong, Keith Fry and Mike O'Hara were brought into the team and Alex Purdie returned after a long injury absence. This was a time when Hakoah's longest serving player in history David Baker, newly arrived from England in 1966, could not get a first team game with Hakoah!

Under the astute leadership of super coach Manny Poulakakis, Hakoah then began a remarkable climb up the ladder and finished a record third with ten wins for the season and as already stated conceded only 24 goals in the 22 match league season.

At the end of the 1966 season, Hakoah had finished only three wins behind the State League champions and won the coveted Dockerty Cup defeating hot favourites Port Melbourne Slavia in the final 4–2, to win the trophy again for the first time in ten years. Hakoah won the Dockerty Cup eight times in all. This was their seventh win.

Hakoah also competed in the Australia Cup series in 1968, and reached the final, but without star keeper Mike O'Hara who had had an altercation with the Hakoah committee chairman John Chaskiel and walked out. The likeable and capable Sandy Henderson, a talented Scottish goalkeeper filled the breach admirably however and later coached the Sky Blues.

The squad in 1966 consisted of Mike O'Hara 'Mad Mick' in goal, full backs George 'Dick' Keith and Jim O'Neil, half backs Hugh Murney, Dick Van Alphen and Alan Stenhouse and forwards Keith Fry, Jimmy Armstrong, Ian Monan, Teddy Smith and Alex Purdie.

The reserves included John Walker, utility defenders Doug Rogers, David Baker, utility forwards Jim O'Neil, Marko Pejovic and Ian Gow. During season 1966, talented Israeli player, Gerri Chaldi returned to Israel.

1966 was indeed a triumphant year for Hakoah Football Club. The dynamic and hardworking Mr. Fred Hutchison was responsible for team fitness and team management and Mike O'Hara and John O'Neill were selected to represent Victoria against leading Italian touring team AS Roma.

The club had an experimental policy aimed at developing juniors through the reserves, with the aim of replacing imported players in the senior team with home grown players.

The reserves in 1966 included players from the juniors and Hakoah–Ajax and with this new system finished a creditable seventh and gave the committee encouragement to continue this recruitment system.

The reserve team also reached the semi-finals of the Harry Armstrong Reserve Cup competition, in which after a scoreless draw they were beaten by Croatia in the replay.

In this game veteran Bill Rowley, sustained an ankle injury which ended his career.

Mr. Harry Sutherland completed his tenth year as Manager-Coach of the reserves after serving the club as an outstanding and popular player. His loyalty to the club was unequalled.

Another ex-player, Ken Waugh, was also involved as an assistant to Harry Sutherland in the reserves.

At the end of the 1966 season, Dr Henry Baytch retired as president of the club and he was replaced by prominent business personality, Mr. George Weinberg.

A common theme throughout the mid 1960s was Hakoah's determination to build its youth program and reserve teams into competitive units. The club was determined to build for the future and by doing this it placed great emphasis on youth and depth.

Season 1967, was the fortieth year of the clubs existence. By this stage, Hakoah had claimed every major honour in the game and had some of the games greatest personalities in its ranks.

At this stage the club was successfully coordinating an excellent working committee with an enthusiastic, talented and strong combination of on-field talent.

The first team was definitely an unashamed effort to buy success, but behind that squad was the depth and commitment of the younger players and a committed coaching staff.

Prior to the 1966 and 1967 record breaking sky blues seasons, the early sixties up to 1965 saw the club struggle at the foot of the table, and 1965 saw Hakoah winning only 3 games in their first ten! Leaving the club at the wrong end of the ladder in 3rd last place!

CHAPTER SIX

Boom or Bust

Hakoah Melbourne Football Club had now been established for over thirty years and its achievements had been seen by other clubs as a bench mark.

A remarkable number of players from Hakoah had regularly been drawn to represent Victoria and Australia and the standards the club set were always very high.

In 1963 the club had surprisingly only escaped relegation by a single point, but typically the club's wise and courageous administrators did not despair as they set about rebuilding the first team squad.

After the unprecedented heady successes the club had achieved in the 1950s, the club began to realise that it could not dwell on the past and it needed to rebuild its team otherwise risk being left behind as the standard of other Victorian soccer clubs began to rise.

Hakoah's administration set out to rebuild and the task was a long and difficult one. Throughout 1964 and 1965 the job went on. In 1966, as already stated the club was again chasing the pace-setters and finished third in the league as well as winning the Dockerty Cup for a record seventh time.

During the rebuilding phase, many players were brought in and tried. Some failed to hold their places, others returned overseas or retired through injury.

The Hakoah club, at its peak in the mid to latter part of the 1960s had players on its books that were, and still are today, considered some of the most famous names in Australian soccer history.

They include, Mike O'Hara (Republic of Ireland), George Keith (Scotland), John O'Neill (Captain) (Republic of Ireland), Hugh 'Shug' Murney (Scotland), Dick Van Alphen (Netherlands), Alan Stenhouse (Vice-Captain) (Scotland), Keith Fry (England), Jimmy Armstrong (Scotland), Ian Monan (Scotland), Johnny Anderson (Scotland), Teddy Smith (Australia), Alex Purdie (Scotland), David Baker (England), and Hans Petersen (Netherlands).

The story of Hugh 'Shug' Murney is a most interesting one as he arrived from Scotland in 1964, as an ex-Celtic player with excellent credentials.

His career later saw him being named as one of the players of the decade in the mid 1970s and his effect on the club and the game was truly inspiring.

As already stated, 1966 saw the debut of two brilliantly talented 19-year-olds in Jim Armstrong and Mike O'Hara. Then David Baker became the third world class recruit, making his league debut in 1967. All three players went on to have very distinguished careers in Australian football.

The Hakoah club coach, the late Mr Manny Poulakakis is remembered as a legend, a man of vision and great depth of thought, and considered at the time to be Victoria's top coach. Following his departure from the sky blues Manny Poulakakis coached South Melbourne Hellas to three championships and was coach of the successful Sydney Hakoah team for two years. He was one of the most personable men of his time.

In 1966, the Hakoah club was attracting as many as 9000 spectators to games such as the one against South Melbourne Hellas in April 1966. A gate that exceeded some League One and League Two clubs playing today in the English Football League!

The club at the time was very systematic and far-sighted in its visions of the future. While the senior team was made up of players predominantly recruited from Scotland, and the UK, the reserve team aimed to nurture the finest young talent it could possibly obtain.

Individuals were coached and nurtured through the reserves and a professional approach to educating players about the technical aspects and team work required by the club was seen as an approach that would make Hakoah powerful for many years to come.

The Champion of Champions club as Hakoah was known during the 1950s was looking to establish itself again as the best club in the country.

In 1970, the club sold Jim Armstrong to South Melbourne Hellas, after having established him as one of the best strikers in Australia.

Legendary Hakoah stalwart Hugh Murney was sold to Lions, in the same year.

Those two aforementioned transfers proved to be the beginning of a more difficult time in the clubs history as the rampaging team of the '60s began to disintegrate.

In 1971, the club finished fourth last, which was an inglorious result for a club with such a proud pedigree. Hakoah clearly lacked depth, but unearthed a prolific goal scorer in the form of Mike Clarey from England in 1971. But even with Mike Clarey in its ranks the sky blues never again found the magic that was created in the golden era of the mid sixties.

Late in 1971, Israel's national team toured Australia for a series of friendly matches against Australia. One of the players in that tour party was a twenty-four-year-old forward named Yehoshua Faigenbaum who was a player with Hapoel Tel Aviv. In 1977, Faigenbaum, was persuaded to join Hakoah along with Shraga Topolonski.

CHAPTER SEVEN

The Death of a Legend

In 1977, Hakoah Melbourne had a disappointing season, finishing ninth in the first year of a weakened Victorian State League that had been ravaged by the disappearance of several Victorian clubs that had joined the Philips National Football League.

Hakoah's problems were compounded when their star keeper Mike O'Hara was enticed to join Footscray J.U.S.T. Soccer Club in the newly formed National Football League.

A small playing staff and a change of coach mid-season did not help matters and the season ended dismally for the once great Hakoah. Hakoah, however, did salvage something from the 1977 season when the club had the gratification of seeing one of its ever present players David Baker, win the Rothman's Victorian State League Best & Fairest Medal for a second time, and another player, Mick Rainey, won a newspaper's best player award.

At this time in the clubs history, the club was being run on a very small shoestring budget and was having great trouble in retaining existing players and attracting high calibre new players due in major part to the devastation caused on the Victorian State League by the formation of the Philips National League.

The club however, true to its history was innovative until the very end. This was shown by a bid to try and woo back members of the Jewish community to its games. To this end Hakoah experimented in

1978 with the import of two former Israeli international players to its playing staff.

Hakoah in fact in 1978, was playing its last roll of the dice in a desperate effort to try and bridge the gap between its club ambitions and the lack of connection with the Jewish community, which had been the hallmark of its success in the post war years, but which now was virtually non-existent, and had to be somehow resurrected.

In the 51 years of its existence in 1978, the main aim of the club had been to keep the traditional name of Hakoah as the symbol of Jewish sports activity in Melbourne. Hakoah was justifiably proud of being the only Jewish sponsored soccer club in Melbourne.

The club was now struggling to avoid relegation in its final years which was a great indignity to a club which had until then had such a proud and successful history.

Hakoah was now only considered by its opponents and the sports commentators of the day to be a middle of the road Victorian State League club that only had a 'feather duster' attack that struggled to score goals. Yet despite this weakness in attack, Hakoah still continued to turn out a team with an impeccable defence and tenacious midfield. The Hakoah defence in 1977 finished the season with the clubs best goals against record in its history, despite finishing well down the table, thanks in major part to the return of Irish keeper Mike O'Hara from Footscray J.U.S.T. and the brilliance of central defender David Baker. For his performance in the Hakoah goal in 1977 the Dublin born Irishman was voted goalkeeper of the season by the Melbourne press and selected for the Victorian State team that played English First Division club Middlesbrough at the close of 1977.

Despite these individual highlights, the clubs problems were further exacerbated by the lack of spectator support due to the more glamorous attraction of the new Philips National League.

While the Hakoah club still saw itself as a proud symbol of Jewish sport and was still very much seen as such by the general Melbourne community, it was having trouble attracting members of the community to watch its games. By now the clubs glamour had well and truly eroded within the community, and to make matters worse the younger supporters that the club were endeavouring to win back, were being swayed in numbers to Australian Rules Football as never before.

Kurt Defris was the longest serving of the current administrators at this time, but there are others who deserve special mention. John Chaskiel, for example, had been chairman of Hakoah for 10 years and Kadish Korman had been vice-president and treasurer for almost as long. Jack Skolnik was one of the strongest early presidents. Other prominent Hakoah leaders included Vic Gross, Eric Erdi, Dr Henry Baytch who became a life member of the Victorian Soccer Federation and of course the current VSF Chairman, Michael Weinstein, who was still on Hakoah's committee.

The clubs declining years from 1977 to its final demise in 1981 was a sad time for many who had represented Hakoah in a myriad of different ways over considerable time. A truly great football club since 1927, Hakoah Melbourne Football Club was to become only a glorious memory of the past for the younger Jewish population emerging into adolescence and ultimate adulthood in Melbourne.

There still existed however, the hard blue blood Jewish and non Jewish supporters who held on until the very end. If the club had been successful at this time, it still would not have ensured the clubs survival because the simple fact was that the community the club aspired to attract to its games simply had no interest in the club, whether it was winning or losing.

That in essence was the greatest sadness!

In 1980, the club held a testimonial game for David Baker at Middle Park. An all-star line-up assembled to pay tribute to the man who had become one of the most respected players the Victorian State league had ever seen.

Well known players like Jim Mackay, Jim Armstrong, Ray Pocock and Ged Bannon were amongst some of the players that came to pay tribute to David Baker.

David Baker was in fact the epitomy of the true professional footballer, true to his club for the total duration of his lengthy football career. David Baker had given fourteen years of his life in soccer to Hakoah Melbourne Football Club. His remarkable effort for the sky blues over this time reflected the fact that David Baker had given his heart, soul and total commitment to a club that he truly loved and respected! David Baker had started with the club in 1966 and played for fourteen consecutive seasons, relatively injury free until 1980.

With his two Rothman's Best & Fairest medals in 1975 and 1977 and more than 153 games for the club, he was the most respected individual anyone could ever wish to have play for their club. He was Mr. Reliable in the Hakoah defence and stood tall marshalling his team from the sweeper's position in fine style.

His competitiveness and fairness was truly exemplary. He rarely conceded any fouls on opponents, never lost his temper and was probably one of the most competitive players ever to play the game. He was an inspiration to anyone who ever came close to him.

The club was briefly rejuvenated again in 1980, with the introduction of universally respected Fred Bunce the former Watford UK player as coach. The depth of the team at youth level was astounding in the previous year, with the Under 19's winning the championship against teams like Juventus and South Melbourne Hellas. The club failed however to allow the majority of these talented youth players make the transition to the higher level of the first and second grade teams, and instead chose to persist with imported veterans who did not provide any scope for the teams future development.

Instead the committee again chose the import route and brought to Hakoah two new recruits from Scotland in Richard McLunie and Stan Webster, both strikers.

Chris Kent was also retained as a bigger than normal money player.

Hakoah lost its Dockerty Cup semi-final to Croatia 6–1 in September 1980.

The team was: Mike O'Hara, Sean Rooney, (David Baker), Steve Gadsby, Anton Dosen, Gerry Edmondson, Jed Bannon, Ian McNeill, Stewart Blair, Bill Jordanou, Graham French and Chris Kent.

After this match veteran Hakoah keeper Mike O'Hara confided to Soccer News chief reporter Les Shorrock, and quote, 'This is only a shadow of the Hakoah I used to know.'

In early 1981, Hakoah's evergreen goalkeeper Mike O'Hara left Hakoah for the last time, signing for Victorian State League club George Cross. Mike O'Hara's transfer to George Cross was due to an issue with Hakoah's new coach Bill Allison who had taken over from former Watford and Ringwood City Wilhelmina star Freddie Bunce, who had himself resigned after a dispute with Hakoah Chairman, Dennis Krongold.

In 1980, the Hakoah reserve team won the Victorian State League Reserve Championship with the depth in the club huge, and eighteen senior squad members.

Hakoah Melbourne Football Clubs last season in the Victorian State League in 1981 as a sole Jewish entity saw the club finish 7th in the 12 team table conceding 41 goals in the process. On record the highest goals against statistic in the clubs history! The last match Hakoah Soccer Club ever played as a sole entity in its own right, was against Sunshine City on September 6, 1981 at Chaplin Reserve Sunshine, in the final round 22 of the 1981 Victorian State League season. Hakoah lost the last match it ever played 0–1.

So history now records the last team Hakoah ever fielded. It was: David Slack, Danny Davidson, Bill Jordanou [Les Nagy 82], George Hannah, Sean Rooney, Les Thomson, Graham French, Jimmy Wilson, Steve Gadsby [Colin Allison 58], Stan Webster. The Coach was Bill Allison.

The magnificence of fifty four years had gone forever.

On November 28th 1981, Hakoah announced that it had merged with South Melbourne Hellas to form a second team for South Melbourne Hellas which would compete in the State League and act as a feeder club to the South Melbourne national league team.

On November 28th 1981, at one second past midnight, Hakoah Melbourne Association Football Club failed to exist! It was but an illustrious memory!

The price paid for 54 years of history was $35,000! The merger had been an ongoing elongated affair between the two co-tenants of Middle Park from the middle of the 1981 season.

The two great clubs had shared Middle Park from 1961 until 1981 on equal terms, but now Hakoah had sighted financial deficit and lack of crowd support as the two prime reasons for the amalgamation of the club, which was forced to accept the offer from South Melbourne Hellas. With considerable hindsight, no blame could be laid upon those responsible, given the unprecedented situation that these men had to deal with. And the old Hebrew observation rang true, 'Creditors don't wait, they just take so be the creditor.' Unfortunately, Hakoah Football Club was not the creditor, and so the history book of arguably the greatest club in Victorian Football was closed forever!

The Hakoah squad that had competed in the final 'All Hakoah' 1981 season consisted of: Fryzer, Slack, Davidson, Hannah, Jordanou, Thomson, Gadsby, Nagy, Rooney, Wilson, French, Kent, Allison, McLunie and Webster. The coach was Bill Allison.

Ironically, one of Hakoah's final matches prior to its dissolution in late 1981 was against George Cross, where Hakoah's greatest post war keeper ever, Mike O'Hara resided. Mike O'Hara as history now records had the last word, with his team George Cross defeating his 'beloved Hakoah' 2–1.

When the club merged with South Melbourne Hellas at the start of 1982, an important era ended in Jewish sport in this country, as the merger was more a takeover than a merger, as is often the case in a cruel corporate and sporting climate. In any event, the history of the proud Hakoah Soccer Club was lost forever. But the magnificent memories were not!

In the years between 1965 and 1982, Hakoah's history was proudly displayed for all to see in its clubrooms at Middle Park.

All club pennants and pictures were hung on the walls for all to see. Jewish news and other press clippings were carefully cut out and framed, proudly hanging on the walls for all spectators and club visitors to see. It was a veritable pictorial history of the once mighty Hakoah Soccer Club.

Mysteriously in 1982, soon after the merger was announced, a fire wiped out the old Hakoah clubrooms and the clubs history was lost forever. No one had taken responsibility for the priceless historical history of the club to be collected. Consequently this valuable historical memorabilia was lost to all future Jewish generations.

Hakoah had shared the Middle Park ground for twenty years in 1981 with South Melbourne Hellas and as the South Melbourne team continued to advance with the support of the Greek community, Hakoah simply sank into oblivion!

Kurt Defris did what he considered to be 'the only honourable thing' when he came to terms with Hellas. And so Hellas–Hakoah soccer club was born into the Victorian State League in late 1981.

'Everyone could see that the writing was on the wall,' said Defris, a reference to Hakoah's overdraft and guarantees totalling $48,000. 'We have done what we could in the past 55 years. The interest in Hakoah Soccer Club no longer is there. At least we have kept the name "Hakoah" flying in soccer circles. The Greek people have treated us almost like brothers. It took us a few months, in fact about a year, to convince our people that we wouldn't be eaten up by a merger. I'm a man who goes with the times and it would have hurt me had we gone out with a bang by being declared bankrupt. For us, amalgamation was the only solution, the only honourable thing we could do.'

The new club was headed by President Jim Diamataris. John Chaskiel, a long standing Hakoah committeeman, and Peter Dourin, were vice-presidents. Chris Papas was treasurer and the general committee numbered 14. Kurt Defris was voted secretary-manager, continuing an unbroken administrative connection with Hakoah, which started in 1947, a unique record in Australia.

At 73 Kurt Defris remained active and alert. His ability to analyse, debate and influence was invaluable over countless committee meetings in a variety of sports. Honoured by the Order of Australia in 1978, life membership of the Victorian Soccer Federation and the Victorian

Table Tennis Association and life presidency of the Victorian Ice Hockey Association, his record is a monument to successful sports administration.

The young Kurt Defris was a dashing winger in the Austrian First Division. His proudest playing days were in 1931 when he was transferred for about $A20,000 from Fair Unitas to the famous Hakoah–Vienna club. During the Second World War he escaped Hitler's persecution of Jews by fleeing to Shanghai in China. There he became chairman of the Jewish Recreation Club which boasted about 20 clubs in the Jewish Soccer League and some 6,000 registered players.

In 1946 he came to Australia and played about half of the 1947 season with Hakoah before taking up an administrative post. Kurt Defris also excelled at table tennis. During his stay in Austria he ranked consistently in the top 10 in the country and was a national representative. His wife was ranked number three in the world after the 1936 world championships. His success and knowledge as a player in both soccer and table tennis were integral to his success as an administrator in these sports. Kurt Defris saw about ten Hakoah presidents come and go, among them Jack Skolnik, Dr Henry Baytch, Les Erdi, Victor Gross, Ned Spicer, Manny Unreich and Dennis Krongold. Kurt Defris greatly admired the first president of Hakoah, Jack Shatin, and valued his friendship with Fred Halpern, Michael Weinstein, John Chaskiel, Kadish Korman, Fred Weider. Henry Greenfield, Dr Ian Kaufman, Henry Fromer, the young budding lawyer Peter Pryles and innumerable former Hakoah committeemen and supporters.

Kurt Defris was a pragmatist in the classic mould. He could reminisce about the former greatness of Hakoah then suddenly spring back to the modern day, candidly outlining the reasons behind the club's increasing economic hardship and eventual amalgamation. Not for him simply fond memories. Hakoah survived under the unstoppable, unflappable Kurt Defris.

The words that follow from Kurt Defris AM, have the same resonance today as the day he uttered them in 1981, read on:

'For years now we have relied upon the backing of the Jewish business community,' he often said. 'Up until about 1965 we were one of the best supported clubs in Victoria but our support dwindled quickly. The old guard died, their descendants didn't become interested in soccer because of the diverse interests prevalent in modern day youth, and the competitiveness of Australian Rules Football. In a way we contributed to our own demise because we neglected our juniors until recently.'

'When I came to Hakoah we played at Royal Park, then we moved to Fawkner Park. Our next home ground was near the Exhibition Buildings and then we became the first club to play at Olympic Park. That was before the stadium was built. In the '50s we played at St Kevins Oval in Toorak until a successful propaganda campaign was carried out by a leading Melbourne radio personality who didn't want to see diverse ethnic groups playing soccer in Toorak. In 1958 we returned to Olympic Park and in 1961 we moved to Albert Park.'

Slowly but surely, stone by stone, the Middle Park stadium evolved. We are indebted to the late Senator Pat Kennelly who was our patron and chairman of the Albert Park Trust. He was instrumental in building our stadium. Of course, we shared the ground with Hellas and I want to stress that there has never been the slightest clash over the use of the ground. And the players I have seen over the years! Who could ever forget them? Players like Hugh Murney, Jim Armstrong, The clown prince Mike O'Hara, Harry Sutherland, Harry Roessler, Jacky Roessler, Joe Gottesman and of course our most famous captains, Tom Jack and John O'Neill. Dick van Alphen, Dave McIntosh and Milan Vesovic are others who readily come to mind. Gentlemen all, and from time to time they come back to watch Hakoah. You know I estimate that maybe 60 per cent of our players finished their careers with us. That says something good about them and about our club, eh?'

Those were the words of one of the greatest Jews who was ever directed by Yahuah to live on this earth. To Mr Kurt Defris AM, all Australian Jews and non Jews alike involved in sport are deeply indebted.

Thousands of Victorian soccer followers, Jews and non Jews, are acquainted with the sight of the diminutive Kurt Defris walking along the touchline with his trusty fold up chair, endeavouring to select a good vantage point just seconds before the kickoff of a Hakoah match. The analogy between that sight and the 'Peanuts' cartoon character Linus with his security blanket in tow is irresistible. That chair could well have joined Hakoah around about the same time as Kurt Defris. Just as the chair is symbolic of the man, the man himself symbolises everything we know as Hakoah Association Football Club.

Sport for most human beings is leisure. For Kurt Defris it was beyond a shadow of a doubt his total life commitment.

CHAPTER EIGHT

The Formation of Maccabi

The Maccabi club evolved from the Hakoah Ajax club that was affiliated with Hakoah Melbourne until 1977.

Season 1999 marked the 21st year of the Maccabi–Hakoah Soccer Clubs existence. The club was created in 1978 by a small group of Jewish players with a passion for the game and through these men the club flourished to become a club which is still competing and progressing through Football Federation Victoria.

In 1976, a group of young Jewish soccer players decided to form a Jewish soccer team. The decision to form a team was inspired by a number of ex-Mount Scopus College boys who had completed their High School education in 1975 and were determined to try and keep their team together after two successful years of interschool competition at Mount Scopus.

Amongst these players were such names as David Efron, Michael 'Dixie' Diamond, Morrie Kalkopf and Alex Zwier. They later recruited players from Yeshivah College which included David 'Boobie' Kraus, Dov Paneth and Harry Greenberg amongst others. The formation of the two school sides then went on to become the nucleus of Hakoah–Ajax Thirds which then soon after became Maccabi–Hakoah in 1978.

In the formation of Maccabi–Hakoah, two people were most instrumental in forming the team. Henry Zelman, who was a dedicated soccer player all his life, recruited Danny Fridman from the State

League and with the talent and enthusiasm of these ex-collegians, they formed a strong club with its own strong Jewish identity, which was a success from the start.

Larry Goldman joined the club as the first club President and the club was on its way. Amongst the early legendary players were names like David 'Boobie' Kraus, Michael 'Dixie' Diamond, Robbie Roth, Morrie Kalkopf, David Efron, Bradley Wein, Alex Zwier, Stephen Bloch, Jonathan Munz, Max Lichtenbaum and Philip Serry.

The club thrived on brotherly camaraderie and spirit, which flowed throughout the complete squad. There were no major sponsors or huge budgets. The club was built on the back of players who really had a passion for the game and were all willing to do whatever was necessary for the club, whether it was menial tasks like washing shirts or line-marking grounds. There was never any shortage of participants willing to help out for the good of the club.

Maccabi–Hakoah commenced its playing life in the Industrial League before becoming a foundation member of the Amateur League in 1979. In 1980, the club dominated the competition, often recording double figure scores against its opponents. The club finished runners-up in the league in 1980, missing out only on goal difference but they won the Amateur League Cup defeating Meadow Park in front of a large crowd at Olympic Park.

One of the most amusing moments in the clubs history was when the club won the Amateur Cup in 1980. This game was a curtain raiser game to the Dockerty Cup final at Olympic Park. After winning the game the trophy was awarded to Danny Fridman, as club captain. After Danny received the trophy, his first reaction was to hold the trophy aloft and as he did so he was greeted by an almighty cheer from the 20,000 crowd, who were simultaneously cheering Melbourne Croatia onto the ground for the start of the main game, being the 1980 Dockerty Cup Final. What was amusing was that Danny didn't realise what the crowd was cheering for, as he thought that Maccabi had won the crowd over with their greatest ever display and this great moment of glory for the club.

After the excellence of 1980, Maccabi–Hakoah continued in the same vein, by winning in 1981 no fewer than three major trophies in the one season. The club was dramatically strengthened in 1981 with the arrival of Clive Barrett who was probably the best player the club had at that time, as well as being the clubs first South African born player. His inclusion to an already powerful line-up saw the club win the Championship in the Amateur League Division One with 40 out of a possible 42 points. The Victorian Amateur Club Championship included victories over Bendigo College 2–0, and the Amateur Club Cup defeating Kooyong Rangers 3–1.

A truly remarkable achievement by any standard!

In 1984, the strength of Jewish Soccer was so strong that with the vision and influence of Henry Fromer, it was decided to split the Maccabi–Hakoah club into Maccabi and Hakoah. This brought about the establishment of a Hakoah team with great ambition to push the club into the higher leagues and revive the glory years of the former Hakoah.

At its peak, the Hakoah and Maccabi teams would have had about 80–90 registered Jewish soccer players between them. In 1986, the Hakoah team won the championship of Provisional League Division Two. In the same year, Steven Freund won Amateur League Player of the Year with Maccabi.

The Maccabi club, like their illustrious predecessor Hakoah Melbourne, went through a difficult time after it had reached its peak, when in the late 1980s a shortage of players almost saw the club dissolve. During this traumatic period it was the incredible hard work of captain coach Stephen Pugh that kept the club alive when player numbers were in sharp decline.

The club managed to survive and went on to greater glories including a sensational first time ever win over NSW Maccabi in a carnival competition on the Gold Coast in 1990/91. This was a time when nothing was left to chance in the clubs total commitment to win a carnival gold medal. A win against Sydney had continually eluded the club for its whole history. No expense was spared including the flying in and out of Stephen Bloch for two games from Melbourne-Gold Coast during the carnival, because Stephen Bloch was unable to stay with the team for the complete carnival due to work commitments.

This carnival victory along with another back to back victory, that included a come from behind equalising goal against NSW, in Melbourne, in 1991–92 were among the finest moments the club ever experienced.

In recent years, the club has been going through an extensive re-building phase.

As many players from Israel, Russia and South Africa have come into the team and many of the older players have been forced to retire. Because of these factors the club culture and playing style has changed.

As the club now competes into the new century, it is an ideal time to reflect on the best team of the past, which includes many current players.

Maccabi Victoria senior team
best ever all star line-up (1978–2016)

	Phil Serry		
Michael Diamond	Boris Seroshtan	Bradley Wein	Greig Rabinowitz
Fima Gulko	Eddie Zolotarev	Clive Barrett	Stephen Bloch
	Andrew Freund	Justin Scrobogna	

Best coach: Danny Fridman

Whilst many outstanding players are not included in this all time best Victoria Maccabi line up, it is simply because of the extreme difficulty in determining who was best at what he did and the success that came from it during that period. With the line of difference being infinitesimal

Exclusion of great players like Simeonne Pollack, David Carrick, Henry Zelman, Jonathan Munz, Martin Fromer, Max Lichtenbaum, Nathi Aroni, the Meleck brothers and Steven Freund, takes nothing away from these Jewish heroes, all of whom assisted in making Maccabi Victoria a first class football team.

In 1995, the squad included, Andrew Freund, Greig Rabinowitz, Eddie Zolotarev and Zvi Kalb. Jonathan Munz effectively moved to President, with Harvey Silver taking a lesser role on the committee. Hugh 'Shug' Murney continued as seniors coach.

Today, Maccabi has teams competing in age groups ranging from 7–15. The senior club has more than sixty players to choose from for its Firsts, Reserves and Thirds. There is a feeling from within the club that the best years of the club are yet to come, with the influx of new immigrants from South Africa, many Israeli players and a number of talented young junior players rising through the ranks.

The club owes a great deal of gratitude to its generous former benefactor Jonathan Munz, who allowed the respective club committees to focus on improving the levels of talent within the club whilst removing the financial challenges from outside.

The future looks extremely promising for the Maccabi Soccer Club in the next 3–5 years and the challenge is there for everyone connected with the club to take the club to a higher glory.

CHAPTER NINE

Maccabi–Hakoah: The transformation

In 1983, two players arrived at the club who have had a profound influence on it ever since.

Whilst arriving from different countries, with different aims and ambitions at different stages of their lives, they nevertheless both combined to form the nucleus of a successful drive towards a more ambitious level of soccer for Maccabi Victoria Football Club.

The two players were Michael Sher and Fima Gulko.

After the 1983 season which saw Maccabi–Hakoah finish third in the Amateur League, a decision was made to form two Jewish teams with distinctly different ambitions.

One was to be called St Kilda Hakoah, in a bid to revive the glory years of the old Hakoah team, whose history was tragically removed after the sale of the club to South Melbourne Hellas in late 1981 and the ensuing fire that destroyed its clubrooms.

The other team would be called simply Maccabi and would remain a Sunday club, less ambitious, but nevertheless proud of its standing success and staunchly committed to the religious ideals of only playing on Sundays with an all Jewish team.

The ambition of St Kilda Hakoah in 1984 was fostered by the enthusiasm of its new club president, Mr. Henry Fromer and the incredible depth which was now available in playing personnel.

St Kilda Hakoah began its new life in Provisional League Division

Four, while Maccabi remained in the Amateur League in 1984. Michael Sher and Fima Gulko were magnificent in their endeavours in a season which saw the club challenging for top place most of the season.

One of the lowest points in Jewish soccer history happened in 1984, when the Meleck brothers were given lengthy suspensions after assaulting the referee one afternoon at Middle Park against Monbulk.

Wild scenes erupted late in the game when the referee sent a second St Kilda Hakoah player from the ground with 15 minutes remaining.

St Kilda Hakoah was losing 2–0 midway through the first half, when Shimon Melek was sent off and the team with ten men looked in a hopeless position.

In the second half, St Kilda Hakoah looked a vastly improved team, but its inability to finish and questionable refereeing decisions added to the team's frustrations late in the game. St Kilda Hakoah finally managed to open its account, and with fifteen minutes left, Ronny Sher hit the cross bar with a fierce shot and John Munz missed the easy rebound.

Tensions then erupted when Michael Sher was sent off the ground for no observable reason, reducing St Kilda Hakoah to nine men. Players and spectators reacted with a barrage of abuse and threats and the situation was further aggravated by an incident involving Moshe Melek behind play.

The referee promptly left the field followed by several outraged and hostile St Kilda Hakoah players and the game remained incomplete at 2–1 in Monbulk's favour.

The infamous incident, remembered by those who witnessed the event, as the 'Monbulk Fiasco' involved a central agitator, Moshe Melek in one of his infamously bad tempered tantrums that saw him manhandle the referee, and threaten to kill him if he didn't restart the match. As an all in brawl broke out, Shimon Melek, who had previously been sent off, came into the centre of the ground to defend his brother, grabbing a corner flag as a weapon on his way to the melee, and also threatened to kill the referee if he decided to continue with his intention to abandon the game.

Brothers Shimon and Moshe Melek were suspended from all competitions in Australia until December 1987 and December 1985 respectively after being found guilty of assaulting the referee.

The suspensions at the time were unbelievably heavy and led to further controversy at the Perth Carnival which was held in 1984–85.

In light of the suspension handed down to the Melek brothers, NSW had refused to allow Victoria to select Moshe Melek in its carnival team. In response, the Victorian team as one, threatened to boycott the carnival which was going to be used as the selection trial for the Maccabiah games in 1985.

Victoria was finally forced to drop Moshe Melek from its squad and went on to Perth losing to NSW in an all too familiar fashion, by the odd goal 1–2.

After returning from the carnival in excellent form St Kilda Hakoah players began the 1985 season solidly and posted some excellent results.

The name 'Hakoah' was well and truly alive again as the team began a new era in professionalism and enthusiasm under the guidance of a former Hakoah State League coach Bill Allison.

It was only the second full season that the club had played together. Hakoah finished in a creditable mid table position and set themselves up for a challenge at the league title which was to follow in 1986.

In 1986, it all came together for St Kilda Hakoah. Moshe Melek returned from suspension, Michael Sher returned after a serious knee injury and the team had an incredible depth of young and experienced talent.

Michael Sher was on fire all season, scoring freely and in the process recording several hat tricks in a 23 goal scoring spree season!

Members of the squad were: Fima Gulko (Captain), Simeon Pollack (Vice-Captain), Moshe Melek, Chaim Rozanski, Michael Sher, Leonid Braude, Ron Sher, Phillip Serry, Danny Klotz, Jonathan Munz, Alon Cohen, Max Lichtenbaum, Martin Fromer, Ronni Avni, Avi Ezra, Boris Tsun. Coach: Bill Allison.

At seasons close, St Kilda Hakoah had played 26 games, won 17 of them, drawn 7, and lost only 2. Scoring 56 goals and conceding only 25.

Michael Sher scored 23 goals and Leonid Braude scored 10. In the same year Steven Freund won player of the season at Maccabi.

This was truly the Hakoah ghost of the past now back in full cry!

The season was a personal milestone for Michael Sher and an extremely gratifying experience for Henry Fromer, who had almost single handedly created the team and took justifiable great pride and satisfaction in seeing his burning ambition fulfilled. The St Kilda Hakoah squad was then further strengthened prior to the 1987 season with the arrival of well recommended Eddie Zolotarev and Nathi Aroni.

Maccabi Australia interstate carnival history

This report includes the Bernie Gold article dated 5th September 2002.

It took 22 years to achieve, but the world game known globally as Association football (originally and incorrectly dubbed as soccer by the United States gridiron football fraternity to eliminate public confusion with its own code) eventually came to fruition and became part of Australia's regular Maccabi sports carnivals as an invitation event in 1976–77.

Historical records show an Interstate Jewish soccer challenge match was played as far back as 1929 between NSW and Victoria in Sydney which was won by NSW and two matches were played in January 1947 at Olympic Park between Western Australia and Victoria with Western Australia winning the first game 2–0 and then combining with a Queensland composite team to win the second game 7–0.

Despite a number of attempts to have it included in the sports program it took another thirty years before it became an official carnival sport.

Although soccer was not a carnival sport, Jewish interstate challenges were held regularly during the 1950s between Melbourne and Sydney Jewish teams with Sydney usually claiming victory.

In 1959 a Sydney Jewish team by the name of Kadimah Progress defeated Victoria Maccabi 6–4.

Throughout all this time the major Jewish sports club in Victoria was Hakoah which initially fielded an all Jewish soccer team in 1927 and flew the flag for the sport both pre and post World War II before coming to its ultimate demise in 1981 through a forced merger with South Melbourne Hellas.

The Sydney Hakoah Soccer Club became even more successful entering as a foundation member of the Australian National League in 1977 and winning multiple championships after having dominated in the NSW State League for a significant number of years until it too ultimately folded in the mid 1980s.

In 1968, the two sides met in a two legged final of the Australia Cup (virtually the national championship) with the Sydney team winning 3–0 and 3–1 at a time when the current Victorian carnival team coach and Hakoah club legend, Mr Hugh 'Shug' Murney was in his prime playing in central midfield for the vanquished Hakoah Melbourne. Other legendary figures in Alex Purdie, Dick Van Alphen and Jim Armstrong also participated in this major final but could not influence the outcome.

Australia's decision to field a soccer team at the 1977 Maccabiah Games in Israel precipitated it becoming a carnival sport.

A mid-year competition was held in April, 1976 between WA and NSW with the visitors causing a huge upset by defeating the home side 2–1. Players from the Victorian team also took part in the trials for the Maccabiah, including club stalwart Danny Fridman, who participated in an Australian Maccabiah team victory in a practice match against Sydney Hakoah as part of their preparations for the Maccabiah in 1977.

The first official carnival match took place in 1976–1977 in Brisbane with NSW reversing the mid-year result and winning 2–1. Harold Finger scored both goals against WA.

Members of the victorious NSW team included George Adler, Harold Finger, Phillip Filler (former Maccabiah Australia President), Eddie Kapel, Graham Lane, Ron Lilling, Ray Lodge, Peter Markovitz, Peter Nadel, Bernie Pollack, David Rutner, Ron Silvers, David Strchler, David Tussie, Gary Weiss and Phil Wolanski. Phillip Green was team manager.

Victoria entered a carnival team for the first time in 1977–78 at the NSW carnival but was easily defeated by the home state 7–2.

That side was Bill Alt, Michael Brown, Michael Diamond, Stephen Dorevich, David Efron, Steven Ehrenreich, Morrie Kalkopf, Joe Katz, David Kraus, Michael Kraus, Harold Lederman, Benny Mikowski, Paul Lelba, Stephen Nowal and Bradley Wein.

The 1978 carnival in Adelaide between NSW and Victoria saw the two teams deadlocked at 1–1 at full-time before NSW won in a penalty shoot-out.

In 1980, Victoria scored a break-through 2–0 victory against NSW in a midyear challenge in Melbourne aided by the legendary Clive Barrett who scored – and dominated the game and Max Lichtenbaum who scored the other. The match was extremely controversial and dominated by on and off the field incidents.

The successful Victorian team was Phillip Serry, Michael Kraus, Max Lichtenbaum, Bradley Wein, Michael Diamond, David Efron, Clive Barrett, David Kraus, Alex Zwier, Danny Fridman and Stephen Bloch. Danny Fridman was coach and Larry Goldman was team manager.

NSW dominated at all carnivals until WA finally made the break-through in 1984–85 in Western Australia with home ground advantage prior to selections for the Maccabiah Games in Israel in 1985, for which Alex Zwier and Jonathan Munz were selected from Victoria and Michael Sher was controversially overlooked after a stellar league season as top goalscorer for Hakoah II in their initial league season in 1984.

The Victorian's had to wait till the inaugural Gold Coast Carnival in 1990–91 for their first official Australian Maccabiah victory, when Jonathan Munz led the team to victory as coach after illustrious career coaches such as Miron Bleiberg, Ernie Merrick and Branco Culina had in earlier years failed to secure the illusive prize.

The Victorians won 6–0 against NSW in the final to take their first ever carnival gold medal aided by the spectacular acrobatics of up and coming striker, Andrew Freund and a youthful Eddie Zolotarev in midfield. Both sides had earlier beaten WA 3–1 in the preliminary rounds and Sasha Sudakov scored a hat-trick in the final against New South Wales.

The team was: Anthony Harris, Nathi Aharoni, Alex Musman, Moshe Meleck, Ron Paneth, Harvey Silver, Eddie Zolotarev, Fima Gulko, Harry Zaitman, Sasha Sudakov, Andrew Freund and Stephen Bloch.

Victoria Maccabiah also won a mid-year carnival in Melbourne 3–2. John Foxman scored twice and Andrew Freund scored the other goal.

The team then went on to make it back to back gold medals after a stunning come from behind 3–3 draw in Melbourne the following year, which was enough to give Victoria their second major trophy in driving rain on the last day of 1991.

Many Jewish soccer player's career highs and lows have been experienced at Australian Carnivals. Some of the players noteworthy of mention through the years include: Clive Barrett, Michael Swibel, Phil Wolanski, Danny Fridman, Gary Weiss, David Kraus, John Foxman, Andrew Freund, Justin Scrobogna, Greig Rabinowitz, Michael Sher, Phil Filler, Hadley Missell, Eythan Rubinstein, Jonathan Pillemer, Stephen Bloch, Avi Ronan, Ron Lilling, Jonathan Munz, Shane Fuhr, Nathi Aharoni, Michael Diamond, Eddie Zolotarev, Boris Seroshtan, David Efron, Avi Moshe and many others.

The sporting rivalries and camaraderie developed from these challenges over the best part of seventy five years were the very embodiment of what the sport is all about, and has been the enjoyable subject of countless Jewish coffee house debates and conversations and has left moving and enduring memories on all those who have been privileged to participate.

In this year of 2017, Maccabi Victoria is the most powerful and progressive sports club within the state of Victoria, with its central headquarters in Caulfield a suburb of Melbourne. Maccabi Victoria, now boasts an astounding 23 different sporting and recreational clubs, with over 4,200 active playing members, and more than 600 regular volunteers. Maccabi Victoria has a staggering 11,000 members, parents, family and friends statewide.

The Association Football arm of Maccabi Victoria, is a well supported and integral component of the Maccabi Victoria club, with its senior teams and its junior teams playing in the official Victorian Leagues under the rules and regulations of Football Federation Victoria. The club representing Maccabi Victoria is known as North Caulfield Maccabi Football Club.

It is now North Caulfield Maccabi Association Football Club that continues the magnificent traditions set by the once mighty Hakoah Melbourne Football Club from 1927 to 1981.

Long live Maccabi Victoria Sports Club and long life to all who have the honour of wearing the shirt of North Caulfield Maccabi Association Football Club.

Gentlemen you have very large boots to fill.

CHAPTER TEN

Forward with Honour

After the ignominious demise of the great Hakoah Melbourne Football Club in 1981 and the consequent end of a glorious era in Jewish sport in the state of Victoria, the newly formed St Kilda Hakoah and Maccabi clubs had quite literally been built on the pyre of the Hakoah Melbourne Football Club phoenix, and had risen as the new phoenix with unique features and the new freshness of youth.

Season 2002, marked the twenty fifth anniversary of the Maccabi club and it is a credit to the club that it has managed to forge its own history by stepping out from under the wings of the Hakoah Melbourne phoenix ashes.

With over 4,200 active playing members of Maccabi Victoria in 2016, there are high hopes that this club through its association football arm, North Caulfield Maccabi Football Club, can move forward with honour and emulate the feats of the great Hakoah Melbourne Football Club in the years to come.

Looking back with great hindsight, it is apparent that where Hakoah Melbourne F. C. failed, was its inability to bridge the gap between the old influx of post war immigrants and the descendants of those immigrants.

The 'new' generation became more absorbed into mainstream society moving away from the traditional ethnicities and into mainstream Australian society.

In consequence this led to the club failing to create and maintain a sustainable junior club, which would have seen the natural progression of talented juniors to senior ranks. In addition, dwindling supporter numbers which started in the early '70s and ended with the clubs ultimate demise in 1981, gave the club little hope for the future. These were the major reasons that the once mighty and revered Hakoah Melbourne F. C. became extinct.

It is quite an ironic twist that as we view Jewish soccer in the new century, it is taking on quite a reverse shape to the club that existed over thirty five years ago.

Today it is the influx of immigrants from every corner of the globe that are moving the club forward. The junior numbers at North Caulfield Maccabi Football Club are bursting at the seams and the parents of these juniors are fanatically supportive of the respective junior teams.

These juniors are ultimately going to progress through the club ranks and into the senior team with greater competition for places a certainty.

It is also a sign of the times that women's association football has taken off like a whirlwind around the globe, with teams appearing throughout Australia. North Caulfield Maccabi women's football is a very good example of this new gender world phenomenon! As both genders progress through junior ranks at North Caulfield Maccabi Sports Club, their parents, relatives and friends will most certainly take a keener interest in the club, and further impressive growth of senior players, supporters and club resources is a forgone conclusion.

The next task for the club is ultimately a home ground of high quality with facilities for supporters, players and friends of the club. The current playing amenities are a credit to the local city council and all those concerned with the high standard of ground and change room maintenance.

Once the club manages to establish a broadening of facilities on a grander scale, it is certain that a larger number of elite players will be produced and the club will then have the opportunity to climb to its ultimate potential of competing in the highest Victorian league where it belongs.

In essence, North Caulfield Maccabi Football Club must now move forward with honour and dedicated persistence in order to create the sort of performances that a club aiming for the highest level should achieve, 'win and win again and they will come' has never been a more appropriate saying as far as this club is concerned, for if it takes up the challenge now and works through the junior ranks to develop top class youth, then there is no telling how far the club can go with its current forward looking administration, influx of new players and strong junior growth.

CHAPTER ELEVEN

2017: The New Age of Association Football in Australia

Statistical data from Federal sources reveals that association football in Australia in 2017 is marginally ahead of both Australian Rules football and Rugby League football in terms of attendance figures. And more importantly further statistics show that more children at both primary and secondary level in all Australian public schools choose association football as their recreational sport ahead of the other two former named codes.

This spectacular information is comprehensively reflective of the magnificent pioneering work of 'the world game' by the various Jewish and non Jewish committee's of clubs like Hakoah Melbourne since 1927, all around Australia, and the continuance and hardships that these clubs and their committee's had to tolerate in the face of rabid racism and anti-semitism regarding the introduction of the great 'world game' into Australian society. The renowned and recently deceased SBS commentator, Les Murray had much to do with the furtherance of the 'world game'. Such men like Les Murray will be sadly missed!

As one singular example, because of the untiring and truly dedicated work over many years by the likes of the stand alone great Mr Kurt Defris AM, the secretary of Hakoah Melbourne A.F.C., Association Football has become the most popular sport in Australia and the world.

Once known as 'wogball' openly shouted aloud in the public domain by the medieval rabid thousands of red neck Australian Rules supporters in Australia, to the denigrating detriment of all new European Australians to the Great Southern Land, the sheer skill requirements of the game and its non violent negative contact of participating players has made this great game the favourite choice for schoolchildren throughout the Australian continent in 2017!

Victoria alone has 55,000 registered junior soccer players and the Australian Football League (AFL) is truly fearful of the competitive threat that association football poses to them as a code.

Australia has already arrived as a major player in the world economy, and the global world. Australia is now also a major player in international association football globally, and as a full member state of F.I.F.A. has already won the Asian cup in 2015! Association football in Australia, as in two thirds of the rest of the world is the number one sporting code period. With a total of 2.2 billion fervent fans globally!

Australia now boasts its own National Football League comprising at this point in time of ten full time professional clubs throughout Australia.

Players are now contracted as full time professionals and command lucrative contracts. From all of this, it is now clear that association football has become the major sport of the Australian nation. Association football is then, in the year 2017, beyond any shadow of a doubt the greatest spectator sport in Australia and the world.

The amount of money in the game today, already shown by the outrageous remuneration paid to even past players like Mark Viduka and Harry Kewell, not to mention the modern day sky high wages of megastars like, Messi, Ronaldo and the arm biting Suarez, borders on absolute lunacy.

Where does all this money come from? That is the question, with Shakespeare's one liner 'to be or not to be' definitely the question!

Australian success on the world stage in defeating countries that 20 years ago would have been only an unattainable dream is now a stark reality.

Australia's victory in the 2015 Asian Cup on home soil was the clear indicator that Australian Association Football has come of age, and that Australia is a serious contender for World Cup success in the future.

Thanks to the early pioneers of Association Football in Australia, epitomised by the great Mr Kurt Defris AM, through his beloved Hakoah Melbourne Football Club in existence from 1927 to 1981, together with the other myriads of dedicated Jewish and non Jewish European immigrants and protagonists of the great world game over considerable time in Australia, Australian Association Football has finally set its own benchmark for all young Jewish and non Jewish Australians to follow. And it is only a matter of time before Australia realises its greatest ambition, which is to win the World Cup. A dream that eventually will one day in the future become inevitably a reality!

An Historical Informatory of Hakoah Melbourne Football Club from the 1930s to the 1960s

In July 1950, Dave McKenzie from a publication called *Sports Novels* described Hakoah as 'one of the most unique organizations in Australian sport' – as the club was an entirely Jewish soccer team headquartered at the time at Olympic Park – the premier soccer facility in Melbourne.

The Hakoah Soccer Club was conceived in late 1927 and held their first committee meeting in January 1928 before competing in their first ever season in the Victorian Amateur Soccer Football Association. The name 'Hakoah' was adopted firstly in recognition and with intention to perhaps emulate in some small way the achievements of the all conquering Hakoah–Vienna which by that time had firmly established themselves as one of the finest clubs in Austria and Europe.

Hakoah pronounced 'Har-Koah', is a Hebrew word meaning strength, and the club throughout the course of its history valiantly justified the optimism of its name.

This was a time when there was a steady stream of Jewish immigrants coming into this country, with the founders of the club being prominent businessmen from Carlton including Josef Shatin, a front rank barrister and solicitor and the Skolnik brothers, leading wine and spirit merchants.

The club had always enjoyed the support of outstanding Jewish men of business its office bearers having included frock and clothing manufacturers, a spinning mills proprietor, a motor trade magnate, a handbag manufacturer, a large delicatessen proprietor, prominent doctors and barristers, wine merchants, shoes and stocking manufacturers and the general manager of the largest store in Melbourne.

The first ever game for the club was against North Carlton at Fawkner Park which Hakoah won 1–0.

1930s

The team proved itself worthy of the patronage of such outstanding supporters by coming up from a minor league to make itself premiers (in four short years) of the third division of the Victorian Soccer League, going through that particular season without defeat.

On thus gaining promotion to the second division, the Hakoah side again went through the season undefeated and won the premiership and promotion to the first grade. The following year the side won the first division premiership, again remaining undefeated in doing so – thus completing an achievement surely rare in the annals of Australian sport.

The man chiefly responsible for this run of unbroken success was Phil Bowman, an Englishmen of Jewish ancestry who back home in England a few years previously had had an extremely promising career with the famed Manchester United cut short by the infliction of a spinal injury. Bowman migrated to Australia and recovered from the injury that had ended his career in the top flight – first taking up the game again in Melbourne with South Yarra.

At South Yarra, Bowman as captain, brought them up from third division to the first division championship – winning each grades premiership en rout before being persuaded to move across to Hakoah.

His association with Hakoah ended in the late 1940s and his achievements with the club were considered legendary – unanimously considered at the end of his career as being the greatest leader the club had in its first quarter century of existence.

A highlight of the Bowman era was when the Hakoah team met the members of the famed M.C.C cricket team during the 1932–33 body-line tour in a highly unique international match at the Old Exhibition Oval with Hakoah running out 3–1 victors against an M.C.C line-up that included Wally Hammond, Maurice Leyland, Bill Voce, George Duckworth, Bill Bowes, Les Ames and Hedley Verity.

Hakoah had throughout its history controversially grappled with the question of fielding non-Jewish players. Whilst the team was an all-Jewish team in its formative years, a fall in the numbers of Jewish immigrants during the depression years forced the club to have to look to players of other nationalities in order to fill its ranks and maintain the clubs momentum.

Thus by the mid 1930s Hakoah became an absolute Foreign Legion amongst sports organizations, the diversity of nationality truly unique in Australian sport.

A typical line-up during this era (with players birthplace in brackets) was a unique snapshot of immigration and absorption during that time and the beginnings of a long and strong association the club formed with player's immigrating from the United Kingdom – particularly Scotland.

The line-up was: Aquilera G. K. (Spain), R. B. Hayden (Aust), L. B. P. Bowman (England), R. H. W Yafee (Palestine), C. H. Roth (Germany), L. H. J. Bowman (England), O. R. C. Yaffe (Palestine), I. R. Orr (Scotland), C. F. Mclvor (England), I. L. Johnstone (Scotland), O. L. Forrest (Scotland).

In Melbourne's centenary year 1934, Hakoah were again premiers of the first grade of the Victorian Soccer League and also winners of the prestigious Dockerty Cup – Victoria's premier soccer award and the Victorian equivalent of the English FA Cup – played at the time at the conclusion of the regular season.

From 1934–1938 Hakoah won three Victorian First Division Championships and a Dockerty Cup.

During the war years, at a time when not only the club but the game itself could have quite easily disintegrated, Hakoah battled on to stay alive, although being forced for reasons of financial and playing strength, to amalgamate with the Moreland club – thus becoming Moreland–Hakoah for a period of time.

The amalgamation proved to be a successful one with the merged Moreland–Hakoah winning the premiership in 1942 and 1944, the Dockerty Cup in 1945 and being Runners Up in the Dockerty Cup from 1942–1944.

After the conclusion of World War 2, Hakoah again profited from a waive of Jewish immigration as they did in their formative years – only this time the numbers were much larger and the benefits of this were that the club was again able to stand alone and thus the Moreland–Hakoah merger was broken at the commencement of the 1946 season.

Hakoah again became an all Jewish club and dropped down a couple of leagues before ultimately climbing back to the first grade of the Victorian Soccer League in 1949. Alby Meier and Issi Petes are known as two fine servants for the club in the late 1940s.

The club was considered a force in the game throughout this initial quarter century of its existence and with limited opportunities for any international and interstate activities at this time, the club was still able to have a dozen of its players honoured by such selection.

Nat Spicer – Profile:

Nat Spicer was famously connected with the Hakoah club as an administrator, committee member, Secretary and President during the 1940s.

Nat was originally a shoe manufacturer, born in London who came to Australia with tremendous enthusiasm to make a success of his life in business and the sport he loved so dearly.

Nat was described as an absolute ball of fire in administrative matters for Hakoah having worked at all his official duties with the vigour of a proverbial beaver. His tremendous enthusiasm even saw Nat set himself the voluntary task of attending to the placing of stops in all the players boots and mending all those in need of repair.

He also took on the self-appointed task of washing the jerseys of the clubs teams and on Monday mornings following a match he had over forty jerseys hanging on his backyard clothes line.

Nat was also a great asset to Hakoah on the playing field with his ability finding him several times selected to take part in matches against various international teams.

His services to the club were most noteworthy and his name was considered a good symbolic sample of what the Hakoah name stood for being strength as Nat Spicer gave as much to the club as anybody possibly could.

Kurt Defris – Profile:

Kurt Defris is well documented and known for being Hakoah's longest serving committee member who gave his heart and soul to the Hakoah club for over thirty five years.

As a youngster, Defris was a dashing winger in the Austrian First Division. His proudest playing days were in 1931 when he transferred for about $AUS20,000 from Fair Unitas to the famous Hakoah–Vienna club at the age of 22.

During the Second World War he escaped Hitler's persecution of Jews by fleeing to Shanghai in China. There he remained active in the sporting community by becoming Chairman of the Jewish Recreation Club – which boasted about twenty clubs in the Jewish Soccer League and some 6000 registered members.

In late 1946, Kurt made his way to Australia and played about half of the 1947 season with Hakoah before taking up an administrative post.

Defris also excelled at table tennis – a sport he no doubt enhanced his abilities in whilst living in Shanghai. During his stay in Austria he ranked consistently in the Top 10 in the country and was an exceptional national representative. His wife was ranked three in the world after the 1936 World Championships.

His success and knowledge as a player in both soccer and table tennis were regarded as having been integral to his success as an administrator in these sports.

Kurt Defris was the stalwart committee person at Hakoah whilst some ten presidents presided over the club. Amongst the Presidents were Jack Skolnik, Dr Henry Baytch, Les Erdi, Victor Gross, Nat Spicer, Manny Unreich and Dennis Krongold.

Kurt had great admiration for Hakoah's first President Mr Jack Shatin and valued his lasting friendships with fellow committee members including Fred Halpern, Michael Weinstein, John Chaskiel, Kadish Korman, Fred Weider, Henry Greenfield, Dr Ian Kaufman, Henry Fromer, Peter Pryles and innumerable other former committee members and club supporters.

Defris was considered a pragmatist in the classic mould who was known to reminisce about former great Hakoah teams whilst never being one to stay stuck in the past and always firmly keeping an eye to the future right up until the clubs final days.

Kurt Defris was a classic survivor who wore the economic hardships of the club harder than most and was frequently required to shoulder responsibility to find much needed funds to keep the club operating at many times when the club was struggling. His survival and Hakoah's survival could be said to be eternally linked and his life was consumed with his love for this club.

Whilst the club continually and consistently performed at an exceptional level – consistently in the highest State League in Victoria, the club suffered through lack of genuine support both in attendances and from the wider Jewish business community and whilst Defris was often very irritated by the situation, he steadfastly held on and often single handedly, pushed and maintained an upward path for this club that he undyingly supported with the most immense passion.

In an interview in the early '80s Defris remarked:

'For years we have relied upon the backing of the Jewish community. Up until about 1965 we were one of the best

supported clubs in Victoria but our support dwindled quickly. The old guard died, their descendants didn't become interested in soccer because of the diverse interests prevalent in modern day youth and Australian Rules Football was more enticing than soccer. In a way we contributed to our demise because we neglected our juniors until recently. When I came to Hakoah we played at Royal Park then we moved to Fawkner Park. Our next home was near the Exhibition Buildings and then we became the first club to play at Olympic Park. That was before the stadium was built. In the 1950s we played at St Kevins Oval in Toorak until a successful propaganda campaign was carried out by a leading Melbourne radio personality who didn't want to see diverse ethnic groups playing soccer in Toorak. In 1958 we returned to Olympic Park and in 1961 we moved to Albert Park. Slowly but surely, stone by stone, the Middle Park stadium evolved. We are indebted to the late Senator Pat Kennelly who was our patron and Chairman of the Albert Park Trust. He was instrumental in building our stadium. Of course we shared the ground with Hellas and I want to stress that there never has been the slightest clash over the use of the ground. And the players I have seen over the years! Who could forget them? Players like Hugh Mumey, Harry Sutherland, Jack Roessler, Harry Roessler, Joe Gottesman and of course our most famous captain Tom Jack, Dick van Alphen, Dave McIntosh and Milan Vesovic are others who readily come to mind. Gentlemen all, and from time to time they come back to watch Hakoah. You know I estimate that maybe sixty percent of our players finished their careers with us. That says something good about the club, eh?'

In 1978, Kurt Defris was the longest serving administrator in the clubs history.

At this time, John Chaskiel had been chairman for 10 years and Kadish Korman had been Vice President and Treasurer for a similar length of time.

Kurt Defris interview in Soccer Action January 27 1982:

> *'We have done the honourable thing in joining our club with South Melbourne Hellas to form the Hellas–Hakoah Soccer Club to compete in the Victorian State League from the start of the season in 1982. Everyone could see that the writing was on the wall, said Defris – a reference to Hakoah's overdraft and guarantees totalling $48,000. We have done what we could in the past 55 years. The interest in Hakoah Soccer club no longer is there. At least we have kept the name "Hakoah" flying in soccer circles. The Greek people have treated us almost like brothers. It took us a few months, in fact about a year, to convince our people that we wouldn't be eaten up by a merger. I am a man who goes with the times and it would have hurt me had we gone out with a bang by being declared bankrupt. For us amalgamation was the only solution, the only honourable thing we could do.'*

Jim Diamataris took over as the new President of the club and John Chaskiel remained with Peter Dourin as the Co-Vice Presidents. Kurt Defris remained as Secretary-Manager continuing an unbroken administrative stretch with Hakoah which started in 1947, a unique record in Australian and world soccer. Kurt was 73 at this stage and his abilities to analyse, debate and influence were considered invaluable over countless committee meetings in a variety of sports including his great loves of table tennis and ice hockey.

The Victorian Ice Hockey Player of the Year Award is until this day struck in his name.

In 1978 he was honoured with an Order of Australia medal and given life membership at FFV the Victorian Table Tennis Association and Victorian Ice Hockey Association.

Thousands of Victorian soccer followers who grew up watching the game in Victoria throughout the Kurt Defris era, were well acquainted with the sight of Defris walking along the touchline with his trusty fold-out chair, trying to select a good vantage point in the terraces just seconds before the kick off of a Hakoah match.

The analogy between that sight and the 'Peanuts' cartoon character Linus with his security blanket almost irresistible. The chair was believed to have joined Hakoah around the same time Defris stepped into the place.

Just as the chair was symbolic of the man, the man himself certainly symbolizes everything that we knew about Hakoah Soccer Club.

Prominent Hakoah past presidents include

- Jack Skolnik (formative years)
- Vic Gross
- Eric (Les) Erdi
- Dr H Baytch (Life Member of FFV)
- Michael Weinstein (past FFV Chairman and Life Member)
- Dennis Krongold

Past Hakoah coaches

- Asa Robbins
- John Kursweil
- Aku Roth
- Dave McIntosh
- Tom Jack
- Manny Poulakakis
- Ted Smith
- Ron Sawecki (1964–65)
- Jim Adams
- Harry Sutherland
- Mike Mandalis
- Milenko Rusmir
- Gerry Chaldi
- Johnny Anderson (1972)
- Alex Purdie & Hugh Murney (1973)
- Sam Meyer (1974)
- Frank Micic
- Bill Allison
- Ollie Norris
- Fred Bunce

Harry Sutherland – Profile:

Harry Sutherland played in England for Leeds United, Exeter and Bournemouth and was player manager of Western League Club Bedford before he came to Australia in 1953 at the age of 38. His first job was with Brighton SC, where as a player coach, he led his new team into the Dockerty Cup Final. The following year Sutherland joined Hakoah, which had been beaten by Brighton in the 1953 cup final and he played at Hakoah from 1954–1957. He stayed as coach but later switched to Altona City which he coached from 1967–1972. He then returned to Hakoah to act as Team Manager in the late 1970's. In 1954 Sutherland scored 31 goals for Hakoah which is understood to be the highest total by a Hakoah first team player in its history.

1950s

The Hakoah team that won four Dockerty Cups in a row from 1954–1957 featured probably one of the oldest forward lines in Victorian top-league history and the youngest goalkeeper. These forwards included Jackie Ressler, Henry Rice and Joe the Czech – all well into their thirties. John Slade was only 16, when he made his way into the Hakoah line-up for the 1954 final only to be replaced in the following season by Aldo Vitti from Juventus.

The 1954 line-up also featured Dave McIntosh who was an accomplished left back from Scotland who later went on to coach the club and a strong robust midfielder from Yugoslavia called Vesovic.

Ressler was one of the great Hakoah stalwarts and his name became synonymous with Hakoah.

Tom Jack was a great Hakoah player during this era and achieved many caps for Australia – finishing his career as a player coach. Other noteworthy Australian internationals during this era included Ralph Piercy (previous club: Chester, England), Syd Thomas (Scotland-Midfielder) and Angus Drennan (Argus Medal Winner – Box Hill 1959 – other previous club ICI Deer Park).

Bill Harburn was also a part of this legendary team in the 1950s. Bill played originally for Bishop Auckland in England and was later tragically killed in the Westgate Bridge disaster. His son Steve also later played as a goalkeeper for the club in the late 1970s.

Frank Moucha – Czechoslovakian full back.

Ted Smith – one of the few players who can boast having played for Australia at the Olympic Games in Melbourne in 1956.

1960s

John O'Neill joined Hakoah in 1965 as a defender, having played as an Irish international.

He played for Preston North End in the English First Division for six years alongside the great Tom Finney, and also won the Argus Medal, later to become the Rothmans Medal for the Best & Fairest Award in 1969.

Alan Stenhouse was John O'Neill's partner in defence in the most powerful team ever to play in the Hakoah colours. Alan Stenhouse played in Scotland for both Motherwell and Cowdenbeath before he joined Hakoah in 1963.

Dick van Alphen was a top player in Holland and with Ringwood Wilhelmina before he joined Hakoah and was capped for Australia. He was one of the Socceroos in the infamous 10 match tour of Asia in 1967.

George Keith was a brilliant full back from Scotland who also went on to represent Australia in 1969 in the World Cup elimination matches. Keith went on to play for Apia Leichhardt and stayed there as a coach.

Mike O'Hara from Luton Town must be rated as one of the most colourful goalkeepers ever to have played in Victoria. 'Mad Mick' played for Slavia in between two stints with Hakoah and spent the 1978 season with Footscray J.U.S.T. in the first season of the National League.

Hugh Murney played in Scotland for Queen of the South and Morton before joining Hakoah in 1964. He played for nine seasons with Hakoah before moving to Albion Rovers, Fitzroy-Alexander, Heidelberg, Park Rangers and then later rejoined the club where he ultimately became team manager.

Jim Armstrong – started his legendary career at Hakoah and after having played three and a half seasons there – he was transferred to South Melbourne Hellas and then ended his career at Juventus. Armstrong was capped for Australia and scored a record 152 goals in State League.

Hakoah: The Story of a Soccer Club

The club known as Hakoah Sports Club has survived depression, war and many other vicissitudes.

It all began in 1927 with the formation of Hakoah Soccer Club, by Aku Roth together with fellow enthusiasts Kalman Rogers, Stan Robe and Jack Shatin. The sporting and social aspects of the new club provided immediate friendly contacts so necessary for newcorners from other lands.

The club, affiliated with the Victorian Amateur Soccer Football Association, went on to win many honours, including First Division Championships in 1934, 1935, 1938 and 1943. The club holds the record for Dockerty Cup successes with eight wins, in 1935, 1945, 1953, 1954, 1955, 1956, 1966 and 1973.

The Reserve team won its League Championship in three consecutive years, 1958, 1959 and 1960, and the Harry Armstrong (Reserve) Cup in 1956, 1958, 1964 and 1969.

The Thirds have also had their taste of successes with Premierships in 1970 and 1971.

Members will undoubtedly remember with a deep sense of nostalgia the names of some of the club's outstanding players through the years – Alby Meyer, Aku Roth, Frank Mclver, Alan Forrest, Tom Jack, Harry Sutherland, Issie Roessler, Joe Gottesman, Milia Vesovic, Ralph Piercy, David McIntosh, Harry Rice and Syd Thomas, each of whom in his own way brought glamour to the club.

The club is currently engaged in a long-term plan for team-building, with special emphasis being on developing local talent from the Junior and Thirds sides under coaches John Anderson, Sam Meyer, Senior team manager is D. H. Copeland, while the Senior team captain is Hugh Murney who took over from club stalwart Alan Stenhouse who retired in mid-season after many years of great service to Hakoah.

A great source of pride to the club have been the enthusiastic performances by Hakoah's four Junior under age teams

Today the Middle Park Soccer Stadium ranks as one of the finest football arenas in Australia, with a splendid all-weather playing surface, and first-class facilities for players, referees, club officials, the Press, and up to 25,000 spectators. In addition, there is a spacious car park.

Credit for this remarkable transformation is shared by the club's Board of Trustees, officials of joint tenant South Melbourne-Hellas, and of course the Chairman. This splendid stadium is proving a valuable breeding ground for future talent. From all indications there are numerous promising players with the potential to make their marks in State League soccer in the near future.

The club's first home ground was the Exhibition Oval, which no longer exists. It then moved successively to Princes Park, the old Motordome (now the site of Olympic Park), St. Kevin's Oval and finally, in 1956, through the courtesy of the South Melbourne United Soccer Club, to Middle Park.

At that time, the Middle Park ground was enclosed by a disused cycling track, with an extremely rough playing surface and virtually no amenities whatsoever for players or officials.

But the Albert Park Committee of Management, with the Honourable Senator P. J. Kennelly, himself a Patron of Hakoah Sports Club, in charge has changed all that.

Many members will also recall two other highlights in the history of Hakoah Soccer Club – the challenge match, played at the Melbourne Cricket Ground, between Hakoah and members of England's cricket Test Team during its 1933–34 visit, and an exhibition match against the Japanese Olympic soccer team at the Showgrounds in 1956.

Article Gallery

KURT DEFRIS

Often referred to as "Mr. Sports" he is Secretary-Manager of the Hakoah Sports Club and the Hakoah Soccer Club, Secretary of the Board of Trustees, Vice-President of the Victorian Table Tennis Association and Chairman of the Hakoah Table Tennis Club, President of the Victorian Ice Hockey Association and Manager of the Hakoah Ice Hockey Club, and Chairman of the South-of-the-Yarra Junior Soccer Federation.

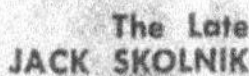

The Late JACK SKOLNIK

A foundation member of the Hakoah Sports Club and its President for ten years during the Fifties and early Sixties.

Hakoah was assigned by VASFA to the lowest grade — the Third Division. Original players in 1928 included *Roth, Willie* and *Charlie Yaffe, Jack* and *Yehudi Skolnik, Nat Spicer, Ted Cohen*, the late *Mendel Slonim, H. Silver, J. Orloff, L. Olbaum, N. Kleinman, G. Winikoff, S. Kaplan*, and *K. Pesch*.

The team manager was *Joe Wexler*, and the club secretary was Harry Spivakovsky.

Michael WEINSTEIN, AM, BEM

Michael Weinstein arrived in Australia in 1950 and quickly became an administrative leader in the sport.

Born in Poland in 1923, he started as team manager of the Melbourne Hakoah Club, was a foundation member of the Australian and Victorian Associations and was the driving force behind the purchase of Victorian soccer's first home in St Kilda.

He also helped to gain Australia's return to FIFA, served for more than 20 years as chairman of the VSF and toured overseas frequently as manager of Australian teams.

During his career, he was a member of the World Cup committee, delegate to the Australian Olympic Committee, ASF vice-president from 1975 to 1986 and is a life member of both the ASF and VSF.

He has dedicated most of his life to Australian soccer and still retains an active interest in the national scene and as a VSF Trustee.

Proud . . .
moved . . .
and humble . . .

GEORGE WEINBERG

WHEN an organisation produces a Year Book, it is customary for the Editor to call upon the President to say a few words, which are usually published under the heading of "The President's Message."

This is not always as simple as it seems. Many Presidents, including myself, follow the wise dictum of Richard Whately, who said: "Preach not because you have to say something, but because you have something to say."

On this occasion, the Editor called upon me at the right time. I certainly have something to say, for I have just read Aku Roth's account of the stirring history of Hakoah. It leaves me deeply moved and tremendously proud.

I am moved because of the gallant efforts and sacrifices of the many people who had the courage and foresight to establish Hakoah and foster its development, often against substantial odds, during the last four decades.

And I am proud for many reasons. I am proud of the many successes which Hakoah has enjoyed, and the respect with which it is regarded in the world of sport.

I am proud of the exploits and the exemplary conduct of the many teams and athletes Hakoah has fielded in a wide variety of sports, both now and in the past.

And I am proud to be one of those chosen to follow in the footsteps of the late Mr. Sam Yaffe as President of the wonderful organisation known as the Hakoah Sports Club. In this connection, my pride is leavened by a deep sense of humility.

The publication of this Year Book offers me a convenient opportunity to thank the hundreds of young men and women who wear Hakoah's colors on the field of sport; to thank the dozens of people who serve as administrators, trustees, sectional leaders, delegates, and advisers — people who selflessly sacrifice time, effort, and money for the advancement of the club and its many divisions; to thank our Patron, Senator P. J. Kennelly, for the home he has provided for the club at Albert Park; to thank the South Melbourne-Hellas Soccer Club for its generous co-operation in the sharing of our home; and to thank the thousands of supporters without whose loyalty Hakoah would fade away into limbo.

This year marks the fortieth anniversary of the club. I shall close by wishing all concerned "many happy returns".

G. WEINBERG

President

it alive, although being forced through sheer necessity to amalgamate with the Moreland club.

The amalgamation proved, however, to be an extremely successful one as regards playing results—the combine winning the premiership in 1942 and 1944, the Dockerty Cup in 1945, and being runners-up for the Dockerty Cup in 1942, 1943 and 1945.

However, with the close of war and the recommencement of Jewish immigration to this country, Hakoah dissociated itself from the Moreland side and again became an all-Jewish club. It has played as such since the 1946 season, and with the complete setting-up again of the Victorian Soccer League climbed to the first grade last season and is hoping to remain there.

The club has been a force in the game in Victoria throughout its existence, having, with the limited opportunities in this country for international or interstate activities, had a dozen of its players honored by such selection.

The Skolnik brothers also gave the game a lift by presenting a cup for annual competition between teams confined to players under nineteen years representing Victoria and South Australia.

The club, too, in contradiction to the usual stories circulated concerning the close-fistedness of the members of its race, has always been noted for its fine treatment of its players.

An outstanding case in point is that of a crack Scottish forward called Johnny Lewis who once won a premiership for Hakoah with a spectacular overhead goal forty yards out from the net.

Johnny later fell upon hard times, and, forsaken by friends and relatives, would have died in a pauper's grave if the matter had not come to the notice of the Hakoah club which immediately made and supplied all funeral arrangements and expenses.

PERHAPS the outstanding character connected with the club throughout its history has been little Nat Spicer, a shoe manufacturer originally from London.

Nat has been an absolute ball of fire in administrative matters for Hakoah, having at various times been committee member, secretary, and president of the club, and having worked at all his official duties with the vigor of the proverbial beaver.

His tremendous enthusiasm has been such that for a number of years he set for himself the voluntary task of attending to the placing of stops in all the players' boots and mending all those in need of repair.

He also took on the self-appointed task of washing the guernseys of the club's teams, and on the Monday morning following a match has had as many as forty-four guernseys hanging on his back-yard clothes-line!

Nat was also a great asset to Hakoah on the playing field, his ability finding him several times selected to take part in matches against various international organisations. He is not now actively connected with the club, but his former services are remembered with deep gratitude.

Hakoah, as has been stated, means strength, and the members of the club have in the past given ample vindication of the fitness of the title.

It may safely be predicted that they will continue on the Soccer field to overthrow the Philistines in true Samson-like fashion, for the national pride that is the mainspring of their organisation makes them truly worthy of the steel of the doughtiest of opponents.

The very first Hakoah side, vintage 1928, an entirely Jewish eleven.

The Birth and Growth of Hakoah

This stirring history of Hakoah is based on the recollections of AKU ROTH

THIS is the story of the conception, the birth, and the growth of the Hakoah Soccer Club, which has developed into the most widely respected club in the Victorian soccer community. Now completing its fortieth year, it is by far the oldest club in the State League, and the only survivor from pre-war days. It is also the foundation upon which the multifarious Hakoah Sports Club was built. So that the long and proud history of this illustrious club could be presented as accurately as possible, the club called upon one of its foundation members, AKU ROTH, an outstanding soccer player and team captain for nearly twenty years, to provide the salient facts for this inspiring narration.

This story begins in the first half of the Twenties, when incidents in Europe provided the example for the establishment of Hakoah in Melbourne. At that time, *Aku Roth* and his twin brother were playing soccer with a prominent team in Germany.

"In 1924, Germany's Jewish community was electrified by the successful tour of an all-Jewish team from Vienna — the famed Hakoah," said Roth. "Hakoah's tour inspired the formation of Jewish soccer clubs throughout Germany.

"When affiliated with their local Associations, these clubs had to start playing in the lowest grades of their respective leagues, in most cases the fifth or fourth divisions.

"Yet they were able to attract players from leading clubs who willingly made the positional and financial sacrifies necessary to join these new Jewish clubs for idealistic reasons.

"I personally left a club which was four times national champion of Germany to join a small Jewish club, but I was only one of many who gladly made the sacrifice."

When Roth elected to leave the growing racial tumult of his native country in 1927, he migrated to Melbourne and was quickly signed by the local champion team Melbourne Thistle.

MOVE TO FORM HAKOAH

But when, toward the end of 1927, a move was made to form a Jewish soccer club, he remembered Hakoah-Vienna and its inspiration of German Jewry, and leapt at the chance to assist in the formation of the proposed new club.

HAPPY BIRTHDAY! 50 YEARS OF HAKOAH

Melbourne Hakoah in 1931: Front row (left-right): Nat Spicer, Joe [illegible]. Second row (left-right): Morrie Slonim, Aku Roth, Jack Skolnik (team manager), Phil Bowman, Paddy [illegible] (Standing). Third row (left-right): [illegible], Willi Yaffe, Jack Grant, Henry Kleinman, Charles Yaffe, Joe Wexler. Fourth row (back): Kalman Goldberg, Samuel Yaffe (president), Kalman Rogers, Harry Spivakovsky, Morrie Belkin.

Melbourne Hakoah celebrates half a century of activity this year during which it became a household name in Australian soccer. One of the founding members of the club, Kalman Rogers, spoke to Jewish News reporter Steven Kalus about the early days.

The real activity of the Melbourne Hakoah Soccer Club started in the late twenties when a group of Jewish migrants, inspired by the tremendous success of the famous Vienna Hakoah, decided to form a Jewish soccer club in Melbourne, so that the name of "Hakoah" be kept alive in Australia.

Several meetings were held by a very enthusiastic group of Jewish soccer players at the Polish club in Neil Street, Carlton, but the first official gathering took place on a Sunday afternoon, outside the Carlton Football Oval where about 50 young Jewish sportsmen responded to an advertisement in the Jewish Herald.

After a short discussion the meeting decided to form and register a Jewish Soccer Club and to name it after the famous Vienna Club "Hakoah." An executive committee was elected with Joe Shatin as chairman, and the following members: Sam Yaffe, Alec Orloff, Norman Shatin, Kalman and Eric Rogers, Jack Skolnik, Harry Spivakovsky, Stan Rosenberg, Sam Goldfine, Henry Goldberg, Bob Fetter and Morrie Belkin.

Training and practice matches were held outside the Princes Park Oval in North Carlton. After trainings we met usually in the garage of one of our supporters Mr Jack Lewinman. Jack's garage also served as a storeroom. All expenses were covered by the players. To equip the team, we also depended on the generosity of the players and supporters.

The first official general meeting took place in January 1928 when the late

plauded and well received by a large number of our supporters. It was also the year when Hakoah affiliated with the Victorian Amateur Soccer Association.

As the years progressed, more accomplished Jewish players joined our club. Amongst them Aku Roth, crack centre-half of the German champion club, F.C. Nuernberg, astute defender Nat Spicer, Ted Cohen, Morrie Slonim, Jehuda Skolnik, George Wasnikof, Chaim Klayman and many others. Throughout the years Hakoah players were chosen to represent Victoria and Australia.

During the past 50 years the main aim of the Hakoah administrators was to keep the traditional name of "Hakoah" as the symbol of Jewish sport in Melbourne and Victoria.

The Hakoah of today can hold its head high as the only Jewish sponsored soccer club in Melbourne and so should all the past and present committee members, players and supporters connected with the Blue-Whites.

AKU ROTH (right) with M. SLONIM (left) and JACK SKOLNIK after winning the Soccer Championship in 1931.

The enthusiastic instigators of the move included *Joe Shatin, Stan Rosenberg,* the late *Jack Skolnik, Kalman Rogers, Harry Spivakovsky* and the late *Sam Yaffe.* They were soon to be joined by *Lou Miller, Alec Orloff, Sam Goldfine, M. Hirsch, H. Goldberg, M. Belkan* and *Bob Fetter.*

"There were others of course", said Roth, "But my memory is not what it was and, if I've neglected to mention some of the original founders and committeemen, I beg their forgiveness".

The club was formed, the name Hakoah was adopted, and its affiliation with the VASFA was accepted. Although the existence of the new club was welcomed by the Jewish community-at-large, opposition was encountered in some quarters because of the necessity to play on Saturdays.

THE FIRST PRESIDENT

The first president was the late Mr. Sam Yaffe.

He was an ideal leader", said Roth. was a fatherly figure, a real patriarch

The official opening of the Albert Park Soccer Stadium was an historic occasion. Seen here (from left) were Hakoah's President of the day, Mr. Edward Zola, Mr. Nathan Jacobson, Senator P. J. Kennelly, and Mr. Charles M. Hay.

The team's efforts culminated in a glorious "double" in 1935 when it won both the league championship and the Dockerty Cup.

Apart from Aku Roth, who represented Victoria and Australia on many occasions, Hakoah's squad in these wonderful early years included prolific goalgetters *Frank McIver* and *Alex Forrest*, *Charlie Yaffe*, goalie *Sol Aguilera*, the *Bowman brothers*, *Alf Mackay Nat Spicer*, *Johnny Orr*, *Benny Molinski*, *Paddy Hayden*, *Sol Halperin*, *Tom Harrison*, *Fred Pollock*, *George Hawks*, *Jock Lurton*, *Andy Lang*, *Johnny Johnstone*, *Clarrie Power*, *Walter Huck*, and others whose names were well-known at the time — *Lewis*, *Wise*, *McCluskey*, *Armstrong*, and *Bardas*.

PRIMITIVE CONDITIONS

Matches in those days were played on all kinds of rough-and-ready pitches. Players stripped in sheds or in the open. Showers were practically unheard of. Hakoah was one of the first clubs to obtain an enclosed ground — the Exhibition Oval, which no longer exists.

It then moved successively to Princes Park, the old Motordrome which was the original site of Olympic Park, St. Kevin's Oval, then finally to its present home in Albert Park.

AN ENTERPRISING CLUB

Roth recalls well the line of presidents who succeeded Sam Yaffe — *Michael Pitt*, *Harry Lapin*, *Nat Spicer*, *Tony Rubinstein*, *Jack Skolnik*, followed by *E. Zola*, *Dr. Henry Baytch* and current President *George Weinberg*.

BIGGEST SOCCER FIXTURE FOR 1934 SEASON

Hindmarsh Game Should Be Even

CREDIT TO COACH

CAPTAINS' OPINIONS

HAKOAH

KINGSWOOD

SOCCER RIVALS DRAW AGAIN

Sunshine and Footscray Cup Battles

SOUTH YARRA DOWN

SUNSHINE and Footscray Thistle have battled for three and a half hours in an endeavour to decide which shall pass into the second round of the Dockerty Cup. As no decision has been reached they will now have to meet on neutral ground for at least another 90 minutes.

HAKOAH DEFEATED

SOCCER RECORD MISSED

1934

Footscray Still in Danger Zone

Nine Goals in Principal Match

Preston Defeats Hakoah

HAKOAH AND KINGSWOOD TO MEET AT HINDMARSH

Big Interstate Soccer Match

(By "Penalty")

SOCCER enthusiasts will be well catered for on Saturday, when the Hakoah team from Melbourne will meet the leaders of the South Australian Soccer League—Kingswood—in a special challenge match on the Hindmarsh Oval.

Race For Soccer Honors Be

By Nimrod

1934

THE race for the senior premiership appears to be between Hakoah and Caledonians, the premier team and Dockerty Cup winner respectively last season. Caledonians have an easy game with Box Hill at Olympic Park today, but Hakoah may be fully extended to win at Preston.

HAKOAH'S CUP TEAM

1934

GOVERNOR AT SOCCER

DOCKERTY CUP FINAL

Hakoah and Caledonians to Meet

Record of the Clubs

A. ROTH S. WEIR

SOCCER SIDES FIGHT FOR DIVISIONS

Relegation Or Promotion?

By "ONWARD"

With the first and second division soccer premierships practically ended, interest in the league contests on Saturday will centre in the relegation and promotion issues in which Brighton and South Yarra (first division) and South Melbourne and Heidelberg (second) are involved.

BRIGHTON'S JOB

LESSON IN TEAM SPIRIT

JUNIORS FOR N.S.W.

Soccer

HAKOAH WINS CUP FINAL

The two outstanding soccer teams of the year, Caledonians and Hakoah, contested the final of the Dockerty Cup at Olympic Park this afternoon. Last year the same clubs also appeared in the final, and after a drawn game, the Scots won the replay by an odd goal.

Hakoah won the toss and Caledonians started against the wind toward the river goal. Hakoah was first to make progress. A nice pass from Lewis to McCluskey ended in the latter testing Morgan with a cross shot.

THE FIRST SCORE

UNUSUAL INCIDENT

HALF TIME

CALEDONIANS, 2; HAKOAH, 1.

SCORES EQUALISED

AN ACROBATIC GOAL

FINAL SCORE

HAKOAH, 4; CALEDONIANS, 3.

SCHOOLBOYS' TRIAL

Win In Cup Final Gives Hakoah Soccer Double

By Nimrod

HAKOAH reached the height of its ambition on Saturday, winning the Dockerty Cup from Caledonians by 4-3. This, the Division One championship, gives it a double success, achieved by only six other clubs since the start of the present soccer regime in 1908.

THE game on Saturday was one of fluctuating fortunes and thrills. After Hakoah had had the better of play for the greater part of the first half, it was the victim of circumstance, and crossed over a goal in arrears.

Unusual Incident

There was a quick transfer to Caledonians' territory, and it was then noticed that a linesman was signalling. The referee stopped play, went over to the touch line to consult the linesman and then gave the Scots a penalty kick, from which Johnstone netted.

Hakoah players seemed upset by the incident. Caledonians attacked vigorously and Peter Young, gaining a good shooting position by pertinacity, sent in a rising shot that had Aguilera beaten.

Another Reverse

McCluskey dashed away on the Hakoah right and crossed the ball accurately to Forrest. In a flash it was in the net.

Two minutes later McIver sent forward for Forrest to crash through, and although he was brought down full length, there was sufficient power behind the ball to carry it past Morgan for the equaliser.

Acrobatic Scoring

Lewis was lying on his back, but got his foot round the ball and pulled it over himself and into the net.

The Players

Schoolboys' Trial

OCCER WINDS UP SEASON

1935

School Champions At Middle Park

By "ONWARD"

ALTHOUGH several first division and reserve games are outstanding the executive of the Soccer Association have had to cancel the remaining fixtures because of the problem of securing grounds. Tomorrow's game at Middle Park is between the combined champion teams and the Rest.

The cancellation does not affect the championship or relegation, but certainly gives weight to the plea that the divisions be limited to eight clubs.

The constitution of the competitions for next season will be discussed at the annual revision of rules meeting on Monday, October 21.

WONTHAGGI'S AIM

During the visit to Wonthaggi last week-end of metropolitan teams opportunity was taken to discuss the future of the code there.

For several years it has been the object of a Wonthaggi club to play in the metropolitan competitions, but so far the application has not been entertained.

The suggestion has been made that enough teams be raised at Wonthaggi to run a competition there, and that from these teams one side be selected to play for the Dockerty Cup.

That course would give the miners a chance of again lifting the cup, but would it find favor with the other entrants?

Shepparton, Yallourn and Mildura districts would have to be extended the same privilege—in fact, any group of clubs could combine to make one good side.

Some years ago it was found that the Wonthaggi team was selected in this way, but the practice was stopped and is not likely to be allowed again.

The fame of the Hakoah club has spread, and Tasmania is anxious to be visited by the champions next year.

SCHOOLBOYS' GAME

The schoolboys will wind up their season with a contest between the combined champion teams, the University High School and Tottenham versus The Rest, at Middle Park at 3 p.m. The selected teams are:—

CHAMPIONS.—Steed, Gester, Yon, A. Leslie, Murray, Hunt (University High), Bird, Chalmers, Ferguson, Bernard, Beard (Tottenham). Reserves: Neville (Tottenham), Wilson (University High).

THE REST.—Timmons, Stewart, Harris (Preston), Dawson (Albert Park), Wilson, Boyd (Middle Park), R. Leslie, Webster (University High), Alexander, Todd (Geelong Road), Demaine (Coburg High). Reserves: Markie (Middle Park), Sparks (University High). Teams meet at Middle Park station, 2.30.

Three Left In Running For Soccer Premiership

1935

By Nimrod

THE fight for the soccer premiership has been narrowed down to Footscray Thistle, Caledonians and Moreland, Hakoah having been able only to share the points at Moreland on Saturday. Both Thistle and Scots had narrow escapes, defeating Brighton and Coburg respectively by the only goal scored in each match.

[illegible]

Soccer Cup Final Sets Record

1935

Same Teams Meet This Year

By Nimrod

THE meeting of Caledonians and Hakoah in the final of the Dockerty Cup competition at Olympic Park today will create a new record for the Victorian soccer championship. It will be the first occasion on which the same teams have met in successive years in the final.

If Hakoah loses, it will be the first time that a team has appeared in the final in successive years and been defeated on both occasions.

It does not always follow that the best teams of the season reach the final, but generally one of them does. Two years ago when Brighton carried off the trophy it was opposed by St Kilda, the division two champion, but Brighton was not in the running for division one honors. Last year Hakoah won the division one championship with the loss of only two points. This year it has surrendered [illegible].

Same Last Year

CALEDONIANS have given away six points and the additional one lost has also given Hakoah top place. The teams were in the same positions last year when the Scots sprang a surprise in the re-play. Extra time was necessary to end the game on the second occasion, but it will surprise if this occurs again. Judging the Scots on their performance last week South Melbourne was unlucky to be defeated.

Few Successive Winners

WINNERS in successive years are limited to three clubs — Carlton 1909 and 1910, Williamstown-Yarraville 1912-13, and Footscray Thistle 1929-30. Melbourne Thistle was joint holder with [illegible] United in 1914 and won the cup in the following year. No team has won the cup for three years running.

Much will depend on Morgan, G. Weir and Beats, the Caledonian defence, whether the cup will remain with the club, but the full-backs will require to change their methods of last week if the Hakoah forwards are to be held.

It will be necessary to make the ball the objective and not the man, as against South Melbourne. The playing [illegible] will be soft and this is more likely [illegible] Hakoah than Caledonians. McIver [illegible] Bowman and Forrest is difficult to stop. [illegible] Hakoah will win [illegible].

The juniors and schoolboys have finished their tournaments and the trophies have been won as follow:—Junior Cup, University H.S. Old Boys; Section A championship and Selmon Cup, South Melbourne A; Miller Cup, South Melbourne B; Section B championship and Salthouse Cup, Prahran.

In the schoolboys' competitions, University High has won the Dunkling Shield, Glen Sheppard Cup and Clelland Cup. Tottenham has carried off the Bartlet Shield. In the secondary schools' competition, in which University High, Melbourne High, Northcote High and West Melbourne Technical took part, the championship was decided on Wednesday when University High defeated Melbourne High 7-1. Marshall scored six goals for University High.

PROGRAMME AND TEAMS

Dockerty Cup Final. — Caledonians v. Hakoah, kick-off 3 p.m.; referee, J. Parker.

Schoolboys' Trial.—Blues v. Reds, kick-off 1.45 p.m.

Caledonians.—Morgan, G. Weir, Beats, Mayne, S. Weir, J. Young, F. Young, Paulsen, B. Gray, Johnstone, Hughes.

Hakoah.—Aguilera, Yaffe, Mayney, J. Bowman, Roth, Rice, McCluskey, Lewis, McIver, Orr, Forrest.

As the colors clash, both teams have been ordered to change. Caledonians will play in claret with blue sleeves and Hakoah in dark blue.

First Soccer Games Today: Champions At Olympic Park

April 4th 1936

By Nimrod

THE Victorian soccer season opens this afternoon, but the programme will not be as drawn because of two Division 1 games and a number of reserve contests being postponed. Moreland was looking forward to making its start in Division 1, but, as Preston's players are engaged in cricket finals the game will be played at a later date.

THE withdrawal of Navy means that Brighton is also disengaged, so that the two games in which the promoted clubs were to have played will not now take place.

At Olympic Park

LAST year's champion team, Hakoah, will open the campaign at Olympic Park against Footscray Thistle. From the abundance of talent possessed by these clubs a first-class match should result.

Hakoah suffered only one defeat last season when Footscray beat it [illegible] on the same ground. It will be a big surprise if Hakoah again suffers defeat.

Hakoah has chosen 14 players to be ready for final selection, and may prefer Fenn, the newly acquired custodian, to Aguilera. Hayden returns to the back division after a season at South Yarra, and should make an ideal partner for Mackie.

McCluskey hopes to get a transfer to Footscray Thistle, and is not likely to play for Hakoah. In that case, the choice for the extreme right position will lie between Arber and Hawkes, providing the latter signs on before the game. With Roth helping again, big scores should be registered by Lewis, McIver and Forrest.

Footscray's Last Line

McKelvey, who has seen service with a number of clubs, will be Footscray's last line and, in association with Smith and Macauley, should make a resolute defence. The trio will find plenty to occupy their attention at Olympic Park, especially if Hakoah's sharp-shooters are on the target.

Baxter, the South Yarra centre man, will lead Thistle. If in form, he will be hard to hold.

South Melbourne will have W. Morton from Footscray, Stevenson from South Yarra, and Currie, late of Windsor, in the side to meet Caledonians. All should be an acquisition to the club. South will be the only Division 1 club operating at Middle Park as the Scots are sharing Olympic Park with Hakoah for their home games.

Several of Caledonians' last year's team will not be available for this game. G. Weir has signed for Nobels, but may return to the Scots for the next game. Morgan, the custodian, has gone elsewhere, but in securing Brown from Moreland the position should be capably filled. The contest should be an even one.

TODAY'S FIXTURES

Division One. — Hakoah v. Footscray Thistle, at Olympic Park; Coburg v. South Yarra, South Melbourne v. Caledonians.

Division Two. — Nobels v. Geelong, Heidelberg v. Box Hill, Brunswick v. Collingwood, Sunshine v. Camberwell, Spotswood v. Prahran.

Division Three. — North Melbourne Presbyterians v. St. David's, Sandringham v. Melbourne Manx.

Division One Reserves.—Caledonians v. South Melbourne.

Division Two Reserves. — Geelong v. Nobels, Box Hill v. Heidelberg, Collingwood v. Brunswick, Camberwell v. Sunshine, Prahran v. Spotswood.

Juniors.—Section A: Hakoah v. Prahran A, University H.S.O.B. v. Brighton A, Brunswick v. Collingwood, South Melbourne A v. Northcote H.S.O.B.

Section B: Heidelberg v. Footscray Thistle, Moreland v. Preston, Prahran B v. South Melbourne B, South Melbourne C v. Brighton B.

SELECTED TEAMS

Hakoah. — Aguilera, Fenn, Hayden, Mackie, Bowman, [illegible], W. Yaffe, Arber, Lewis, McIver, [illegible], Forrest, McCluskey, Hawkes. [illegible] N. Rosenberg.

STURT AND PORT THISTLE TO MEET IN POZZA CUP FINAL

Soccer Season Closes on October 3: Young Carnival Teams

By CORINTHIAN

One important district soccer match will remain to be played at the finish of the interstate carnival. The season will close with the first division Pozza Cup final between Sturt and Port Thistle. The game will be played on [illegible] ground on October 3.

Sturt, already holding the Palace Cup, will naturally enter the Pozza Cup final with determination to bring off the double event, while Port Thistle will be equally determined to crown [illegible] cup success the sudden improvement in form which came to them towards the middle of the season.

[illegible]

With the [illegible] interstate carnival for the English Association trophy in full swing, soccer followers are [illegible] football of outstanding quality.

New South Wales and Victoria are to be commended for having decided to give young teams an opportunity, and there is no need to regret the absence of some of the more experienced men who have made great names for themselves in the eastern States.

GROWTH OF GAME

[illegible]

HARD FIGHT BY STURT

[illegible]

HAKOAH 7 V. PRAHRAN 0

1936

[illegible]

Soccer Problem Still Unsolved

By Nimrod

1956

SATURDAY'S first division results made the soccer championship problem more complicated than ever. Home teams had a very bad day and only Hakoah annexed full points. Moreland gained a meritorious victory at Footscray and placed itself in line for the premiership. In fact on games played Moreland is in a better position than the leader. Coburg's defeat of South Melbourne also places it in a favorable place that may lead to the top.

HAKOAH, in the match against Brighton, seemed at one period as if it was going to be the victim of [illegible] by the referee on the offside law.

Both Brighton's goals were the result of players being allowed to go on when [illegible] offside and in consequence Brighton was able to cross over on even terms. [illegible] goals were scored during the first half. Hakoah got the first as the result of a penalty kick taken by Hayden. This was given for Fitzgerald tackling Molinski unfairly inside the penalty area. The second goal came from a shot by Molinski.

Hutton got the benefit of feeding Macdonald and then converting his centre into a goal. Just before the interval the scores were levelled by Campbell, who was offside with two other players of his side, but in spite of Hakoah's strong protests the goal was allowed to stand.

[illegible] was upset by Calderwood, and the referee placed the free kick just outside the penalty area. [illegible] and Arber feeding Orr, the veteran [illegible] the ball into the net well out of [illegible].

Ten minutes from the end Warburton [illegible] through the Brighton defence and [illegible] hard into the net. [illegible] played a [illegible] game for Hakoah [illegible] team. [illegible]

Smith Ordered Off

SMITH, the Footscray Thistle captain and right full back, was ordered off by the referee after [illegible] minutes had gone in the second half of the game with Moreland. It happened after an altercation between Smith and Ziebell, the Moreland centre forward. At the time Moreland was in the lead and held it to the end.

Johnny Johnstone made his first appearance for Footscray since his transfer from Caledonians and signalled it by scoring both Thistle goals.

During the last [illegible] minutes nothing was scored.

South Easy Victory

IN spite of the penalty of the deduction of two points Caledonians are well placed to annex the championship. A weakened South Yarra side could make no impression on the strong Caledonians' defence and at half-time the visitors led by four goals.

Bob Gray was responsible for four of the seven goals. He scored the first two, the fifth, and the seventh, the other three being shared by Mayne, Paulsen and F. Young.

Barnes and Cook in defence put up plenty of resistance for South Yarra but received little support. Mayne and Paulsen were outstanding for Caledonians.

South's Run Broken

SOUTH MELBOURNE'S run of success was broken by Coburg at Middle Park and its prospects of obtaining the championship are remote.

Coburg played a similar system to South, but played it better and established a two goals lead. Currie and Stevenson equalised, but Coburg, finishing stronger, got the winning goal with more than 15 minutes to spare.

Scores And Scorers

Dockerty Cup Re-play.—Collingwood 2 (Caterall 2) d. Sandringham 0.

First Division.—Moreland 3 (Knowles 2, Ziebell) d. Footscray Thistle 2 (Johnstone 2); Caledonians 7 (R. Gray 4, Mayne, Paulsen, F. Young) d. South Yarra 0; Hakoah 4 (Hayden, Molinski, Orr, Warburton) d. Brighton 2 (Hutton, Campbell); Coburg 3 (Deakeford, Gillie, Warnock) d. South Melbourne 2 (Currie, Stevenson).

Soccer Team From New South Wales Here for Carnival

TO TAKE PART in THE AUSTRALIAN SOCCER CARNIVAL which will begin tomorrow, the Victorian and New South Wales soccer teams arrived in Adelaide today. The New South Wales team at the station.

THREE MATCHES ARRANGED

Plans for Soccer Carnival

ARRIVAL OF TEAMS

By Corinthian

NAVY OUT OF SOCCER COMPETITION

Programme Curtailed

HONOURS TO AUSTRALIA

Indians Please

Although India showed much the better footwork, speed, and combination, it lost the fifth soccer Test match against Australia—at the Melbourne Cricket-ground—by 3 goals to 1.

India Scores First

Brighton Wins Cup

The Brighton-Moreland Salmon cup contest, which was the curtain-raiser, was won by Brighton by one goal to nil.

HAKOAH EXPECTED TO RETAIN SOCCER LEAD

By "ONWARD"

With the completion of the seventh round of first division soccer games on Saturday, all clubs will have met each other once, and no matter how the matches go Hakoah will enter on the second half of the programme at the head of affairs.

Game For Second Place

FEWER MIGRATIONS BY SOCCER MEN

Games Open On Saturday

By "ONWARD"

With no provision made for continuity of soccer players' services with one club from one season to the next, it becomes an annual event for some players to seek new quarters. Others remain loyal to one club throughout their playing careers, and these are generally found to be the backbone of the game.

NOBELS POWERFUL

CUP FINALISTS TO MEET

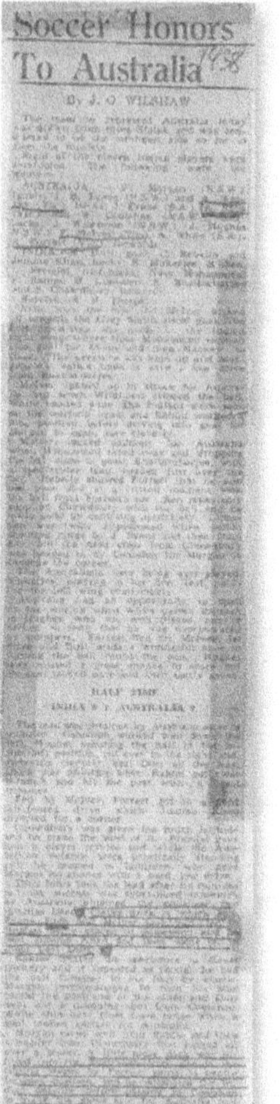

Soccer Honors To Australia

By J. O. WILSHAW

HALF TIME

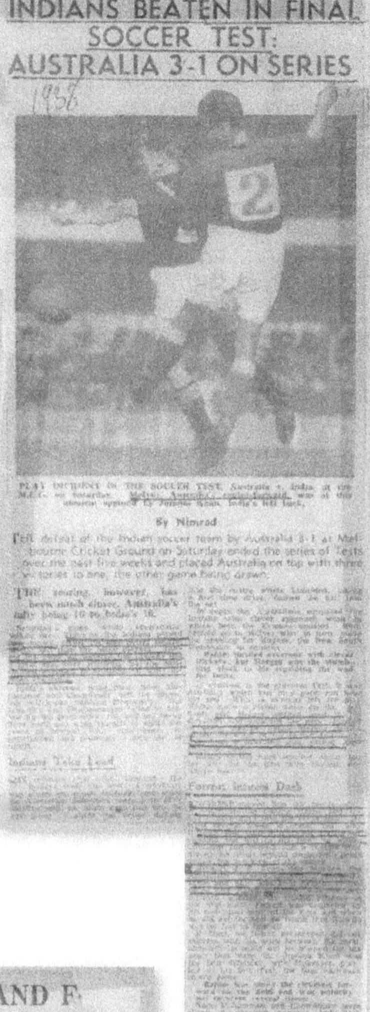

INDIANS BEATEN IN FINAL SOCCER TEST: AUSTRALIA 3-1 ON SERIES

By Nimrad

The defeat of the Indian soccer team by Australia 3-1 at Melbourne Cricket Ground on Saturday ended the series of Tests over the past five weeks and placed Australia on top with three victories to one, the other game being drawn.

The scoring, however, has been much closer, Australia's tally being 16 to India's 18.

Indians Take Lead

Forrest Injured

TEST CRICKETERS SHOW SOCCER FORM—AND F

Judaean League of Victoria

Charity Soccer Match

HAKOAH v R.A.A.F.

NORTH MELBOURNE FOOTBALL GROUND

Sunday, 25th June, 1944, at 3-15 p.m.

PRECEDED BY JUNIOR MATCH

HAKOAH JUNIORS v COMBINED JUNIORS

AT 1.45 P.M.

DISPLAY BY JUDAEAN GIRLS' GYMNASIUM,
Accompanied by West Coburg Citizens' Band.

Proceeds in aid of Jewish National Fund, United Jewish Relief Fund and a Patriotic Fund nominated by R.A.A.F. Team.

ORGANIZING COMMITTEE:

L. ABRAHAMS, President. N. SPIZER, Org. Secretary.
B. ABRAHAMS, Treasurer. MISS S. HONIG, Secretary.

S. Werthiem, A. J. Fayn, N. Marks, M. Zonenberg, A. Makemoff, G. Mavitz, D. Altshul, Mrs. M. Solomon, Misses E. Phillips, M. Pahoff, R. Gorr.

CHARITY BALL at MONASH HOUSE, TONIGHT

8 p.m. till 12 p.m.

Proceeds in aid of above Funds.

HAKOAH

Colours: HAKOAH: Blue and White

HAKOAH GOAL

POWER

Right: A. SPICER

Left: L. TAYLOR

Half-Backs:

WALLACE ROTH WOLFFS

Forwards:

GREER WEISS A. MYER

EDGEL FAIRWEATHER

Reserve: FRASER

Referee: L. ARMSTRON

Linesmen: C. CARTWRI

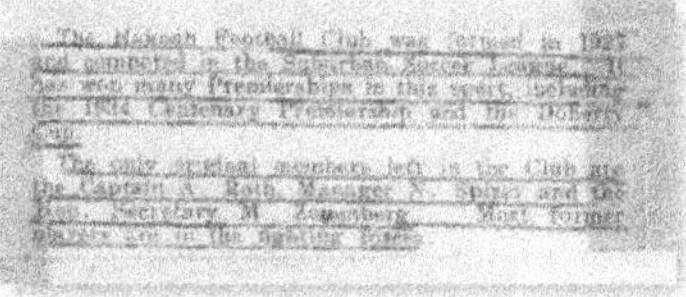

The Hakoah Football Club was formed in 1927 and competed in the Suburban Soccer League. It has won many Premierships in this sport, including the 1934 Centenary Premiership and the Dockerty Cup.

The only original members left in the Club are the Captain A. Roth, Manager N. Spizer and the Hon. Secretary M. Zonenberg. Most former players are in the fighting forces.

SOCCER TEAMS' WRONG TACTICS COSTLY

Eight In Third Cup Round

By "ONWARD"

Whoever was responsible for playing Meckey at left-half and centre-forward in the Hakoah soccer team on Saturday made a present to Collingwood of at least four goals, which probably would not have been scored if the international full-back had been in his proper position.

[illegible]

FOR THIRD ROUND

[illegible]

334

A CHARITY SOCCER MATCH

In aid of the U.J.O.R.F. Youth Section

HAKOAH v. MORELAND

These two well-known teams will meet at

The Olympic Park

on

SUNDAY, 13th OCTOBER

1946, at 2.45 p.m.

THE TOM JACK ERA

Hakoah perhaps reached its greatest heights in the mid-Fifties, a period now recalled as "the *Tom Jack* era". Jack led Hakoah to four Dockerty Cup wins in a row, from 1953 to 1956.

Those were the days of *Harry Sutherland, Syd Thomas, David McIntosh, Milia Vesovic, Joe Gottesman, Harry Rice, Ralph Piercy, Issy Roessler, Bill Harburn* and *Aldo Vitti*.

The Reserve team also won many laurels in these latter years, winning its League Championship in 1958, 1959, and 1960, and the Harry Armstrong Reserve Cup in 1956, 1958 and 1964.

The junior teams have also had their share of successes.

A HOME AT LAST

After 35 years in a wilderness of muddy paddocks and primitive playing conditions, Hakoah at last found a home at Albert Park in what is now one of the finest soccer stadiums in Australia.

It is well-equipped with first-class facilities for both players and officials.

JOSEPH SHATIN

TOM JACK

Joe Shatin was one of the founders of Hakoah Sports Club. Tom led Hakoah to four Dockerty Cup wins in a row—a grand era for the club.

It would have been gratifying if the team had won the league championship in this, the fortieth year of the club's existence. It hasn't done so, but its supporters can be very proud of its high position on the ladder, and its performances in a very hard State League.

The progress achieved in the past four seasons was carefully planned and successfully implemented by the Committee. Now the additional task of preparing players for the future is proceeding, and Hakoah's youthful Reserve team is showing the results of the coaching they receive by producing technical soccer that is a delight to watch.

Their capable coach is a former Hakoah player of 1952, *Jeff Davis*, and to him must go the credit for the improvement in individual ability and co-ordinated teamwork now being displayed by these youngsters.

I feel sure that, with the progress made to date, plus the keen desire to do better that is evident at every level in the club, a very bright future can be predicted for Hakoah.

At the risk of being branded over-optimistic, I am prepared to suggest that Hakoah is on the brink of an era such as it enjoyed years ago when its team was regarded as "the champion of champions".

— *FRED HUTCHISON.*

This was the soccer team which brought Hakoah back into the top division in 1950 after a sojourn in the Second Division. BACK ROW (from left): Johnny Kurzweil, Joe Lachmann, Sergio Bassi, Tom Jack, Kurt Defris (Secretary), Milia Vesovic, Karl Marischel, Frank Brachta. FRONT ROW: Joe Olshina, Issy Peters, Fred Lester, Franto Moucka, Jackie Roessler.

Friday, May 2nd., 1952 "THE AUSTRALIAN JEWISH NEWS" Page Five

HAKOAH HITS THE FRONT

5:0 WIN OVER SANDRINGHAM

SOCCER LEADERS

Melbourne Hakoah's fine 5:0 win over Sandringham took the Jewish team to the top of the Victorian Amateur Soccer Football Association's 2nd division ladder.

Pictured above are (from left to right) standing: Alex and Bill Olszyna, Joe Lachman, Fred Lester, Frank Roubal, Jonny Kurzweill (captain/coach) and Mr. K. Defris (manager). Front row: Karl Mashrischel (v.c.), Issy Peters, Frank Lorenzoni, Isidor Ressler and Harry Bader. Frank Moucka, Paul Pechout, Frank Werther and Joe Gottesman (not pictured) have also played in some games.

Forward line oldest in the league

The following year, Sutherland joined Hakoah, which had beaten Brighton in the 1953 Cup final, and he played there in 1954, '55, '56 and '57.

He stayed on as coach but later switched to Altona City which he coached from 1967 to 1972.

Now he's back with Hakoah as team manager.

Sutherland's 31 goals in 1954 still stands as the highest total by a Hakoah first-team player.

The Hakoah team that won the Dockerty Cup four times in a row featured probably the oldest forward line in Victorian top-league history.

Inside forward **Henry Rice from Scotland, winger Jackie Ressler** and Czech ball artist **Joe Gottesmann** were well into their thirties.

Ressler was one of the great Hakoah stalwarts. His name became synonymous with Hakoah.

John Slade was only 16 when he played in the 1954 Dockerty Cup final. Regular goalkeeper **Klassic** was dropped to make room for Slade who acquitted himself well.

However, Hakoah later got **Aldo Vitti** from Juventus and Slade had to play second fiddle again.

Dave McIntosh, a left back, was an accomplished Scottish player who later coached Hakoah and **Milan Vescvic** was a strong, robust wing half from Yugoslavia.

Two Hakoah greats who have since died were full back **Bill Harburn** and **Tom Jack** who was capped many times for Australia and was also Hakoah's player-coach.

Harburn, who played for Bishop Auckland in England and whose son Steve played goalkeeper for Hakoah and Sandringham, died in the West Gate Bridge disaster.

Hakoah had three more distinguished Australian internationals – **Ralph Piercy, Syd Thomas** and **Angus Drennen**.

Piercy, a brilliant outside left, played for Chester in England and guested for many of the top English clubs during the war.

Syd Thomas, from Scotland, played on the wing or at half back. He was with Harry Sutherland at Brighton before both switched to Hakoah and he played for Victoria as well as Australia.

Angus Drennen won the Victorian Argus Medal while with Box Hill in 1950. He also played for ICI Deer Park and was a fine half back for Hakoah.

Another great player of that era was Czech full back **Frank Moucka**. Going further back into the late forties, we remember **Alby Meier** and **Issi Peters** as fine servants of Hakoah.

The greatest player of more recent times was defender John O'Neill, an Eire international who joined in 1965. O'Neill spent six years with Preston North End, playing alongside the great Tom Finney, and was also with Barrow where a broken leg almost ended his career. He won the Argus Medal in 1969.

O'Neill's partner in defence was **Alan Stenhouse,** who played in Scotland for Motherwell and Cowdenbeath before joining Hakoah in 1963.

Dick van Alphen was a top player in Holland and with Ringwood Wilhelmina before he switched to Hakoah and was capped for Australia. He was one of the Socceroos who returned unbeaten after a 10-match tour of Asia in 1967.

George Keith, the brilliant full back from Scotland, also went on to represent Australia and to play in the 1969 World Cup elimination matches. Keith transferred from Hakoah to APIA where he also coached.

Mike O'Hara from Luton Town still rates as the most colorful goalkeeper Victoria has had. He played for Slavia in between two stints with Hakoah and spent the 1978 season with Footscray J.U.S.T. in the Philips League.

Hugh Murney played in Scotland for Queen of the South and Morton before joining Hakoah in 1964. He had eight memorable seasons with Hakoah and then coached Albion Rovers, Fitzroy-Alexander reserves, Heidelberg and is currently coach of Park Rangers.

And what about **Ted Smith?** He was one of the select few who can boast of having represented Australia at soccer in the Olympic Games.

It was in Melbourne in 1956, the only time Australia has contested an Olympic soccer tournament.

And Hakoah is the club that gave the great **Jim Armstrong** his start in Australian soccer in 1956. He had three and a half seasons there before transferring to Hellas and then to Juventus. Armstrong, who was capped for Australia, retired recently after scoring a State League record 152 goals.

Hakoah of the late sixties, standing from left: Dick van Alphen, Mike O'Hara, Hugh Murney, George Keith, Ian Moran, Jim Armstrong. Front: Alex Purdie, John O'Neill, Ted Smith, Keith Fry, Alan Stenhouse.

Hakoah's 1952 squad, standing from left — M. Kodak, J. Kurzweil, Lachmann, S. Bassi, T. Jack, K. Defris (secretary), M. Vescvic, M. Marishel, Werther, W. Copeland. Front — M. Breitberg, I. Peters, F. Lester, F. Moucka, J. Ressler.

1953

"THE AUSTRALIAN JEWISH NEWS" 10/53 Melbourn

Hakoah Changes Its Name

NOW HAKOAH SPORTS CLUB

By BEN ALEXANDER

At the annual meeting of the Hakoah-J.R.C. sporting club last week, the meeting decided, after a long spirited discussion to change it's name from Hakoah-J.R.C. to the Hakoah Sports Club.

The meeting, which was held at the Caulfield Hebrew Centre, was attended by nearly 50 members and observers. The Senior vice-president Mr. T. Rubinstein occupied the chair in the early absence of the president Mr. Jack Scolnick, and continued in that capacity throughout the evening.

After Mr. Basil Isaacs president of AJAX, was welcomed Mr. Kurt Defris gave a brief report on the club's financial position. He praised the table tennis and basketball sections for their splendid bank balance, £59 and £22 respectively, and gave mention to the respective treasurers, Mr. Norman Silberberg and Mr. Sam Komesarook.

Mr. Defris stated that the Soccer section in the past year had "made ends meet," but he hoped with the enclosed ground and the increased membership, the section would in the coming year gain substantially.

"COACHING" CHALLENGED

Discussing the treasurer report, Don Finkelstein, a player queried the £59/12/- on the balance sheet allotted to coaching fees, and put the question to the president Mr. Jack Skolnik whether Johnny Kurzweill a player, ras received that amount. If so, he must be classed as a professional and therefore ineligible to play competition.

Mr. Skolnik said he would go into the matter.

Presenting the Managers' report Mr Kurt Defris gave the 3 teams' performances in the season just completed.

He stated the first team, which had been promoted to first division for this season, had an excellent year winning 18 games to 2, kicking 92 goals to 29, finished second behind Moreland on the premiership, and showed excellent team spirit.

Mr. Defris paid special praise to forwards, Gottesman Kurzweill, and Roessler, half line Peters and Kodak, and backs Lester and Maehrischel. Kurzweill got special mention to his handling of the captaincy.

In mentioning the results of the international series last lear, Mr. Defris stated that Hakoah officially would not help to form the Israel team this year.

He remarked also on the reserve and junior teams as having a very successful year.

Mr. Defris went on to say that, Hakoah, should be hououred and proud of having Dr. Evatt and Mr. Cleary as patrons of the Club, and credit for this achievement should be given to the president Mr. Skolnik.

Mr. Defris stated that Hakoah have now leased St. Kevin's Oval in Toorak for the coming season and outlined the ground's amenities.

He also stressed the necessity of good behaviour by all concerned to enable Hakoah to get the groiund for future years.

Mr. Norman Silberberg, representing the table tennis section, gave a brief outline of the table tennis sections stating that teams had been very successful in competition play, membership had grown to the limit, the club's finances are in a happy position, and predicted a bright future for the club.

Mr. K. DEFRIS, re-elected Team Manager

OTHER HALL?

He however stressed grave concern in the Caulfield Hebrew Centre's reluctance to give the club the use of the rooms for more than two nights. He stated the possibility may arise when Hakoah finding two nights insufficient may have to find another hall.

Mr. Don Finkelstein (Basketball) gave a bright report of that section's progress, stating a very successful first year with an excellent record in competition and finances very stable. He also made a plea for more support at the competition games.

Mr. Basil Isaacs (President Ajax) congratulated the outgoing committees on their hard work put in through the year and stressed his sincere wish that the incoming committee carry on the

He gave special tribute to Mr. Kurt Defris for his most comprehensive typed report and balance sheet, and to Mr. Jack Skolnik on his managemen of the club.

Mr. Clarrie Power, speaking as a member expressed his wish that the club should be made all Jewish again soon. He stated that Hakoah was founded as a Jewish Club and should be carried on as a Jewish club.

Mr. Rubinstein had a difficult time controlling the meeting as there were many interjectors caused, by the tense, pent up feeling of the members there.

PROMISES NOT KEPT

Mr. Don Finkelstein addressed the meeting, and asked the committee why he did not get a game with the first team last year after having been promised to play for the senior side if he did not leave the club.

Mr. Defris answering his question, stated they had all intensions of doing so but he was so much out of form that it was impossible to do so.

A motion to the effect that the Magen David be dropped from the club's colours was defeated and it will now remain.

The members then elected their new committee.

(See last week's Jewish News).

Page Eighteen Melbourne, Friday, April 9th., 1954

(David Fell photo).

Hakoah's senior soccer eleven, which scored 8-3 over Footscray in the season's opening 1st division fixture at St. Kevin's Oval last Saturday. From left to right: (standing) S. Thomas, H. Rice, Mr. K. Defris (manager), I. Raessler, V. Vinezenza, J. Gottesmann, T. Jack (captain-coach), Mr. J. Reich (selector), F. Sutherland, Mr. A. Kun (chairman of selectors). Front: R. Balabanski, P. Clarke, F. Lorenzoni, M. Kodak, M. Vesovic.

The 1954 Hakoah team which won the Dockerty Cup, standing from left: Mr Brown (official), Kurt Defris (secretary), Tom Jack (coach), Pat Clarke, Dave McIntosh, Jack Skolnik (president), goalkeeper Klassic, Syd Thomas, Frank Moucka, Jim Reich (manager), Bobby West (player). Front: Harry Sutherland, Henry Rice, D. Aliempijevicz, Joe Gottesmann, Jackie Ressler, Milan Vesovic.

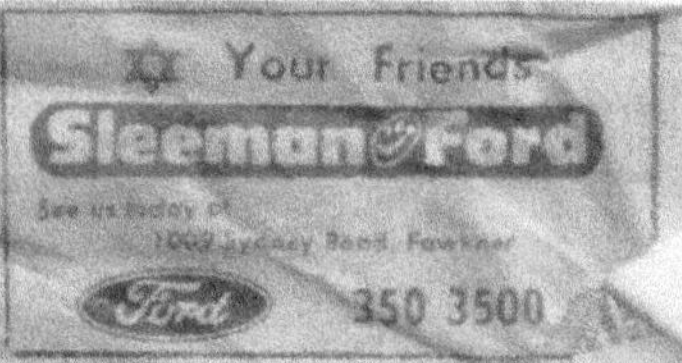

THE DRAW SYNDROME

By JANET COHEN

Poor disposal particularly in midfield and attack, marred Hakoah's disappointing 1-1 draw with Prahran Slavia in their State League soccer match at the Showgrounds on Saturday.

The defence was generally solid but had occasional lapses in concentration and teamwork. The team will not win matches until it combines as a unit.

The midfielders were unable to pass the ball to the forwards.

Finally State player **Mike** [illegible] secured the ball and his powerful shot at goal just missed.

Hakoah had several further scoring attempts with **Stewart** [illegible] and **Billy Jordanou** going close.

Goalkeeper **Bill Whiteside** [illegible] made one fortunate save. Moments later however he could not stop a Slavia forward [illegible]. Slavia led 1-0.

Then a penalty to **Mike** [illegible] resulting in a goal levelled the score at 1-all.

[illegible]

Early in the second half [illegible] **Les Owens** was taken off with a knee injury. His replacement captain **Jerry** [illegible] played a solid game.

Ian Gibson, playing his [illegible]

Hakoah reserves lost 1-2 against Prahran-Slavia.

Goal: Rooney

FIXTURES

Hakoah-St. Kilda v. Sunshine City at Sunshine, 3.00 p.m. Sunday, reserves 1.30 p.m.

Under 14s Saturday Sunshine, 1 p.m.

Under 15s Saturday Sunshine, 2.30 p.m.

Hakoah thirds all-Jewish team will play Keysborough at Keysborough Sunday, 3 p.m.

INTERSTATE SOCCER SERIES

● Pictured is the Victorian side which will compete over the June long weekend against top Jewish sides from W.A. and N.S.W. The teams will be competing for the New South Wales Maccabi Trophy awarded to the top state.

A revival in Jewish interest in soccer is the aim of a "mini-carnival" in Melbourne over the Queen's Birthday holiday week-end (June 10-12).

Three States, Victoria, N.S.W. and W.A. will be represented [illegible]. It is the first Jewish soccer [illegible] in Melbourne [illegible] years.

[illegible]

The [illegible] side will be drawn mainly from Hakoah's all-Jewish side, the thirds.

The Australian Maccabi Federation and Hakoah — St. Kilda soccer club will support and assist the staging of the tournament.

U.K. DON'T PLAY BALL

JERUSALEM (JCNS): Israeli football officials are blaming Britain for Israel's failure to be admitted as a member of UEFA (Union of European Football Associations).

Mr. Michael Aimog, the chairman of the Israel Football Association, told the JCNS [illegible]

FIRST LOSS

Judaean Sunday special C tennis side had its first loss [illegible]

This picture shows Middle Park Stadium, the new home of Hakoah Football Club from 1961 until 1982. At the time of its completion, Middle Park Stadium was a state of the art facility as a venue for association football

The Soccer Club

The Hakoah Soccer Club is necessarily the axis around which the other sport segments of the club revolve.

Its team has been rebuilt many times, but its senior sides won First Division Championships in 1934, 1935, 1938 and 1943. Hakoah also holds the record for Dockerty Cup successes, with six wins in 1935, 1945, 1953, 1954, 1955, and 1956.

The Reserve team won its League Championship in 1958, 1959, and 1960, and the Harry Armstrong Reserve Cup in 1956, 1958 and 1964.

The junior teams have also had their share of successes, and will undoubtedly provide players for the future.

Memberships

During the struggles of the past 33 years, many members of the Jewish community were connected with the Hakoah Soccer Club in one way or another, but its lack of a satisfactory home ground proved to be a discouraging factor.

Now, with a stadium of which any club could be proud at the disposal of its supporters, and a newly rebuilt soccer team that is currently enjoying a fair degree of success, the club is engaged in a membership drive and appeals for YOUR support.

Enclosed you will find a Membership Application Card.

It offers two classes of membership for your personal choice.

Standard Membership—The Season Pass of Standard Membership will entitle you to admission to all events sponsored by the Hakoah Sports Club at the Middle Park Sports Stadium, including all home games of the Hakoah Soccer Club. The donation is $12.

Full Membership—As a Full Member, you will receive a Blue Pass, which will entitle you to all the privileges of Standard Membership, PLUS A RESERVED GRAND STAND SEAT to all home games of the Hakoah Sports Club at the Middle Park Sports Stadium. The donation is $20.

Please fill in the Membership Application Card and send it together with your cheque, to—

Mr. K. Deitz, Secretary-Manager,
Hakoah Sports Club,
110 Westbury Street, St. Kilda.

Hakoah's Club Rooms

● Hakoah has 2,000 square feet of space in its clubrooms at Middle Park for social functions. Picture shows a small section prepared for a meeting of the Committee.

Many thanks to John Punshon, Damian Smith and Yaniv Bleicher

HAKOAH MEANS STRENGTH – And Victoria's brilliant Jewish soccer team lives up to its name

Dave McKenzie *Sports Novels,* July, 1950

One of the most unique organizations in Australian sport is the entirely Jewish Soccer team of Hakoah, the headquarters of which is at Olympic Park in the heart of Melbourne.

Hakoah, pronounced Har-koah, is a Hebrew word meaning strength, and the club throughout the course of its history has valiantly justified the optimism of the name.

The club was formed in 1928 when there was a steady stream of Jewish immigrants coming in to this country, the founders being prominent Melbourne businessmen including Josef Shatin, a front-rank barrister and solicitor, and the Skolnik brothers, leading wines and spirit merchants.

The club has always enjoyed the support of outstanding Jewish men of business, its office-bearers having included frock and clothing manufacturers, a spinning mills proprietor, a motor trade magnate, a handbag manufacturer, a large delicatessen proprietor, an M.L.C. (*), prominent doctors and barristers, wines merchants, shoes and stocking manufacturers, and the general manager of the largest store in Melbourne.

The team proved itself worthy of the patronage of such outstanding supporters by coming up from a minor league to make itself premiers (in four short years) of the third division of the Victorian Soccer League, going through that particular season without defeat.

On thus gaining promotion to the second division, the Hakoah side again went through the season undefeated and won the premiership and promotion to the first grade. The following year the side won the first division premiership, again remaining undefeated in doing so – thus completing an achievement surely rare in the annals of Australian sport.

The man chiefly responsible for this run of unbroken success was Phil Bowman, an Englishman of Jewish ancestry who back home in England a few years previously had had an extremely promising career with the famed Manchester United cut short by the infliction of a spinal injury. Phil had migrated to Australia, and, having recovered from the injury that had finished his English big league career, had again taken up the game.

He performed the same spectacular feat, as captain with the South Yarra club, of bringing them up from the third division to the first division championship – winning each grade's premiership en route-before being prevailed upon to go to Hakoah.

Although his association with Hakoah ended more than a decade ago, Phil's efforts are still spoken of in warm terms by officials, and he is unanimously conceded to have been the greatest leader the club has had in its almost quarter-century of existence.

During the period in which Phil Bowman was its leader, the Hakoah club met the members of the M.C.C. (**) cricket team of the famed '32–'33 body-line tour in a highly unique international match at the old Exhibition Oval, Hakoah running out victorious three to one. The M.C.C. line-up included Wally Hammond, Maurice Leyland, Bill Voce, George Duckworth, Bill Bowes, Les Ames, and the late Hedley Verity.

Shortly after the formation of Hakoah, Jewish immigration fell away (owing to the depression) and consequently the club was forced to look to players of other nationalities to fill its ranks. During the next few years it became an absolute Foreign Legion among sports organizations, the diversity of nationality of its members making them perfectly equipped to man a Saharan fort.

The following constitutes a typical line-up of the team as it was at this time – the place of birth of the players being given in brackets: Goal: Aquilera (Spain), R.B. Hayden (Aust.), L.B. P. Bowman (Eng.), R.H. W. Yaffe (Palestine), C.H. Roth (Germany), L.H. J. Bowman (Eng.), O.R. C. Yaffe (Palestine), I.R. Orr (Scot.), C.F. Mclvor (Eng.), I.L. Johnstone (Scot.), O.L. Forrest (Scot.).

In 1934, Melbourne's centenary year, Hakoah were again premiers of the first grade of the Victorian Soccer League, and also winners of the Dockerty Cup – Victoria's premier soccer award, given to the team victorious in the Cup final series that follows upon the conclusion of the ordinary premiership matches.

During the war years, at a time when the game could have quite easily taken the coup de gras in Victoria, Hakoah battled on to keep it alive, although being forced, through sheer necessity to amalgamate with the Moreland club. The amalgamation proved, however, to be an extremely successful one as regards playing results – the combine winning the premiership in 1942 and 1944, the Dockerty Cup in 1945, and being runners-up for the Dockerty Cup in 1942, 1943 and 1945.

However, with the close of war and the recommencement of Jewish immigration to this country, Hakoah dissociated itself from the Moreland side and again became an all-Jewish club. It has played as such since the 1946 season, and with the complete setting-up again of the Victorian Soccer League climbed to the first grade last season and is hoping to remain there.

The club has been a force in the game in Victoria throughout its existence, having, with the limited opportunities in this country for international or interstate activities, had a dozen of its players honored by such selection.

The Skolnik brothers also gave the game a lift by presenting a cup for annual competition between teams confined to players under nineteen years representing Victoria and South Australia.

The club, too, in contradiction to the usual stories circulated concerning the close-friendliness of the members of its race, has always been noted for its fine treatment of its players.

An outstanding case in point is that of a crack Scottish forward called Johnny Lewis who once won a premiership for Hakoah with a spectacular overhead goal forty yards out from the net. Johnny later fell upon hard times, and, forsaken by friends and relatives, would have died in a pauper's grave if the matter had not come to the notice of the Hakoah club which immediately made and supplied all funeral arrangements and expenses.

Perhaps the outstanding character connected with the club throughout its history has been little Nat Spicer, a shoe manufacturer originally from London.

Nat has been an absolute ball of fire in administrative matters for Hakoah, having at various times been committee member, secretary, and president of the club, and having worked at all his official duties with the vigor of the proverbial beaver.

His tremendous enthusiasm has been such that for a number of years he set for himself the voluntary task of attending to the placing of stops in all the players' boots and mending all those in need of repair.

He also took on the self-appointed task of washing the jerseys of the club's teams, and on the Monday morning following a match has had as many as forty-four jerseys hanging on his back-yard clothes-line!

Nat was also a great asset to Hakoah on the playing field, his ability finding him several times selected to take part in matches against various international organizations. He is not now actively connected with the club, but his former services are remembered with deep gratitude.

Hakoah, as has been stated, means strength, and the members of the club have in the past given ample vindication of the fitness of the title.

It may safely be predicted that they will continue on the soccer field to overthrow the Philistines in true Samson-like fashion, for the national pride that is the mainspring of their organization makes them truly worthy of the steel of the doughtiest of opponents.

* Member of the Legislative Council, the upper house of Victoria's parliament.

** The English cricket team. Their 'bodyline' tour of Australia in 1932–33 was a bitterly fought series of matches in which the English fast bowlers took aim at the batsman rather than the stumps. This was considered by most to be extremely poor sportsmanship.

Top players and eight Cup triumphs

Soccer Action, October 25, 1978

Hakoah, which celebrates its 50th anniversary this year, had its first committee meeting in January 1928, The first game was against North Carlton at Fawkner Park and Hakoah won the game 1–0. Hakoah was officially affiliated with The Victorian Amateur Soccer Football Association.

The club was named after the famous Vienna Hakoah club, which had achieved great success in Austria. Kurt Defris, who has been secretary of Hakoah–St Kilda since 1947, is a former player of Vienna Hakoah. Hans Strohs and Vice President Fred Halpern were also involved with the Austrian club.

The first executive committee of Hakoah–St Kilda was: Joe Shatin (President), Sam Yaffe, Alex Orloff, Norman Shatin, Kolman and Eric Rogers, Jack Skolnik, Harry Spivakovsky, Stan Rosenberg, Sam Goldfein, Henry Goldberg, Bob Fetter and Morrie Belkan.

In the 50 years of its existence, the main aim of the club has been to keep the traditional name of Hakoah as the symbol of Jewish sports involvement in Melbourne. Hakoah is justifiably proud of being the only Jewish-sponsored soccer club in Melbourne.

For many years Hakoah–St Kilda has been the poor relation of Sydney's mighty Hakoah club – but it was not always so. From 1934 to 1938, for example, Hakoah won three Victorian First Division championships and a Dockerty Cup. And from 1953 to 1958 inclusive, it won the Dockerty Cup four years running. In fact, Hakoah has won the Dockerty Cup eight times – more often than any other club.

Kurt Defris is the longest serving of the current administrators, but there are others who deserve mention. John Chaskiel, for example, has been chairman for 10 years and Kadish Korman has been vice-president and treasurer for almost as long. Jack Skolnik was one of the strongest early presidents. Other prominent Hakoah leaders included Vic Gross, Eric Erdi, Dr H. Baytch who became a life member of the Victorian Soccer Federation and of course the current VSF Chairman, Michael Weinstein, who is still on Hakoah's committee.

Hakoah's past coaches have included some of the foremost names in soccer – Asa Robbins, John Kursweil, Dave McIntosh, Tom Jack, Manny Poulakakis, Jim Adam, Mike Mandelis, Milenko Rusmir, Sam Meyer and of course there were also great players. One of the greatest was centre half Aku Roth who came from German club FC Nuernberg and became a regular member of the Victorian team. Gerry Chaldi, now coach of Hakoah in Sydney, played half back for Melbourne's Hakoah for two years in the sixties.

Harry Sutherland played in England for Leeds United, Exeter and Bournemouth and was player-manager of Western League club Bedford before he came to Australia in 1953 – at the age of 38! His first job was with Brighton, where as player-coach, he led his new team into the Dockerty Cup final. The following year Sutherland joined Hakoah, which had beaten Brighton in the 1953 Cup final, and played there in '54. '55. '56 and '57. He stayed on as coach but later switched to Altona City which he coached from 1967 to 1972. Now he's back with Hakoah as team manager. Sutherland's 31 goals in 1954 still stand as the highest total by a Hakoah first team player.

The Hakoah team that won the Dockerty Cup four times in a row featured probably the oldest forward line in Victorian top-league history. Inside forward Henry Rice from Scotland, winger Jackie Ressler and Czech ball artist Joe were well into their thirties. Ressler was one of the great Hakoah stalwarts. His name became synonymous with Hakoah. John Slade was only 16 when he played in the 1954 Dockerty Cup final. The regular goalkeeper was dropped to make room for Slade who acquitted himself well. However Hakoah later got Aldo Vitti from Juventus, and Slade had to play second fiddle again. Dave McIntosh, a left back, was an accomplished Scottish player who later coached Hakoah and Milan. Vesovic was a strong, robust wing half from Yugoslavia.

Hakoah greats who have since died were full back Bill Harbum and Tom Jack, who was capped many times for Australia and was also Hakoah's player-coach. Harbum, who played for Bishop Auckland in England and whose son Steve played goalkeeper for Hakoah and Sandringham, died in the West Gate Bridge disaster.

Hakoah had three more distinguished Australian internationals – Ralph Piercy, Syd Thomas and Angus Drennan. Piercy, a brilliant outside left, played for Chester in England and guested for many of the top English clubs during the war. Syd Thomas, from Scotland, played on the wing or at half back. He was with Harry Sutherland before both switched to Hakoah and he played for Victoria as well as Australia. Angus Drennan won the Victorian Argus Medal while with Box Hill in 1959. He also played for ICI Deer Park and was a fine half back for Hakoah. Another great player of that era was Czech full back Frank Moucha. Going further back, into the late forties, we remember Alby Meier and Issi Petes as fine servants of Hakoah.

The greatest player of more recent times was defender John O'Neill, an Eire international who joined in 1965. O'Neill spent six years with Preston North End, playing alongside the great Tom Finney, and was also with Barrow when a broken leg almost ended his career. He won the Argus Medal in 1969. O'Neill's partner in defence was Alan Stenhouse, who played in Scotland for Motherwell and Cowdenbeath before joining Hakoah in 1963.

Dick van Alphen was a top player in Holland and with Ringwood Wilhelmina before he to joined Hakoah and was capped for Australia. He was one of the Socceroos who returned after a 10-match tour of Asia in 1967. George Keith, the brilliant full back from Scotland, also went on to represent Australia and to play in the 1969 World Cup elimination matches. Keith transferred from Hakoah to APIA where he also coached.

Mike O'Hara from Luton Town still rates as the most colorful goalkeeper Victoria has had. He played for Slavia in between two stints with Hakoah and spent the 1978 season with Footscray J.U.S.T. in the Philips National League. Hugh Mumey played in Scotland for Queen of the South and Morton before joining Hakoah in 1964. He had nine memorable seasons with Hakoah and then coached Albion Rovers, Fitzroy-Alexander reserves, Heidelberg, after which he coached Park Rangers. And what about Ted Smith? He was one of the select few who can boast of having represented Australia at soccer in the Olympic Games. It was in Melbourne in 1956, the only time Australia has contested an Olympic soccer tournament. And Hakoah is the club that gave the great Jim Armstrong his start in Australian soccer. He had three and a half seasons there before transferring to Hellas, and then to Juventus. Armstrong who was capped for Australia, retired recently after scoring a State League record 152 goals.

Kurt Defris saves Hakoah through link with Hellas

Craig McKenzie *Soccer Action,* January 27, 1982

Kurt Defris did 'the only honorable thing' when he came to terms with Hellas. And so Hellas–Hakoah soccer club was born into the Victorian State League late last year. 'Everyone could see that the writing was on the wall,' said Defris, a reference to Hakoah's overdraft and guarantees totaling $48,000. 'We have done what we could in the past 55 years. The interest in Hakoah Soccer Club no longer is there. At least we have kept the name "Hakoah" flying in soccer circles. The Greek people have treated us almost like brothers. It took us a few months, in fact about a year, to convince our people that we wouldn't be eaten up by a merger. I'm a man who goes with the times and it would have hurt me had we gone out with a bang by being declared bankrupt. For us, amalgamation was the only solution, the only honorable thing we could do.'

The new club is headed by president Jim Diamataris. John Chaskiel, a long standing Hakoah committeeman, and Peter Dourin, are vice-presidents. Chris Papas is treasurer and the general committee numbers 14. Kurt Defris is secretary-manager, continuing an unbroken administrative connection with Hakoah, which started in 1947, a unique record in Australian and world soccer.

At 73 Defris remains active and alert. His ability to analyze, debate and influence has been invaluable over countless committee meetings in a variety of sports. Honored by the Order of Australia in 1978, life membership of the Victorian Soccer Federation and the Victorian Table Tennis Association and life presidency of the Victorian Ice Hockey Association, his record is a monument to successful sports administration.

The young Defris was a dashing winger in the Austrian First Division. His proudest playing days were in 1931 when he transferred for about $A20,000 from Fair Unitas to the famous Hakoah–Vienna club. During the Second World War he escaped Hitler's persecution of Jews by fleeing to Shanghai in China. There he became chairman of the Jewish Recreation Club which boasted about 20 clubs in the Jewish Soccer League and some 6,000 registered players.

In 1946. he came to Australia and played about half of the 1947 season with Hakoah before taking up an administrative post. Defris also excelled at table tennis. During his stay in Austria he ranked consistentiy in the top 10 in the country and was a national representative. His wife was ranked number three in the world after the 1936 world championships. His success and knowledge as a player in both soccer and table tennis have been integral to his success as an administrator in these sports. He has seen about 10 Hakoah presidents come and go, among them Jack Skolnik, Dr Henry Baytch, Les Erdi, Victor Gross, Ned Spicer, Manny Unreich and Dennis Krongold. He admires the first president of Hakoah, Jack Shatin, and values his friendship with Fred Halpern, Michael Weinstein, John Chaskiel, Kadish Korman, Fred Weider. Henry Greenfield, Dr Ian Kaufman, Henry Fromer, Peter Pryles and innumerable former Hakoah committeemen and supporters.

Defris is a pragmatist in the classic mould. He can reminisce about the former greatness of Hakoah, then suddenly spring back to the modern day, candidly outlining the reasons behind the club's increasing economic hardship and eventual amalgamation. Not for him simply fond memories. Hakoah survives. Maybe not strictly based upon the support of the Jewish business community but its survival nonetheless.

'For years now we have relied upon the backing of the Jewish business community,' he says. 'Up until about 1965 we were one of the best supported clubs in Victoria but our support dwindled quickly. The old guard died, their descendents didn't become interested in soccer because of the diverse interests prevalent in modern day youth and Australian Rules Football was more enticing than soccer, in a way we contributed to our demise because we neglected our juniors until recently.'

'When I came to Hakoah we played at Royal Park, then we moved to Fawkner Park. Our next home ground was near the Exhibition Buildings and then we became the first club to play at Olympic Park. That was before the stadium was built. In the 50s we played at St Kevins Oval in Toorak until a successful propaganda campaign was carried out by a leading Melbourne radio personality who didn't want to see diverse ethnic groups playing soccer in Toorak. In 1958 we returned to Olympic Park and in 1961 we moved to Albert Park. Slowly but surely, stone by stone, the Middle Park stadium evolved. We are indebted to the late Senator Pat Kennelly who was our patron and chairman of the Albert Park Trust. He was instrumental in building our stadium. Of course, we shared the ground with Hellas and I want to stress that there never has been the slightest clash over the use of the ground. And the players I have seen over the years! Who could forget them? Players like Hugh Mumey, Harry Sutherland, Harry Roessler,

Jacky Roessler, Joe Gottesman and of course our most famous captain, Tom Jack, Dick van Alphen, Dave McIntosh and Milan Vesovic are others who readily come to mind. Gentlemen all, and from time to time they come back to watch Hakoah. You know I estimate that maybe 60 percent of our players finished their careers with us. That says something good about them and about our club, eh?'

Thousands of Victorian soccer followers are acquainted with the sight of Defris walking along the touchline with his trusty chair, trying to select a good vantage point just seconds before the kickoff of a Hakoah match. The analogy between that sight and the *Peanuts* cartoon character Linus with his security blanket in tow almost is irresistible. That chair could well have joined Hakoah around about the same time as Defris. Just as the chair is symbolic of the man, the man himself symbolises everything we know as Hakoah Soccer Club.

What makes Hakoah successful?

WHAT goes on in a soccer club? What are the ingredients that bring success or, when they are lacking, leave a vacuum that induces failure? Perhaps the man best qualified to answer these questions is one who is connected with the club, but is neither committeeman nor player nor coach. Yet he must be close enough to observe all of these in action. Such a man is the Team Manager, and this is what the Hakoah Soccer Club's Team Manager, Fred Hutchison, has to say about the club.

Even in the light of some of the great teams it has fielded during the past forty years, the glamorous names who have appeared on its team sheets, and the large number of players that have been drawn from the club to represent Victoria and Australia, the Hakoah of today can hold its head high.

It's amazing to think that in 1963, only four years ago, Hakoah escaped relegation by a single match point. But, typically, the club's wise and courageous administrators did not despair.

They took stock. They realised that, while they had labored to maintain the ability of the team at a steady level, other clubs had managed to lift the standard of their teams as well as the standard of Victorian soccer. Hakoah's administrators set out to do likewise.

Rebuilding is always a slow and heartbreaking task. All through 1964 and 1965, the job went on. The reward came in 1966, when Hakoah finished third on the ladder and won the Dockerty Cup for the seventh time.

During the rebuilding of the team, many players were brought in and tried. Some failed to hold their places, others returned overseas or retired through injury.

Those remaining can be considered, collectively, as the most experienced group of players in the State League. They include *Mike O'Hara, George Keith, John O'Neill* (captain), *Hugh Murney, Dick van Alphen, Alan Stenhouse* (vice-captain), *Keith Fry, Jimmy Armstrong, Ian Monan, Johnny Anderson, Teddy Smith, Alex Purdie, David Baker, Hans Petersen*, and *Johnny Walker*.

WHERE CUP CAME FROM

The first rounds of the 1964 Dockerty Cup matches will be played on Saturday but many of the players will know little of the man behind the Cup.

He is Harry Dockerty, the 82-year-old founder of soccer in Victoria and president of the Victorian Soccer Federation.

In 1907 "Doc" as he is known everywhere, gave the cup to the sport to help promote the code in Melbourne.

Harry Dockerty, who was born in Scotland, is still one of soccer's most regular spectators and attends the regular Federation meetings at Soccer House.

NO LONGER

Many of the clubs which have won the Dockerty Cup in the past are now defunct.

They include famous clubs like Carlton United, Melbourne Thistles, Wonthaggi Magpies, and Royal Caledonians.

Competition for the Cup has always been fierce. In the 53 years history of the cup, the holders have managed to defend it seven times.

Hakoah is the only club to have ever won it four times in a row—1955, 56, 57 and 58.

The present holders are J.U.S.T., who won it from George Cross in a whirlwind series last year when 23 games were played in 16 days.

Tas. side will not be easy

No State League matches will be played this weekend, but Victoria's top players will not be idle.

The big game will be the Victoria v. Tasmania match at Olympic Park on Sunday afternoon.

The Victorian side may be named tonight.

The match against Tasmania is part of the two-year series to decide the Australian championship.

The Tasmanians did not fare well in the first half of the title last year, playing three games and scoring a draw and two losses.

DRAWN

Two years ago the Victorians went to Tasmania and received a shock when the Tasmanians played a three-all draw.

This year Victoria will play South Australia, leaders for the title, Queensland, and Tasmania.

Present points in the interstate series are: South Australia 5, Victoria 4, NSW 4, Queensland 3, Western Australia 2, Northern NSW 1, Tasmania, 1.

The most vital game will be against South Australia at Olympic Park on June 13.

Watch the ages

IT won't pay to play overage boys in matches conducted by the North of the Yarra Junior Soccer Federa-

These are some of the soccer players of the future—the Under 10 and Under 12 Hakoah-AJAX juniors of 1966.

Also in 1933, Hakoah played Wally Hammond's English Test team at the Motordrome. Although the visiting cricketers included several soccer professionals, Hakoah won 3-1.

During the war years, when enlistments made it practically impossible to field a team, Hakoah united with Moreland for the duration. The combined team won the First Division Championship in 1943, and the Dockerty Cup in 1945.

Aku Roth was still playing at this time — probably a record for length of playing service with a senior club in Australia. Asked about the war years, he became reminiscent.

"The late *Maurice Zonenberg* was our secretary at the time, and a very efficient secretary he was, too", he said. "He arranged charity games for the Red Cross and other organisations assisting the war effort."

Still reminiscing, he recalled the names of other outstanding Hakoah players — *Alby Meyer, Hans Axelrad, Fred Lester* and *Frank Werther* — then apologised again.

"There must be many more, but that's a long time ago and my memory is faulty now", he said.

NEW ARRIVALS

He also recalled the boost received by the club with the arrival in the late Forties of Jewish refugees from Shanghai. These included *Kurt Defris, Erwin Eisfelder* and *Paul Eichler*.

"The name of Defris is now a byword in Victorian sporting circles", he said.

HAKOAH SPORTS CLUB

OFFICE BEARERS

President:
G. WEINBERG

Patrons:
SENATOR P. J. KENNELLY
Mr. A. A. CALWELL, M.H.R.

Immediate Past President:
Dr. H. BAYTCH

Vice-Presidents:
Dr. H. BAYTCH C. M. HAY
S. HANDELSMAN

Life Member:
C. M. HAY

Treasurer:
K. KORMAN

Secretary-Manager:
K. DEFRIS

Sectional Delegates:
Athletics: R. LEVY
Cricket: S. WOOLF
Football: H. DAVIS
Hockey: R. SAPFER
Ice Hockey: P. EICHLER
Soccer: N. SIMON
Table Tennis: K. DEFRIS
Football: H. DAVIS

●

BOARD OF TRUSTEES

Chairman:
S. HANDELSMAN

Secretary:
K. DEFRIS

Trustees:
Dr. H. BAYTCH F. EISFELDER
M. UNREICH M. WEINSTEIN

YEAR BOOK 1967

CONTENTS

Editor:
M. BUCKNER

Contributors:
R. SAFFER K. JAVOR
A. ROTH P. BROOKS
K. DEFRIS
F. HUTCHISON

- English born Hakoah Central Defender
- Australian Under 23 International
- Victoria State Representative
- David Baker earned a coveted place in the Hakoah Football Club all time top 20 legends Hall of Fame
- David Baker is the longest serving Hakoah player in the clubs history, having served Hakoah from 1967–1980. A total of 14 years
- David Baker gained referee recognition for being the best footballer in Victoria state on two separate occasions in 1975 and 1977
- David Baker was made captain of Hakoah Football Club, after which he led by example and showed great leadership qualities
- David Baker was a member of the Hakoah Dockerty cup winning squad of 1966
- David Baker played in the Hakoah Dockerty cup winning team of 1973
- David Baker played as a central defender in the 1977 Hakoah team that broke all previous records for the best defence in Hakoah Football Club history 1927–1981

1975 & 1977

David Baker

Hakoah St Kilda

43 & 32 Votes

Baker is best

By Stephen Quartermain

After fifteen seasons and more than 350 games of top-grade soccer, Ringwood resident David Baker has received the highest tribute soccer can give.

David, 33, plays for Hakoah in the State League.

Recently, he was honored with a testimonial match in recognition of his services to Hakoah since 1968.

David was signed by Hakoah many years ago when he was playing for Yeovil Town in the English League.

After coming to Australia, he immediately established a place for himself in the Hakoah side and from that time on, hasn't looked back.

During his career, David has received many soccer awards and honors and among his best achievements are:

- 7 best and fairests for Hakoah in a row — excluding 1979.
- Victorian representative 8 times.
- Australian Under 23 representative in 1967.

Without doubt, David's best achievements were his two Rothmans Medals in 1975 and 1977. These were awarded for best and fairest in the State League and David is only one of three players to win the coveted award twice.

In winning the 1975 medal, he also set another record when he polled 41 votes in the 22 games — the most votes ever polled in the medal count.

David's other great honor came about when he was playing for Victoria a few years ago.

That day, he played against the Brazilian side, Santos, when a man by the name of Pele was participating.

"That was my biggest thrill apart from the Rothmans," said David." Pele is just a freak, a natural, and watching him play was fantastic."

Up until this year, David, who plays in defence, had about a 300 games in a row run without injury.

However, this year has been a different story and David has just played in his comeback game after suffering a varicose vein injury.

When asked about his future, David said that he believes he still has a lot to offer on the field.

"At a later date, I am thinking about a coaching position, however, at the moment, I can help the younger players in our side on the field by passing down all my experience".

When asked about Victorian soccer, David said that it is definitely going places.

"Soccer in this country is getting better but to be even more successful, it must become more professional." Victorian soccer lacks good coaches, especially in the junior leagues, and for soccer to improve, the kids must be coached properly."

"Soccer is a simple game, the easier you make it, the easier it becomes. If you have the three basic qualities of fitness, ability and enjoyment, then you have the potential to become a good player."

By winning the Ringwood - Croydon - Lillydale Sports Star of the Week Award, David will be a candidate for the final judging of the Eastern Suburbs Sport Star of the Year which carries a Holden Commodore as the major prize.

As well, Bill Patterson Motors of Ringwood and Noel Dight Motors of Lilydale, will provide a monthly prize valued at $100.

David is also entitled to a months free use of the John Driver Fitness Centre in Forest Hill.

Anyone wanting to nominate a sportman for the Sports Star of the Week should write to Stephen Quartermain at 158 Maroondah Highway, Ringwood or ring him on 870 3333.

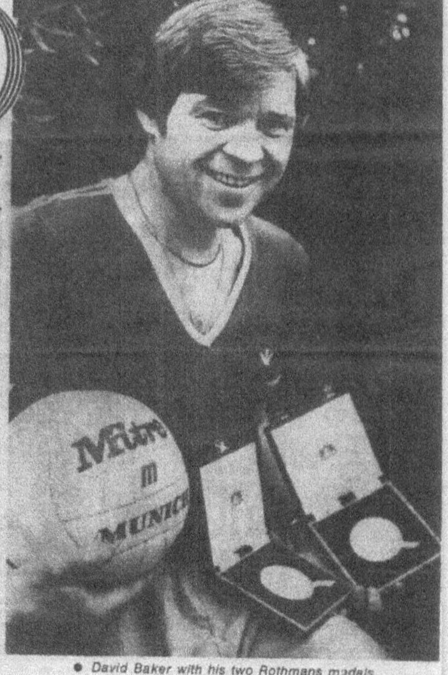

● David Baker with his two Rothmans madals.

Hakoah centre back David Baker (left) receives the 1977 Rothmans Medal from ASF president Sir Arthur George. It was Baker's second

LACK OF SUCCESS MY ONLY REGRET

By DAVID BAKER

Do the simple thing and play within your own ability — they're the golden rules I have stuck by during 13 years with Hakoah St. Kilda.

I have been part of many good Hakoah teams and few that were not so good, but my attitude to the game hasn't changed.

David Baker (centre) watches anxiously as Juventus midfielder (now Preston) Claude Lucchesi shoots at goal. At right is goalkeeper Mike O'Hare.

Guest stars to pay tribute

Jim Mackay, Jim Armstrong, Ray Pocock and Gerl Bannon are expected to make guest appearances for Hakoah St. Kilda against Essendon Croatia in the David Baker Testimonial game this Sunday at Middle Park (March 16).

The four star guest players should boost the attendance at the testimonial for Baker, who has served Hakoah so well for 13 years.

Baker, a true gentleman, is a credit to his club and Victorian soccer. His loyalty and dedication are unmatched in the modern era of Victorian soccer.

Baker has twice won the Rothmans Medal for the best and fairest player in the State League, and has represented Victoria on four occasions.

He toured Noumea with the Australian under 23 team in 1976.

Since joining Hakoah in April 1965, he has made more than 360 first team games.

Baker hasn't been booked or sent off in 13 years of State League soccer — a unique record which shows the character of the man.

Testimonial matches are rare in Australian soccer, as loyalty is easily bought or sold. However, David Baker has displayed genuine loyalty over the past 13 years, and fully deserves to be rewarded with a testimonial.

"Soccer Action" pays tribute to Baker for his consistent service to Hakoah, and wishes him the best of luck in his testimonial game.

The main game will kick off at 2.30 pm, preceded by a match at 1.30 pm between Hakoah reserves and Geelong Croatia.

1966 TEAM THE STRONGEST

When asked to name a composite Hakoah All-star team, David Baker declined, saying the 1966 team was the strongest team and included the outstanding individuals.

"I doubt whether a star player from another year could have got a place in the 1966 team," said Baker. "It was simply too strong, and I spent the season on the outer because of that.

Here is the 1966 team:

Mike O'HARA

John O'NEILL — Alan STENHOUSE — Dick VAN ALPHEN — George KEITH

Teddy SMITH — Hugh MURNEY — Gerry CHALDI

Alex PURDIE — Jim ARMSTRONG — Ian MOONAN

Quiet man David wins gold medal

by FRED VILLERS

DAVID Baker, the quiet man of Victorian soccer, has won the Rothmans gold medal award for the best State League player of 1975.

Two sons

It's easy to write about David Baker. To use words like unassuming champion, loyal servant or club stalwart will immediately paint a picture in your mind, and with David, that picture would be correct.

He played for Hakoah for 14 years after joining the legendary 1966 side, then playing right through to 1981 when the club was enveloped by South Melbourne and he took his cue to retire. Along the way he won no less than seven Hakoah Best and Fairest awards, as well as the honour of the Rothman's Medal awarded to Victoria's best player – twice. In fact, when he won his second in 1977, he won by the highest margin in history. But it all started in less salubrious surroundings.

> 'Basically, I was playing semi professionally in England when Fred Hutchison got in touch with me in '66. I was only 20, but I decided to give it a go for two years. I came out by myself, and I guess it was the sense of adventure that got me on the boat. It only cost £10 in those days, so I didn't have much to lose.'

When the young Baker arrived, it wasn't so much the football, the quality of Middle Park or the crowds that stole his imagination, it was, well, Australia.

> 'When Fred picked me up, we drove down the Esplanade, and I can still remember the bay, the sand and the palm trees. The sun was out, and it was like paradise. I found the people so relaxed and happy, and in those times, Australia was really booming. Most people where I was from didn't have two pennies to rub together, but I used to write home and tell them that if the people here tipped sideways, the money would come flowing out of their ears.'

So what about the football?

> 'I knew nothing about Australia and even less about Australian football. I was told Hakoah was in the State League and a powerful club, but that was about it. I knew the money would be OK and I was told finding a job to help would be easy, so I took the chance. But I was

> pretty impressed when I started training and playing. Middle Park was magnificent, and we had a really good team around '66 and '67 with some great players. So I quickly learnt about Australian Football, and learnt that it wasn't bad.'

After 1967, much of that quality team started to fall apart, and it was the beginning of a slow end, really. Some retired, one or two moved to other clubs with more money, and the Committee was getting tired. Throughout the early '70s, David was the only one that remained, and he witnessed the standard start to drop.

> 'We were still good, and there were always good players coming through, but it wasn't the same. We were always at the right end of the league, but I regret never having won a league championship with Hakoah even though we won other trophies.'

The National League began in 1977, and Hakoah didn't have the funds or the depth of support required to make the step up. They remained in the State League whilst the other top clubs in Victoria joined the new NSL, and took much of the crowd support and interest with them. Wasn't David tempted to move on?

> 'I'd be lying if I said I wasn't tempted over the years, but in the end, I knew I'd always be wondering and asking about Hakoah, so I stayed. The people there were always so good to me, and I was happy there. I always enjoyed my soccer at Hakoah – right until the end.'

And this is where David's wife Margaret picks up the story. After David had stayed his two years, he went back to Bridgewater and brought Margaret and her family back with him.

> 'They were very good to us and helped us settle. Being a part of a club meant instant friends in a new country, and that really helped. I remember one time I had my purse stolen when I was watching a game. We had two young boys at the time, and the money had to go a long way. The club found out about it, then replaced the money for me.

> No questions. It's things like that that kept David at the club all those years. They were good to us – and it wasn't just about the money. They didn't think twice about helping.'

David officially became an Australian with a British passport, and that came around quicker than expected.

> 'I was asked to play in the Australian U/23 team, but to do that I needed to officially be Australian. I didn't think twice about it, and the whole thing was raced through. I didn't even go to the ceremony.'

He also played for Victoria 8 times, including against Pele and Santos.

> 'To leave home for an adventure, then years later play against Pele, well, it's quite a thing.'

David was just coming back from injury when the 1981 merger with South Melbourne occurred. His come back never eventuated, and he hasn't been involved with the game since.

> 'I just knew it was over. No more Hakoah, and my kids were getting older and needed shipping around to their own sports. I had a good run in the game, so I just decided to stop.'

But don't let that mislead you to think there was no emotion involved. Even over 40 years since the young David landed on Australia's sunny shores, emotion still fills his chest when he thinks of the end.

> 'The club gave me a testimonial game not long before all this happened, which was a tremendous gesture. I haven't heard of it happening since with any club. Then one day a few years later, I went down to watch South Melbourne at Middle Park – my home for 15 years. Our clubrooms were on one side, and there's were on the other. Well, ours were just gone. Nothing. I have no idea where the memorabilia ended up, but the rooms were just not there. Gone. Just gone.'

David couldn't watch the match that day, because his mind was elsewhere. It was back in the old clubrooms and back in the good old days. And whilst he was sad for the unceremonious end, he smiled for the memories those days still contain.

- English born attacking mid fielder.
- Hakoah history maker, playing over 205 games in his 12 year career with Hakoah Melbourne Football Club, and in doing so becoming the man who played more games in the star of David shirt than any other player in the history of the club!
- An honoured member of the immortal 20 all time great Hakoah players who entered the hall of fame and walked into history for eternity!
- Steven was the quiet type who said little, but gave much when he entered the arena and took on the best in Victoria for his beloved Hakoah Football Club.
- A truly great man who overcame near insurmountable personal crisis and drew greater strength from the ordeals, marked by his brilliant displays for Hakoah, particularly in the Dockerty Cup Final of 1973 where his midfield mastery tipped the scales for Hakoah in a magnificent 1–0 victory for the sky blues.
- Steve Gadsby, Hakoah legend, true champion!

Peterborough born Steve Gadsby made more appearances for Hakoah AFC than any other Hakoah player in the history of the club, and stands only behind club captain David Baker in years of service with Hakoah Football Club.

Steve Gadsby is credited in official Hakoah confirmed records of playing in excess of 205 games in the Star of David Hakoah shirt.

Steve Gadsby: 12 Years service with Hakoah Football Club.

Picture shows a long legged Steve Gadsby (just left of centre behind opponent) watching the outcome of a heading duel in the 1973 Dockerty Cup Final at Olympic Park, won by Hakoah 1–0.

Picture shows Steve Gadsby collecting his 1973 Dockerty Cup Final winners medal.

Above: Picture shows a young Steve Gadsby (before his moustache, second from right) purposefully observing South Melbourne Hellas opponent George Gillan head for goal in a SM Hellas vs Hakoah 'local derby' at Middle Park in 1978.

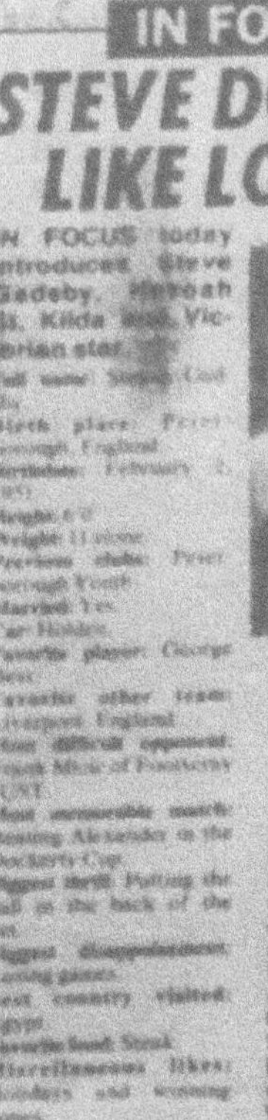

IN FOCUS

STEVE DOESN'T LIKE LOSING

IN FOCUS today introduces Steve Gadsby, Hakoah St. Kilda [illegible] Victorian star.

Full name: [illegible] Gadsby

Birth place: Peterborough, England

Birthdate: February [illegible]

Height: [illegible]

Weight: 11 stone

Previous clubs: Peterborough Youth

Married: Yes

Car: Holden

Favorite player: George Best

Favorite other team: Liverpool, England

Most difficult opponent: Frank Micic of Footscray JUST

Most memorable match: Beating Alexander in the Dockerty Cup

Biggest thrill: Putting the ball in the back of the net

Biggest disappointment: Losing games

Best country visited: Egypt

Favorite food: Steak

Miscellaneous likes: Holidays and winning games

Miscellaneous dislikes: Losing

Favorite TV shows: Benny Hill, Till Death Us Do Part

Favorite singers: Paul McCartney, Mick Jagger

Favorite actor/actress: Charles Bronson, Candice Bergen

Best friends: Judy Gadsby; Sam my dog

Biggest influence on career: Sam Meyer (coach of Hakoah)

Biggest drag in soccer: Waiting for kick-off on match days

International honors: None

Personal ambition: To be successful

Which person in the world would you most like to meet?: Bobby Charlton

- Scottish born Hakoah right half midfielder.
- Hakoah all time top twenty legends hall of fame.
- This tenacious, incredibly gifted and versatile midfield genius Hugh Murney was beyond any shadow of doubt the best wing half in the Victorian state league during the eight years he served his beloved Hakoah Football Club.
- A virtual ever present in the Hakoah team from 1964 until his retirement in 1972, Hugh Murney was a shining light to all his team mates and in particular youngsters coming into the team.
- Hugh Murney played in the all conquering Hakoah team of 1966 that won the Dockerty cup and finished the 1966 season in Hakoah's highest position [3rd] in the clubs entire history.
- Hugh Murney was in the 1967 Hakoah team that holds the current FFV all time record of zero goals conceded at the start of any season. 7½ Matches.
- Hugh Murney was known at Hakoah as a live wire character, with his brilliant Scottish sense of humour and lightning wit legendary. A man of monumental integrity, loyalty and absolute dedication to Hakoah Football Club.

Hugh Murney goes into legendary folklore history by way of *Hakoah Heroes* of being one of the finest human beings to ever wear the Hakoah Football Club shirt!

- Scottish born Hakoah, South Melbourne Hellas, & Juventus striker
- Australian International
- Victoria state representative
- Jim Armstrong, for Hakoah, was undoubtedly the greatest striker of the modern era in Hakoah Football Club's history.
- Jim Armstrong, earned by sheer determination and Scottish grit following personal adversity, an 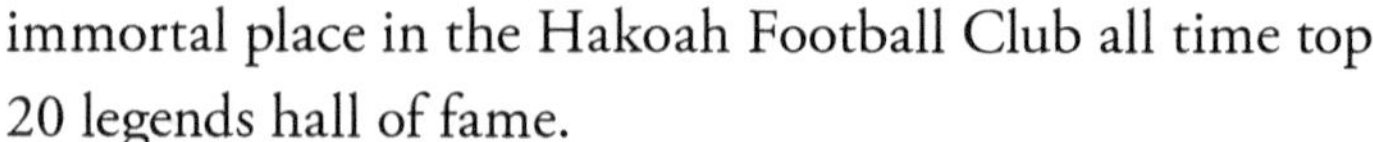 immortal place in the Hakoah Football Club all time top 20 legends hall of fame.
- 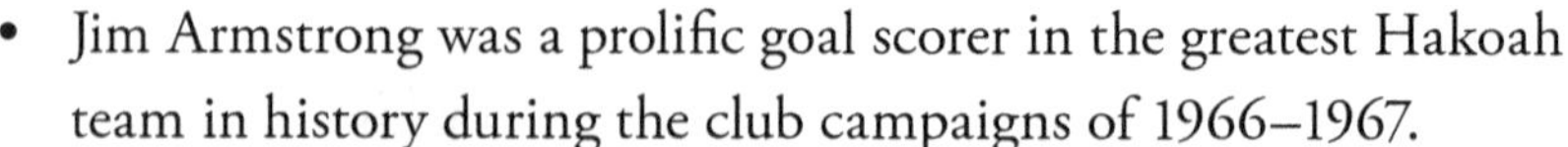 Jim Armstrong was a prolific goal scorer in the greatest Hakoah team in history during the club campaigns of 1966–1967.
- During this time Jim Armstrong scored regularly for Hakoah and according to the press was a feared striker, because he had one of the hardest and most accurate shots in the game.
- Jim Armstrong was a talented professional footballer who played the game fairly, but asked no quarter and gave none!

When you ask people about Jimmy Armstrong, there's a common response to the way he played. Instinctive, unpredictable, dangerous, and did things you can't coach. What ever it was, he scored goals for fun, notching 152 State League goals in his years for Hakoah, South Melbourne Hellas, and Juventus. He became a Socceroo in 1972 and played for his adopted country 5 times. He was selected in South Melbourne's 'Team of the Century', won three League Top Scorer Awards, and still holds a dear place in the hearts of every Hakoah fan.

Fred Hutchison was once again the man who got the Scottish import to Hakoah, but the path to the club was a little different to the others.

> 'I was on the way to Australia on a two year working holiday and to play football. My sister already lived in Australia, and my old boss in Scotland heard I wanted to play. Just before I left, he recommended Hakoah, and got them in touch with me. My Mum had to pay £50 to get me out of my contract with my club in Glasgow, and I paid the £10 to get on the boat. It was the best £10 I ever spent.'

The year was 1966 – the year that one of the great Hakoah teams was forming. But it only took one training session before the Hakoah officials knew they had stumbled onto something special, and made sure to keep their new recruit happy. And after only one game, they were over the moon, when the new kid scored a hat-trick on debut. They got him a job as a PE teacher (with no qualifications), sorted out his accommodation in 'little Britain' in Elwood, and helped make his life comfortable.

> 'They did their best to help me settle, and life was pretty easy. The first coach was Bill Walsh, then Ollie Norris and then Manny [Poulakakis]. We were winning games, and had a good team. I'd never played centre forward before, but when I got here, that's where they played me, and I loved it. I always played with [6 foot 5] Ian Monan, and he helped me get a lot of goals. Middle Park was great, the standard was good, and I didn't even go back to Scotland for a visit for seven years.'

Of course, that was the 'era of the characters' at Hakoah, and Jimmy played his part with typical Glaswegian charm. There was drinking, there were practical jokes, and there was always things happening to keep things interesting.

> 'We had some great laughs, but there were some loonies there too. O'Hara was a nutcase who apparently thinks he's the illegitimate son of Hitler. He was a good keeper, but always on the edge. I remember when the police came to get him from training one day for some

reason, but none of us were completely surprised. Ian Monan was another, but things went pretty bad for him after Hakoah. He came to stay on our couch for a few days with a few of us lads because he'd nowhere to stay, then one day we came home from work and he'd cleaned and made dinner. He said it'd be this way every day if he could stay. But after two weeks, there was no dinner, the place was a mess, and the jar that had the rent money was gone. I've never seen him or heard from him again. I remember another time when George Keith jumped the fence to lay into a couple of guys because they'd pushed into his pregnant wife in the stand and she fell. George wasn't one to rev the crowds up (that was more like Jimmy's job), but seeing what happened to his wife, he didn 't think twice.'

Jimmy stayed with Hakoah for almost 4 years before South Melbourne Hellas came in for him. They offered $5,000 to Hakoah, a sum of money they just couldn't refuse.

'I remember playing for Hakoah against Hellas, and after I scored, I ran in front of the Hellas crowd with my two fingers up at them – and they HATED it as you can imagine. After the game, they stormed the pitch and threw things at us. At me in particular. They were nuts, and I thought 'I'm gonna join these bastards'. I thought I'd like to be playing for those crazy supporters, and not against them. Hakoah got me for nothing, then made $5,000 on the transfer, so they did OK. In the end, Hellas were a bigger club, with big, passionate crowds, and were more professional by that stage. Hakoah didn't hold me back, but it was a bit sad to see that era over.'

So Jimmy moved to the club that shared Middle Park with Hakoah, and he never really played well when he came up against his old team.

'I don't know, maybe they knew me too well. But they were a real bogey team for me for the 7 years I played for Hellas. But there were never any hard feelings towards me or towards Hakoah. The committee were always great, and I'm still in touch with the guys from that time.'

Besides when he played Hakoah, Jimmy's form continued to blossom. So much so that in 1972, Rale Rasic selected him into the Socceroo tour of South East Asia during the Vietnam War. The tournament was called the 'Friendship Games' and was staged as a publicity stunt more than anything else. But it was anything but friendly, and amongst the literal heat of the battle, it was an interesting time to make a debut.

> 'My first game was off the bench, but the first game I started was against South Korea. There were big crowds, and guys patrolling all over the place with machine guns. The game was a bit crazy, and I do remember the guy playing on me kicking me and provoking me all game. So I turned and belted him, and his teeth went flying. The ref didn't see it, but the other players did, and one of their guys did a big karate kick that just missed. It would've taken my head off. Later we played a young Vietnam team, and they were throwing things at us. I was hit in the eye with something and couldn't see for a while. We seriously asked about just going home, but the local officials basically told us it would be harder to get out of the country than it was to get in, so we had to stay. Before the next game, we walked around with a big banner before the match giving our support for South Vietnam and appeasing the supporters. Thankfully it helped ... but what a tour.'

Jimmy's name wasn't included in the 1974 World Cup squad when he was dropped to make room for a third goalkeeper. It's not something he loses sleep over, but something of a 'what if' in his career.

> 'I am a Scotsman who paid £10 to get out here, and because of football, look what has happened for me in this country. The fact that I got to play for my adopted country was and is a huge honour, and I got to do it five times.'

When the National League was about to start in 1977, South Melbourne Hellas were accepted into the new competition. Jimmy, however, wasn't.

> 'One of my only regrets in my career is that I never played in the new National League. I was 31 when Hellas decided they didn't need me anymore. It was a tough pill to swallow.'

Jimmy moved to Juventus in the State League for two years, then in 1980 moved to Shepparton United with fellow ex-Socceroo Jim MacKay for 'good money and as much fruit as we could fit into the car'. Next was Morwell Falcons, then the Amateur Leagues for a bit of fun.

Coaching came next, and Jimmy has plied his expertise at a range of levels from kids through the Victorian State Leagues. These days, he's more likely to be running after his grandkids than footballers, but he still likes being around the game.

> 'Once the game is with you, it's with you. I go to watch Socceroo games whenever I can, and catch up with the guys at different matches. This game brings people together, and more than everything, it's the friendships you make and the fun you have that mean the most.'

Fred Hutchison has had a bigger direct impact on immigration to Australia than even he would recognise. And he definitely had a bigger impact on the quality of Hakoah in the '60s than his humility is prepared to admit. During his years as Manager of Hakoah, he lured no less than 29 British players and their families to our shores, and to the best of his knowledge, only one has returned.

Pictured is the dynamic, legendary and brilliant Yorkshire born Mr Fred Hutchison, who, as team manager of Hakoah Melbourne Football Club, was a catalytic factor in the Hakoah club's great success in the middle to late 1960s

> 'I used to be in contact with the players' unions in Scotland and England, and got access to the transfer lists to see what professional players were available. I would usually look for players who had been at the very top and were perhaps on the way down the leagues as they got older. Australia was very appealing to Brits in the '60s, so it wasn't that hard to strike a chord with the players. The money wasn't great in the British lower leagues then, so players could earn better money playing here when you added on that we'd get them a job and organise an apartment. We were offering players a new life in the sun, really.'

Fred joined Hakoah in 1964, the year after the club narrowly avoided relegation. He was approached by Kurt Defris, who knew the squad needed strengthening, but didn't exactly know who to do it. Fred was his man.

> 'As well as the 29 overseas players, I also managed to get 8 quality

players from other Victorian clubs. One of them was Dick Van Alphen who was a Dutch international playing at Ringwood. Bill Rowley was my first overseas signing, followed by Hugh Mumey – who is still involved with Maccabi to this day. John O'Neill was an Irish international and became our captain, Jim O'Neil was a Northern Ireland international, and we had some Socceroos like Dick Keith, Ted Smith and Jimmy Armstrong. Everyone we brought out were professional players, but some actually couldn't get a regular spot in our team, so we sold them on. Kurt always made sure we made at least a little bit of money on each of them ... and we generally only paid a pittance to get them here from Britain on assisted passage. The Australian Government wanted more and more people back then.'

Fred organised the new entrants' paths through immigration, organised accommodation, found them jobs, assisted with their taxes and even fronted for a few in court cases. It was the type of job that these days would be accompanied by a high flying salary, and plenty of 10% cuts of transfer fees. Back then though, Fred worked full time as a teacher, and only received a nominal fee from Hakoah to cover travel expenses.

'I look back and wonder how I did it all. I got about half the guys jobs as PE teachers, even though none of them were qualified, and spent so much time on the phone and keeping people happy. In the end though, the attention the club gave the players was a major reason why the club became so successful again – the players were happy to be a part of Hakoah and the spirit around the club was incredible.'

Fred first came into contact with Hakoah in 1952 when, as a recently arrived immigrant from England, he began refereeing the top leagues.

'I was a qualified referee in England, so they were happy to have me here. Throughout the '50s, Hakoah were the team in Victoria, so I couldn't help but know them. They were always a pleasure to referee, as well, because even then they had a lot of British players, so it was much easier for me than when I took Slavia or Juventus or JUST. I remember players like Tom Jack who was captain, and captained

> Victoria and Australia as well. Then there was Harry Sutherland, Ralph Pearcey, Bill Harbum, Dave McIntosh, Harry Rice and Syd Thomas. My impressions of Hakoah were good right from the start.'

Fred hung up his whistle in 1959, and became the manager of his local club – Ringwood Wilhelmina – overseeing the development of their new stadium. During this time, the ethnic clubs were increasing in strength, drawing big crowds, and making significant amounts of money – for the Association. A group of like clubs in NSW had already decided to split from the Association and form the NSW Federation, and the 12 State League clubs in Melbourne were considering the same course of action. Fred was instrumental, along with Michael Weinstein. Henry Baytch was the Hakoah delegate.

> 'Basically, the State League clubs were being held back by the Association. But we thought long and hard about following NSW's lead, and really only wanted to do it if the other States were going to as well. Really, we wanted an Australian Soccer Federation to help recognise that the game was changing and needed to progress with the times.'

After an arduous and ugly court room battle, that's what happened, and the game didn't look back. During the argumentative scenes over those years, the Federation wasn't recognised by FIFA, and neither was the Association due to so many international transfers to Federation (ie rebel) clubs that didn't pay appropriate fees to the international body or their European clubs. The Association eventually died out under the weight of public popularity, and the Federation gained FIFA recognition in 1963.

When that all happened in 1963, Fred was doing some soccer journalism with Fred Villiers, before getting the call from Kurt Defris in 1964. He remained at Hakoah until 1970, when work and family commitments became too great.

> 'From the inside, Hakoah always met the expectations I had from the outside. The Committee were always great to work with, and I had a

great relationship with Kurt, Michael Weinstein, Norman Simon and the others. It's really sad to see that the Hakoah name doesn't exist on Victorian soccer fields any more.'

In 2003, Fred was inducted into the Australian Soccer Hall of Fame as recognition of his 50 years of influential service to a variety of facets of the game. He is proud of the legacy he has left the game, and proud of the impact he had on Hakoah in the '60s.

'After a while, players were asking me if they could come to Hakoah, and it wasn't because we paid more in wages than other clubs. But we wouldn't just take anyone, even if they could play. They needed to be the right kind of person to fit in as well. That's what makes a successful team, and that's the Hakoah we built in those times, I will always remember those times very fondly.'

- Mike O'Hara holds a coveted place in the all time top 20 legends hall of fame of Hakoah Melbourne Football Club
- Mike O'Hara gained more 'press' coverage in his 16 year career in Melbourne than any other Hakoah player in history
- Mike O'Hara while playing for Hakoah represented Victoria state against A.S. Roma in 1966 and Middlesbrough in 1977
- Mike O'Hara was also selected to play for the Australian national team versus Scotland in Sydney in May 1967 as Australia's number one goalkeeper

Following is a pictorial tribute to evergreen Hakoah goalkeeper Mike O'Hara, who played his first game in Australia for Hakoah in 1966 as a 19-year-old, and his last game for George Cross in 1981 as a 34-year-old.

SOCCER WEEK

10th JULY, 1974 | 3 HIGH STREET, PRAHRAN | EDITORIAL: 51 9870 | ADVERTISING: 51 9878 | FOLIO NO. 4 | PRICE: 10c

Michael O'Hare Page 2

SOCCER WEEK

FOLIO No. 53 | 30th JULY, 1975.

3 HIGH STREET, PRAHRAN | EDITORIAL: 51-9870 | ADVERTISING: 51-9878 | PRICE 20c (N.S.W., S.A., TAS., 30c)

Our game lacks colour. . .

BRING BACK THE STARS

ULYSSES KOKKINOS ... the South Melbourne Hellas superstar

MIKE O'HARA... the star performer between the posts for Prahran Slavia

THE game of Soccer in Victoria sadly lacks color and most of all stars.

That's why every effort should be made to bring back two of the most colorful players Victorian fans have ever seen in the local game — ULYSSES KOKKINOS and MIKE O'HARA.

Ex South Melbourne Hellas striker has been out for a couple of weeks with a groin injury and his team badly needs him. Kokki, the Greek superstar, adds that little extra to the game that other players do not have and he also brings in the fans — the lifeblood of the sport.

With luck, Koki will be back next week for Hellas in the big game against Footscray JUST. This is a match which is likely to pull in a good crowd because both teams play attractive football.

Kokki told Soccer Week: "I miss playing with Hellas. The team has been playing badly in recent weeks. When I return I'll be 100 per cent fit. I'm sure we'll beat JUST."

We asked him why he had only scored one goal for Hellas this season. "I've found it very difficult to score this season. So too have my teammates. If I score I have to make the goal. I have to work very hard to make it. I don't know what's wrong with the team. We've only got eleven players and if someone gets injured there are no replacements."

Kokki said he had only played five league games this year. The team missed Andrew Savage when he was on his honeymoon recently and now Peter Bourne was overseas visiting his sick mother.

"We've been beaten twice by Alexander and if they don't win the championship this year they never will," said Kokki.

Mike O'Hara, the Prahran Slavia goalkeeper, is another colorful player who has been out of the game too long. "The Cat", as he's known in soccer circles, is our most entertaining keeper.

He adds some of the color that is missing every weekend in State League games. His antics in goal are a delight to watch.

O'Hara is back, ready and willing to fight for a place in the first team but he has to prove he's better than Billy Whiteside. We know The Cat is purring to get back in top company.

He's been training hard and claims he's fitter now than he was during his best years in the mid-60's.

Soccer needs players like Kokkinos and O'Hara. The goalless draws which keep popping up are dull enough. A little entertainment on the soccer field goes a long way to lift this game of ours from the doldrums.

Let's bring them back soon for the sake of soccer and its dwindling crowds.

And by the way, please don't let's see any more GTV9 Live Soccer games like we saw last Saturday between Moorabbin United and Fitzroy United Alexander with both teams wearing stripes.

More than 90 per cent of viewers have black and white TV sets and we heard none of them knew who was who. In future when there is a clash of strip for the sake of sport, one team MUST change.

Let's have some intelligent thinking from all concerned please.

Big Croatia supplement inside

ΣΧΟΛΙΟ ΤΟΥ ΠΑΝΟΥ ΓΕΩΡΓΙΟΥ - ΣΕΛΙΣ 15.

Jugoslovenska scena st. 14.

REGISTERED FOR POSTING AS A NEWSPAPER CATEGORY B

Vol. 3 No. 5 WEDNESDAY, MARCH 1, 1978 — 250 Spencer Street, Melbourne, ph. 60 0421 — Victoria, NSW 50 cents Other States: 60 cents

JIMMY GREAVES FOR AUSTRALIA?

Jimmy Greaves, the great forward who represented England 57 times, wants to play in Australia.

Greaves, 38, has sent a telegramme to the Philips Soccer League, whose season kicks off on Saturday, offering his services to any club that wants him.

The former Chelsea and Tottenham Hotspur striker was top scorer in the English First Division six times — 1958-59, 1960-61, 1962-63, 1963-64, 1964-65 and 1966 [illegible]

[illegible]

Another famous English player, **Charlie Cooke** of Chelsea, may also come to Australia.

South Melbourne Hellas president **Sam Papasavas** telephoned Cooke last week, when he heard that the Scottish international had been put on Chelsea's free transfer list.

However, the Los Angeles Aztecs have also contacted him.

Cooke, once a winger and now a midfielder, has represented Scotland 16 times and played about 300 games for Chelsea.

He has also played for Crystal Palace and in Scotland for Aberdeen and Dundee.

Jimmy Greaves

McKay State coach

Former Scottish international Duncan McKay has been appointed coach of the Victorian State team.

Victoria will meet Derby County and the Bobby Charlton All-Stars in May, and Hajduk Split in July.

McKay's appointment as State coach comes only two weeks after he was sacked as coach of State League club Essendon-Croatia.

He played 13 games for Scotland and more than 200 for Glasgow Celtic before coming to Melbourne to join the now defunct Croatia club in 1965.

Together with **Billy Vojtek, Jimmy Mackay, Horst Rau, Hugh Gunn, Frank Bot, Tommy McMeechan, Bill McIntyre** and **Brian Adlam**, he was one of the stalwarts of the great Croatia team that won the 1968 championship, Dockerty Cup and Ampol Cup.

From 1972 to 1974 he was back in Scotland, keeping coach Celtic's [illegible]

[illegible]

As State coach, McKay succeeds **Ron Smith**, who has quit his job as Victorian Director of Coaching and returned to England.

A pictorial tribute to Mike O'Hara whose flamboyance has made him one of the institutions of Victorian soccer.

Fairbrother may take legal action

A legal battle looms over the transfer of Barrie Fairbrother from Mooroolbark to Brisbane Lions.

[illegible]

"There is no way Mooroolbark will get one cent for me. I'll stand out of soccer rather than see the club get any money from my transfer."

[illegible]

However, Fairbrother is going to appeal against the ASF Executive decision and, if necessary, take legal action so he can transfer for free.

Continued page 14

O'Hara on show at St. Albans

State goalkeeper Mike O'Hara of Hakoah has signed for Footscray J.U.S.T. to replace Dennis Boland who has yellow fever and will be out for at least two months.

[illegible] **Steve Adamidis.**

O'Hara will play for J.U.S.T. against Green Gully Ajax at Green Gully Reserve, St. Albans, in a practice match tonight (Wednesday) at 8.30 pm.

[illegible] **Mando Pistoresi** [illegible] **Zoran Ilieski** and **John Nicolaides.**

AUSTRALIAN SOCCER FEDERATION

(MEMBER OF F.I.F.A.)
(MEMBER OF OCEANIA FOOTBALL CONFEDERATION)
155 KING STREET, SYDNEY, N.S.W., AUSTRALIA

TELEPHONES: 25 8443
28 9009

TELEGRAMS & CABLES: FOOTBALL SYDNEY

SECRETARY:
IAN A. MCANDREW, A.A.S.A.

16th May, 1967.

Mr. M. O'Hara,
c/- Mr. J. Alam,
16 Greenview Court
EAST BENTLEIGH VIC.

Dear Mr. O'Hara,

We confirm our telegram of today's date informing you of your selection in the Australian National Team for the forthcoming match versus Scotland to be played on 28th May, 1967, at the Sydney Showground.

Arrangements have been made for you to travel to Sydney by Ansett-ANA Flight 8 departing Melbourne 8.00 a.m. Tuesday 23rd May, and returning from Sydney on Monday 29th May, at 5.00 p.m. on Ansett-ANA Flight 27.

You are requested to collect your flight tickets at Ansett-ANA Counter Melbourne Airport Terminal, on Tuesday 23rd May.

Arrangements will be made for you to be met at Sydney Airport on arrival, although in the event of unforseen circumstances it is requested you report to the Australian Team Manager, Mr. G. Bayutti, or the Australian Coach, Mr. J. Venglos, at 10.00 a.m. on Tuesday, 23rd May, at the Randwick House Motel, 2a Allison Road, Randwick, at which your accomodation has been arranged.

For your information, any loss of wages incurred by you due to loss of employment for these seven days will be reimbursed by the Australian Soccer Federation to the extent of $10.00 per day.

Please remember to bring your Australian National Team clothing including your National Team blazer.

In the event that you cannot comply with our requests please contact this office as soon as possible.

Yours sincerely,

Ian A. McAndrew
Secretary

1966 Olympic Park, Melbourne, Australia – Victoria State versus A.S. Roma (Italy).

Mike O'Hara cradling the ball following an A.S. Roma attack. The game played at Melbourne's Olympic Park, drew a crowd of over 36,000 people. Almost all were Italians. Such was the crowd that spectators spilled onto the touchlines with the linesmen running up and down within the playing area! Note that some spectators are actually standing or sitting in precarious positions on the main stand roof!

picture: Laurie Schwab – *The Age* – 1966

Victorian goalkeeper Mike O'Hara with A.S Roma goalkeeper Fabio Cudicini at the official reception, following the Roman's game against the Victorian State Team in 1966. O'Hara stood at 5 feet, 11 inches tall which made Cudicini about 6 feet, 7 inches! O'Hara asked what Cudicini thought of the unique Australian Rules Football game after the A.S Roma contingent had watched a match at the Melbourne Cricket Gound (MCG). Cudicini replied, 'It is like animal warfare, and a game for barbarians and savages.'

picture: Laurie Schwab – *The Age* – 1966

'The abusive, abrasive but brilliant Hakoah keeper Mike O'Hara bellows at his defence after a defensive error allowed Juventus striker Eric Norman to score.' – *Laurie Schwab 1966*

The 'all conquering, all powerful' 1966–1967 record breaking Hakoah team

Top row (*left to right)*: Dick Van Alphen (Netherlands), centre half; Mike O'Hara (Republic of Ireland), goal; Hugh Murney (Scotland), right half; George Keith (Scotland), right back; Ian Monan (Scotland), centre forward; Jim Armstrong (Scotland), inside right. Bottom row (*left to right)*: Alex Purdie (Scotland), left wing; John O'Neill (Republic of Ireland), left back; Teddy Smith (Australia), inside left; Keith Fry (England), right wing; Alan Stenhouse (Scotland), left half.

'This was the greatest team ever to play under the Star of David' – *Laurie Schwab, Melbourne Age Journalist, 1985*

The formidable trio of Hakoah players who dominated the Victorian Premier League in the 1960's, and who made Hakoah Football Club the most feared opposition in the competition in 1966–1967. Picture: Left to Right: The Magnificent 'Tiger' Hugh 'Shug' Murney, 'The Clown Prince' Mike O'Hara, and at far right 'The Human Goal Machine' Jim Armstrong! A Hakoah Committee member is also pictured.

picture: Laurie Schwab – *The Age* – 1967

The picture at left shows Hakoah's star midfielder Hugh Murney bracing himself against the 'flying' Hakoah keeper Mike O'Hara. The centre picture shows the referee warning O'Hara about his dangerous tactics! Picture at right shows O'Hara, already spoken to by the referee and ready to go again!

pictures: Laurie Schwab – *The Age* – 1967

Hakoah still on top

by MARTYN HARRIS

Hakoah, with their depleted side, staged a fine battle to hold Juventus to a 0-0 draw, at St. Kilda Cricket Ground.

Juventus only had themselves to blame for their first half misses and their lethargic play in the second half.

The Hakoah defence has still not conceded a goal this season and this was their toughest assignment so far.

Juventus will have to improve on today's performance if they are to be considered for the title.

Irrespective of tomorrow's game between Hellas and Melbourne, Hakoah will still retain the top spot.

If the Australian selectors were watching today they could not fail to be impressed with the performance of Hakoah keeper, Mike O'Hara.

JUVENTUS. — 1 Voight, 2 Sonsini, 3 Gentry, 4 Luckhurst, 5 Della Rocca, 6 Closs, 7 Barbazza, 8 Corti, 9 Torcque, 10 Millar, 11 Bell. Reserves: McDonald, Malloy, De Marchi, Ballarin.

HAKOAH. — 1 O'Hara, 2 Keith, 3 John O'Neill, 4 Murney, 5 Van Alphen, 6 Baker, 7 Fry, 8 Smith, 9 Monan, 10 Jim O'Neill, 11 Rogers. Reserves: Walker, Conley, Armstrong.

Referee: Stafrace.

Estimated attendance at St. Kilda Cricket Ground 4700.

Hakoah suffered a setback before the start when Purdie (flu), Stenhouse (injured) and Armstrong (injured) were all pronounced unfit. Armstrong was named as a reserve.

Scott, who is still recovering from last week's injury, was missing in the Juventus line-up.

Hakoah kicked off in wet conditions and attacked through Fry on the right wing but Gentry cleared for Juventus.

Rogers to John O'Neill on the left and the full back centred where Monan's header was saved on the line by Voight.

Corti put Torcque clear but O'Hara raced from his goal to smother the centre forward's shot.

Juventus pressed hard and Barbazza crossed hard and low from the left but Torcque just failed to connect.

Play swung to the other end where John O'Neill again centred and Monan rose high above Voight but his header went wide.

The Hakoah defence was at full stretch and conceded three corners in two minutes.

But finally a header from Luckhurst was saved by O'Hara.

Baker at left half was playing well in his first game this season for Hakoah.

He tackled Bell strongly when the winger looked dangerous.

The Juventus forward line were interchanging positions with both Bell and Barbazza at times playing on the left wing.

Van Alphen still appeared groggy as he again missed his kick but O'Hara was on hand to collect and clear.

Juventus attacked again when Bell beat Van Alphen and passed to Corti but John O'Neill intercepted and cleared a dangerous situation for Hakoah.

Hakoah were not giving up and John O'Neill raced upfield to send in a cracker from 25 yards. Voight punched out and Monan headed goalwards, but Voight again saved.

HALF TIME. — Juventus 0, Hakoah 0.

Jimmy Malloy took the field in the second half for his first game of the season for Juventus when he replaced Torcque.

Drama occurred on the touch line after Dick Van Alphen had taken the field. Hakoah officials appeared to want to replace him as he was not fully fit but the referee ruled that he could not be replaced.

Hakoah opened well with a move involving Monan, Smith, Fry and Murney but Murney's 20 yard drive was saved by Voight.

Luckhurst and Della Rocca clashed heads near the touch line and play was held up for two minutes while Luckhurst received attention.

Juventus, sensing victory, swarmed into attack and Luckhurst slipped a fine pass inside John O'Neill to Barbazza but O'Hara raced from goal to dive at the winger's feet and save.

Seconds later, Luckhurst came through in the inside right position and flashed a right foot drive inches wide of the far post.

Hakoah came into the attack, Murney passed to Rogers but the outside left shot over.

Then following a right wing corner, Jim O'Neill first-timed the ball high over the bar.

Closs, at left half for Juventus was their driving force behind most of their attacks.

With Juventus getting lethargic with loose marking Hakoah began to get on top.

First Murney had a shot blocked and then Monan got in the way of Jim O'Neill's pile driver.

Fry volleyed a pass from Rogers inches over the bar for the narrowest of misses.

Juventus had slowed down to walking pace which was hardly understandable in view of their position on the ladder.

Van Alphen was still groggy following his first half injury but was managing to cope with Malloy without much trouble.

Fry beat Della Rocca and Sonsini as he raced down the left wing but over-ran the ball for a goal kick to Juventus.

In the dying minutes, Hakoah played safety first soccer, endeavoring to keep possession of the ball at all times and when in doubt kicking into touch.

FINAL: Juventus 0, Hakoah 0.

Jim O'Neill gave away a free kick 20 yards out when he obstructed Corti.

From the kick, Corti chipped the ball brilliantly over the wall of defenders but Barbazza on his own, with only O'Hara to beat, completely missed the kick.

Hakoah were playing well in mid field through Murney and Baker but only Monan, who was beating Della Rocca every time in the air, looked dangerous up front.

Torcque appeared at least three yards off side as he broke clear but then collided with Van Alphen.

It was fully three minutes before Van Alphen was on his feet and then he left the field, but returned shortly afterwards.

Fry looked dangerous on the right wing for Hakoah as he beat Gentry and cut inside but his shot was easily saved by Voight.

Van Alphen fumbled and Torcque took advantage to race clear but O'Hara narrowed the angle and stopped his shot and Torcque hit the rebound wide for a bad miss by Juventus.

It was now all Juventus as again Torcque had a great chance in the inside position but O'Hara, in top form, dived to his right to save.

In a brief Hakoah raid a header from Jim O'Neill went over the bar.

O'HARA —THE GIFTED GOALIE

By LEN STONE

"Everybody likes an entertainer. Mike O'Hara, the former clown prince of goalkeepers, is now more serious minded but I hope he hasn't lost his showmanship."

TEMPERAMENTAL Mike O'Hara, one of the best four goalkeepers I have seen in Australia over the last 22 years, is back with Hakoah St Kilda.

The fit, fresh-faced O'Hara, who is endowed with considerable skill, natural ability and a fine physique, which all adds up to being an ideal goalie, disappeared last season without telling his club.

But all is forgiven and he has been received back in the fold with open arms.

O'Hara joined Hakoah some years ago and performed well enough to play for Victoria against Roma, at Olympic Park, before a record crowd. I felt he did not get the array of representative honors bestowed on lesser keepers at the time.

He soon came under the notice of colleague Fred Villiers because of some really remarkable saves which were often mixed with colorful antics. The man was obviously news and Fred was quick to call him "clown prince of goalkeepers."

Certainly O'Hara could not be better described. The label stuck and the unpredictable keeper often demonstrated he was one of the best in the country.

Predictably, Mike fell out with Hakoah, joined Slavia, eventually had a dispute with them, return to Hakoah, suddenly took off, trained with the famous Arsenal in London, — they liked what they saw of him — then just as suddenly returned to Australia and naturally is Hakoah's keeper for 1977. And hopefully for many years to come.

Although O'Hara left without permission and Hakoah felt hurt — they are now only too glad to have him back between the sticks. After all, he is O'Hara.

Emotional, comic, clown, genius, unpredictable, erratic, brave, lucky, agitated, inspiring, what's the difference. That's O'Hara.

He improves with age — like good wine. The former Swindon Town professional, was highly-rated in England before he even thought of Australia.

Fortunately he is in Victoria for good. Soccer here can do with a personality like the clown prince.

Success or failure depends entirely on the gifted player himself. While in England last year, not only Arsenal but also new-look Mansfield Town recognised his undoubted ability. Mansfield wanted to sign him on the spot.

But O'Hara whose charming wife is Australian, preferred finally to settle here. I do hope O'Hara, a far more serious-minded keeper than before he left, has not foresaken his showmanship. Everybody likes an entertainer.

If O'Hara gets on with his job as Hakoah custodian, he should do well enough to be among the honors that eluded him before.

I'm sure soccer fans hope the spectacular, confident and courageous O'Hara will treat us to many fine acrobatic saves and good goalkeeping for a long time to come.

MEET OHARA 'The Cat-Like Keeper.'

MIKE O'HARA, that great goalkeeper with a leap like a cat, is back in top form with Prahran Slavia and he's aiming for a job as State keeper.

If Mike has his way he'll get the job — and the way he's playing he deserves it. Just take a look at Slavia's figures. They're very impsoing.

Their defence — and their keeper — have proved they are the best in the League. No other club has such a fine record — four goals in their net in nine games!

As well as Mike, the club has full backs Jim Tansey and Jim Train, and three of the best mid-fielders in the business — Jim Campbell, Steve McCoombe and John Howie.

We know a good defence doesn't win games but Slavia have sizzled this year under the astute coaching of Johnny Sanchez and his assistant Kaz Kowalec. What a great combination they've produced.

In nine games Slavia have won seven, drawn one and lost one with 15 goals scored and only four against. The only team to knock them off was Hellas in a real thriller at Olympic Park — and this by the odd goal.

O'Hara has only played in six games for Slavia this season. He had to fight his way to the top to prove that he was a better keeper than Lou Ivanhoff but in the six week's Mike's been in goal, he's let in two.

O'Hara came to St Kilda from English club Swindon Town. He played with Hakoah for two seasons and then was out of the game for a year "because I asked for more money and they wouldn't pay me."

Said O'Hara: "I think I'm good enough to make the state side. I really do. If I get in the state team I'll stay in this time. I won't let the side down."

At 26, Mike says the hardest side he plays against in State League is Hakoah and the striker he fears most is Mike Clarey. "This team creates openings out of the blue," he added.

O'Hara believes he's playing his best football now than ever before. He has had a great career being the youngest goalkeeper ever to play in English League. This was when he turned out for Luton Town in second division at the age of 15-and-a-half years. He has also played for Bournemouth.

As a boy he played for Ireland Schoolboys. He received three caps when he was 14, against Scotland, Wales and Northern Ireland.

O'Hara is one of Australia's most colorful goalies. He provides plenty of action on the field and gives the fans value for money.

Mike says his concentration has improved 100 per cent and he gives great credit to Kaz Kowalec for the way he's helped him achieve this.

If there is any player in the League who is heading for State honors, O'Hara must be in the running for his fine saves in Slavia's goal during the past six weeks.

His long blonde hair has become a popular sight on GTV9's "Live Soccer" on Saturday's.

Mike O'Hara

Mike O'Hara coming home

Colorful goalkeeper Mike O'Hara of Hakoah will return to Melbourne on November 6.

He has been in England trialling with Arsenal and a couple of second and third division clubs.

He is coming back because his wife is expecting a baby.

O'Hara, long known as the Clown Prince of the State League because of his animated antics between the sticks, was playing brilliantly for Hakoah before he left about half way through the season.

Mike O'Hara, disgusted, walks back to pick up the ball after Peter Shilton (background) had scored.

O'Hara at Arsenal

"Soccer Action" has heard from Mike O'Hara — former Hakoah (Melbourne) goalkeeper who went to England recently.

O'Hara said in a letter to us that he had been training with English club Arsenal for the past five weeks.

O'Hara said in his letter: "I have been told by Jimmy Rimmer, Arsenal's number one 'keeper, I have a lot of ability once my angles are worked out.

"Until I came here it was my courage alone that made me look good, but Rimmer has taught me how to play goal.

"There will be a few surprises when I get back to Australia.

"Paddy Sloan — the ex-Arsenal pro — is well known around here, and how he didn't get a top coaching job in Australia is beyond my comprehension.

"It was Paddy who told me to come to England and get top coaching, and that with my guts, I'd walk into the Australian team."

They tell me..

ARSENAL'S Jimmy Rimmer may have helped Australia find a new goalkeeper for their national team.

Mike O'Hara, 24, who plays for Melbourne club Hakoah, trained with the Gunners for a while following the recommendation of former Arsenal professional Paddy Sloan.

Before he left, O'Hara praised Rimmer for his encouragement.

He said: "Jimmy has taught me many new things about the game and I can promise the folk back home a few surprises when I return."

LUTON have followed Watford in a bid to sign Joe Kinnear, former Spurs defender, given a free transfer by Brighton.

DAVE DRYER Sports Travel have one, two and three-day tours available for England's World Cup qualifier with Italy in Rome on November 17.

ROTHMANS Football Yearbook 1976-77 is full of facts and is top value for £2-50. Publishers are Queen Anne Press.

Players of the Week

Hakoah goalkeeper Mike O'Hara and Juventus midfielder Claude Lucchesi are our Ampol Cup players of the week.

Each of them wins a dinner for two at the North Steak House, 355 North Road, South Caulfield (tel. 58-6150).

The best player from every Friday and every Saturday double-header is chosen by our experts for the night out at the steak house.

The restaurant is run by Jimmy Milisavljevic, a member of the 1974 World Cup squad.

Mike O'Hara

Soccer thrills

By "OFFSIDE"

Hakoah's new soccer coach, Manny Poulakakis maintained his winning run last week-end, when the blue-whites scored their second successive win for the season.

Hakoah won 2-1 over Wilhelmina in a close and thrilling game at Middle Park.

It was the blue-whites' second game and second win under new coach Poulakakis.

In a game full of incidents the main topic was the clash of Wilhelmina's former international de Bruikere against Hakoah's Dutch centre-half Dick van Alphen.

This game finished in a ding-dong battle, with Hakoah leaving the field as well-earned victors.

Van Alphen was the master of the Hakoah defence, with both wing halves, Stenhouse and Murney at their best.

MANY SAVES

Hakoah goalkeeper O'Hara played a thriller and excelled himself under pressure. His saving during the last ten minutes proved goalkeeping at its best.

A good crowd of nearly 1200 spectators, mostly Hakoah supporters, cheered the players.

At several stages the play became affected with fouls, but referee Strafaci had the game well in hand.

Hakoah's first goal was scored in the 28th minute when Monan's rebound was converted by agile Ted Smith, the hardest working man in Hakoah's forward line. Half-time 1-0.

After lemons, Hakoah attacked, but it was after 20 minutes when Alan Stenhouse broke through and a bombshell from 35 yards found the net.

From then on Wilhelmina looked dangerous and in the 80th minute, after a scrimmage in front of the Hakoah net, a self-goal gave the Dutch team their score.

The last 10 minutes saw Wilhelmina on top, but the outstanding performance of O'Hara saved Hakoah two very important points and ninth place on the ladder.

Goalies get themselves into all sorts of acute angles . . . and Hakoah's Mike O'Hara is no exception. Here he thumps the ball away as he hits the ground in the match against Hakoah last week-end. Hakoah full back Ken Waugh looks on.

SOCCER NEWS

and SOCCER LIFE

THURSDAY, SEPTEMBER 8, 1966

Vol. 4, No. 160 Price 10c

MIKE THE FUNNY MAN

Meet Hakoah's goalkeeper Mike O'Hara, the clown of Soccer. Mike is perhaps the greatest character in the game today. He is demonstrative, exuberant, boisterous and colorful. Soccer News photographer Uwe Kuessner trained his camera on Mike at Olympic Park on Sunday. These two shots and pictures on Pages 4 and 5 are the result.

CLOWN-PRINCE OF SOCCER

This is how you will probably meet Melbourne Hakoah's goalkeeper — comedian Mike O'Hara this Saturday night at Hindmarsh.

Mike has been described as demonstrative, exuberant, boisterous, entertaining and perhaps the greatest character in the game today. The No. 1 Clown of Soccer.

"The antics of Mike O'Hara are at times highly dangerous and an invitation to oposing forwards to cut him down to size," said Jim Cook of Melbourne Soccer News.

Will Juventus forwards accept this invitation when they face Mike at Hindmarsh is a matter of speculation.

I think they will, and my money will be on Juventus to win and restore some of the prestige they lost in Melbourne when South Melbourne Hellas beat them 1:4 in the Australia Cup match in October last year.

If there is any restoration of prestige to be done, here is the opportunity!

ZAC DRAPAC

Hakoah holds on to soccer leadership

By Vincent Basile

Hakoah retained the leadership of the State League soccer by defeating last year's premiers, South Melbourne Hellas, 2-0 at Middle Park on Saturday.

Juventus, runner-up last year, completely outplayed Alexander to win 4-0 at the St. Kilda Cricket round yesterday.

Much of the credit for Hakoah's win went to goalkeeper Mike O'Hara, who played a spectacular game to save at least three goals.

O'Hara is the only goalkeeper in the league still unbeaten after four championship games.

Also worthy of mention, however, are Hakoah defenders John O'Neill and Dick Van Alphen, who kept close check on the Hellas' forwards, especially in the first half.

THE REAL O'HARA

Mike O'Hara, Hakoah's 20-year-old clowning goalkeeper, is quite a funny man on and off the field.

Few Australian Soccer circles know he hold's a British record. And that he's played against English World Cup Cup skipper Bobby Moore.

Next Thursday you'll read all about the real O'Hara — the player who brought color to Middle Park ground last season.

You'll read it in Soccer Profile which comes to you from the pen of Fred Villiers.

● Don't miss Soccer News next Thursday. It's your best buy in the round-ball game — 10 cents all leading newsagents.

ORDER YOUR COPY NOW!

Soccer

STATE LEAGUE LADDER.

	P.	W.	D.	L.	F.	A.	Pts
Hakoah	6	4	2	0	10	0	10
Juventus	6	3	2	1	10	7	8
Croatia	6	3	2	1	11	8	8
Footscray	6	4	0	2	8	11	8
Melbourne	6	3	1	2	8	6	7
PM-Slavia	6	3	1	2	7	9	7
SM-Hellas	6	2	2	1	10	7	6
Polonia	6	3	0	3	10	8	6
Alexander	6	2	0	4	8	15	4
Lions	6	1	1	4	5	9	3
P. Makedonia	6	1	1	4	8	15	3
George Cross	6	1	0	5	4	12	2

PT. MELB.-SLAVIA 0 lost to ALEXANDER 2 (Brown, Bisas). Best. — PM-Slavia: High, Cook, Schroit. Alexander: Economides, Brown, Kourkoulass.

LIONS 0 lost to FOOTSCRAY-J.U.S.T. 1 (A. Razi). Best.—Lions: Schwartz, Houston, Carmichael. Footscray: Fode, King, Rice.

JUVENTUS 0 drew with HAKOAH 0. Best.—Juventus: Della Rocca, Cibas, Corti. Hakoah: Van Alphen, Keith, O'Hara.

Coach's special trip

Australia's Soccer coach, Josef Venglos, today will make a special trip to Melbourne to watch two players who have come strongly into calculations for the international matches against Scotland.

The players, Mike O'Hara, a goal-keeper, and Jim Armstrong, a forward, both play for Hakoah club.

Venglos will watch them playing against Juventus today.

O'Hara and Armstrong are among the six Victorian players selected to play in a series of trials in Sydney on Tuesday and Wednesday.

The others are Billy Cook, of Slavia, Billy Rice, of JUST, Hammy McMeechan, of Croatia, and 20-year-old Attil Abonyi, of Melbourn HSC.

South Australia's tw representatives will b the forwards, Stev Herczeg and Tomm McColl, from Adelaide' Juventus club.

The 19-year-old goal keeper from the Cracovi club, Peter Mitchell, wil be Western Australia' only representative.

Northern NSW (New castle) will be represent ed by the forme Australian internationa Bruce Morrow, Hor Schneider, of Wallsenc and the 18-year-old wing er, Peter Pont, from th Awaba club.

The Merton Rover centre half, Gary Catcl pole, will be the onl Queenslander in th trials.

Czechoslovakia World Cup Final goalkeeper Willi Schroif and Mike O'Hara in Vienna. Willi was in goal for the Czechs against Brazil in a 1962, 1–3 defeat.

The Hakoah Melbourne (Hakoah – Hebrew for Strength) contingent at the Victorian State Soccer Player of the Year award, Melbourne 1977. Left to right: Mr Kurt Defris, OA; Mike O'Hara (hand on Kurt Defris' shoulder); Johnny Chaskiel 'Mr Gritty'; David Baker, winner; Michael Weinstein; Mike Rainey.

Mike O'Hara diving at the feet of South Melbourne Hellas Striker Ullysees Kokinnos while playing for Hakoah Melbourne. This skill along with many others, had been taught to Mike as an art form by his beloved hero Uwe, who would place the ball one side of a cow in a field and make him dive under the cow to get to the ball. One had to be lightning fast, or else a flailing hoof could cause injury. After this drill, diving at a human's feet was a 'piece of cake.' **picture**: Laurie Schwab – *The Age* – 1967

THE CLOWN GOALIE IS BACK!

One of the State eague's most olorful characters, ormer Hakoah goalie Mike O'Hara s back in action.

The "Clown Prince" of soccer — he earned this nickname because of his antics on the field — signed for Slavia in a surprise move last Friday.

He went straight into the first team for the game against Melbourne on Saturday and, showing much of his old skill, kept his goal safe in a scoreless draw.

In the past many people wrote off O'Hara as a top goalie because of his temperament, but there was always plenty of skill in his game when he cut out the clowning.

If he can keep his head this time and get on with the job he should go well. Reports have it that he is a reformed character. If so, he could put himself among the top-flight keepers.

Hakoah officials would not disclose the fee paid for O'Hara but it was reported to be a "reasonable" four-figure one.

Before joining Hakoah in 1966, O'Hara, now 23, was on the books of Luton, Swindon and Bournemouth in England.

Left picture: Steve Walker, Essendon Lions strong and robust centre-half approaches with serious intent on Hakoah keeper O'Hara after Walker received a blow to the head from the Hakoah keeper. O'Hara tries to explain!

Centre and right pictures: O'Hara back in the fray!

pictures: Laurie Schwab – *The Age* – 1967

DON'T STOP THIS GOALIE FROM ACTING

IN TOUCH

with Fred Villiers

EVERY sport has its character. Boxing has loudmouth Cassius Clay, athletics Percy Cerutty, and cricket, Freddie Trueman.

In Melbourne, Soccer has Mike O'Hara, the 19-year-old Hakoah goalie.

Mike is a likeable type with plenty of talent.

He recently arrived here from English third division club Swindon Town.

He's Irish and many Pressmen have dubbed him "The Wild Irishman".

Mike waves his arms and shouts as soon as something goes wrong on the field.

But he doesn't really know he's attracting the crowd's attention. It's all part of his make-up. He's always been like this ever since he first kicked the round ball in his schooldays.

Hakoah coach, Manny Poulakakis, has been quite worried about Mike's antics. He's even asked him to calm down and not get excited on the ground.

But I don't think Mike will ever change. In fact I'd hate to see him reform because he's bringing a little much-needed colour to Melbourne Soccer.

He was so excited recently when told that he'd been chosen for the State League squad against the visiting Romans that he couldn't sleep the following night thinking about his chances of being between the sticks at Olympic Park in front of the big crowd.

The goalie, Norm Hobson, Victoria's number one choice, injured a leg a few days before the game. Could Norm hold out for the full 90 minutes?

Mike thought he would and he'd miss his great chance. The big day came, and Hobson's other leg was injured in the second half. O'Hara came on as deputy goalie.

Like always, he played well for his side — and he played well for the crowd too.

MELBOURNE have done it at last. They actually had a bigger crowd for a Soccer match than Sydney — and that's saying a mouthful!

Last Sunday the Roma v. N.S.W. crowd was 32,000. In Melbourne the previous week 35,000 fans saw the game.

Is Soccer in Victoria on the up and up and down?

Come in Green Paper scribes for your comment.

NOT many men in Soccer work through the night burning the midnight oil for no financial reward. But you can find them if you look long enough.

I found one last weekend — Victorian Referees' Selector George Yelland.

He was listing the referees for a full round of Junior Cup, league and country games.

It's not an easy job with ground changes and referee rejections, but he finished his work at 2.45 a.m., . . . "all for the love of it."

Wish we had a few more chaps like George in the game.

With the soccer World Cup dominating the sporting scene in England in 1966, the soccer bosses are not taking any risk of dental troubles for the players.

Every player with a chance of appearing in England's World Cup squad will be given a thorough dental check-up.

This is just one of the precautions which are being taken to make sure the England team go into the fray with the fittest players the country has ever produced.

On the last two tours by England there have been incidents of toothache.

So now, a dental surgeon will be on hand throughout the build-up to the Cup matches and during them.

Vs Juventus (Melbourne) April 29, 1967

Following this match Mike O'Hara was selected in the Australian Squad versus Scotland. **picture**: Uwe Kuessner

More 1967 State League action at St Kilda Cricket Ground as Mike O'Hara, Hakoah's goalie, dives to stop the ball. Dick van Alphen, former Dutch international, Australian and Hakoah centre half, covers him. Picture: Uwe Kuessner

SOCCER SCENE
WITH NORMAN COUZENS

ANOTHER good win for Hakoah, now unbeaten in four soccer league games this season, means the heat is really on for the Middle Park men.

In topping the table with eight points they have scored 10 goals and conceded none, a record which is a challenge to the other clubs.

From now on every game will be a needle match with their opponents going flat out to be the first to penetrate the solid Hakoah defence.

And Hakoah can't afford to ease up. Juventus are only one point behind and waiting a chance to snatch the lead.

In Saturday's 2-0 win over champions Hellas, goalkeeper O'Hara staked another claim for a place in the State squad.

He has a reputation as a showman but always does a workmanlike job. This time he stopped three almost-certain goals with daring saves.

Ο Ο'ΧΑΡΑ ΘΕΛΕΙ ΝΑ ΠΑΙΞΗ ΣΤΗΝ ΕΛΛΑΣ

Ο γκολκήπερ της Χακόα Μίκη Ο'Χάρα επισκέφθηκε τα γραφεία μας την περασμένη εβδομάδα και μας είπε ότι ενδιαφέρεται να μεταγραφή στην ΕΛΛΑΣ. Ήδη έχει κάνει σχετικές συζητήσεις με παράγοντες της ελληνικής ομάδος. Σε ερώτησή μας γιατί θέλει να μεταγραφή απήντησε ότι η ΕΛΛΑΣ είναι μεγάλη ομάδα και θα του αρέσει να συμπεριληφθή σε αυτήν. Υπάρχουν, πρόσθεσε, και οικονομικοί λόγοι. Η μεταγραφή του όμως θα εξαρτηθή από τις απαιτήσεις που θα προβάλη η Χακόα. Και φυσικά από το ενδιαφέρον που θα επιδείξη η διοίκησις της ΕΛΛΑΣ...

It seemed that everytime Mike O'Hara wore the Star of David 'miracles' occured. There was talk of O'Hara joining the fine Greek club South Melbourne Hellas, but the price offered of $10,000 was not enough to secure the fiery Irishman away from his self stated, 'Beloved Hakoah'.

It's O.K., ref., he's still breathing. (Hakoah players are Keith and van Alphen.)

They call him Melbourne's noisiest Soccer player. It's Hakoah goalie, Mike O'Hara, beefing out instructions to his team-mates in the match against Juventus on Sunday. Juventus centre-forward, Eric Norman, had just put the ball into the net. So Mike had plenty to grumble about! **Action shot by Uwe Kuessner.**

Mike O'Hara, Hakoah's keeper calls for a stretcher after 'accidentally' colliding with an Essendon Lions striker!

pictures: Les Shorrock – Chief Reporter *Soccer Action* – 1967

O'Hara taken to hospital

HAKOAH St Kilda's rilliant goalkeeper Mike 'Hara failed all ttempts by State eague champions eorge Cross to beat hem at Middle Park, esterday.

In doing so O'Hara roke a finger in his left and and had to be taken o hospital.

His deputy, 16 year ld Albert Amici, perormed superbly to nable Hakoah to finish he game in a goal-less raw.

The Cross had little to lay for having already won the league title. But they tried — and failed — to break through the strong Hakoah defence led by Mike Rainey and David Baker.

Far too many of their shots went wide. Also shots by Hakoah's Bill Nagy went astray. He was replaced by Alec Marshall.

It didn't take Marshall long before he hit the woodwork but time ran out and his side had to be content with sharing the points.

Man of the match — Mike O'Hara (Hakoah).

EVERY metropolitan newspaper advertised the Hakoah-George Cross State League match as being played at Middle Park today.

But it was played yesterday and as a result only a handful of people saw the match.

Kurt Defris, Hakoah secretary-manager said last night: "We lost about $600 as a result of the game not being advised as a Saturday match."

It appears the round was the seventh State League round which had been postponed because of an international game.

At the time Hakoah was set down for Sunday but because South Melbourne Hellas are playing Canberra City at Middle Park today it had to be brought forward.

The VSF informed newspapers of the change during the week. Some received the information too late for publication while others ignored it.

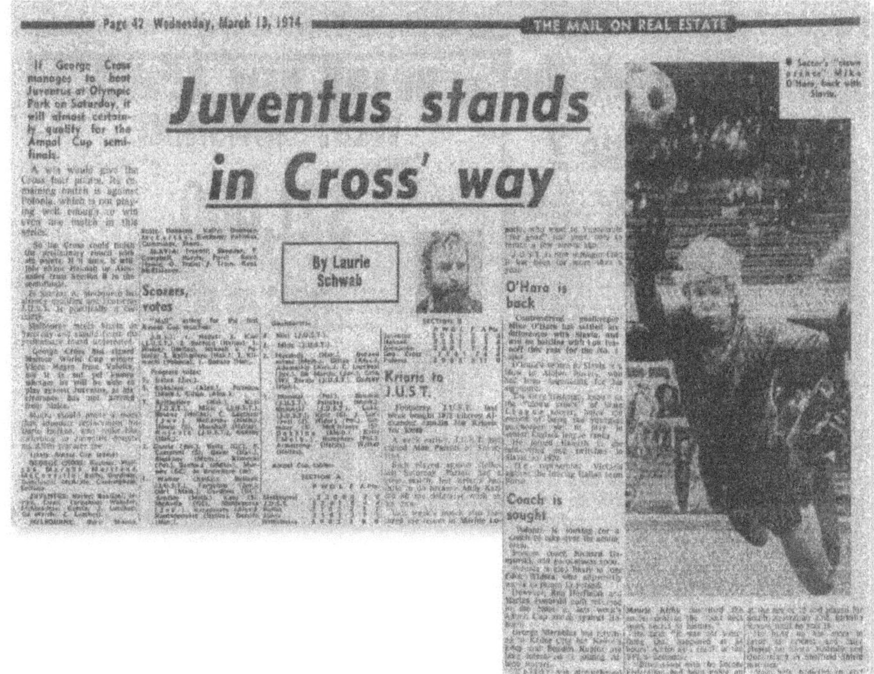

Page 42 Wednesday, March 13, 1974 — THE MAIL ON REAL ESTATE

If George Cross manages to beat Juventus at Olympic Park on Saturday, it will almost certainly qualify for the Ampol Cup semi-finals.

Juventus stands in Cross' way

By Laurie Schwab

Scorers, votes

O'Hara is back

Kriaris to J.U.S.T.

Coach is sought

Soccer's "clown prince" Mike O'Hara, back with Slavia.

Age Sports writer Laurie Schwab never misses an opportuninity of giving the thousands of soccer fans a look at Melbourne's own 'Clown Prince' of goalkeepers, the current Slavia Melbourne custodian Mike O'Hara.

picture: Fred Villiers – *The Age* – 1978.

34 MELBOURNE TRUTH, SATURDAY, JUNE 25, 1977

The Truth about the **VICTORIAN SOCCER SCENE** *with STEVE GRANT*

PRESTON FIGHT FOR DRAW

A BRAVE fighting display by Preston earned them a great draw in the mud at Collier Street ground against Hakoah, on Sunday.

It was a thrill-a-minute match played in shocking conditions.

Both teams proved they are the State League's best mudlark specialists and the 2000 crowd enjoyed every minute of it.

The only disappointment was the loss of Hakoah's forward David Stuart who broke his collar bone three minutes after kick-off when he collided with Frank Campbell.

But his replacement, Mike de Placido, soon made his presence felt with the opening goal in the 38th minute. He turned on the ball in a goalmouth melee and hammered it high over the head of Peter Laumets, the Preston and Victorian keeper.

The ball struck the inside of the crossbar and bounced back into the net.

Twenty-two minutes into the second half Preston levelled the score with another great goal from John McQuade. But it was made by Bill McClement who was on the left wing. He sent over a perfect cross for McQuade to shoot past Mike O'Hara who gave one of his best performances this year.

Preston have not lost a game since former Aston Villa star Jim Adam took over as coach from Mike de Bruyckere two weeks ago.

Had it not been for Tommy Fox (a little overweight and slow on the ball) and John Bernard hitting the post, they would have won the points.

Steve Beech lost his boots in the mud but slushed through the puddles showing good ball control in a difficult situation.

I have never seen Bruce Roberts hit the ball so hard as he did on Sunday. One shot almost beat Laumets but he just managed to hang on to the slippery ball as it skimmed off the mud in front of him.

★ *MIKE O'HARA . . . he gave one of his best performances in goal for Hakoah. His captain, David Baker (right) shields the ball from an opponent.*

Not his day

"WARM UP and get on". Those were coach Ron Smith's instructions to Mike O'Hara, Victoria's reserve goalkeeper at Olympic Park yesterday.

With only 10 minutes to go, Victoria was trailing Middlesbrough by three goals and O'Hara was thrust into goal after spending a cold 80 minutes on the bench.

But he was soon in a hot spot as the English First Division club zeroed in to score a fourth goal through striker Graeme Hedley.

O'Hara had plenty of action in his brief appearance, as these Clive Mackinnon pictures show. LEFT: He leaps in a spectacular effort to deflect a shot and BELOW he sends two Middlesbrough players sprawling to the turf.

Soccer farce at Park

By JIM BARKER

VICTORIAN soccer was humiliated at Olympic Park yesterday by English First Division club Middlesbrough.

As entertainment its rating was near zero, as a soccer match it was a farce and as a promotional exercise a disaster.

The score, which is just for the statisticians, was Middlesbrough 4, Victoria 0.

The Victorians could not have played worse and the Middlesbrough performance was little better.

Victoria had too many players who appeared to be lost and could not find their way back into the game.

It wasn't funny for the 6300 spectators who paid almost $20,000 to see a soccer spectacle.

In fact, Victoria's only positive contribution was to mesmerise Middlesbrough into playing almost as badly.

Surely this debacle marks the end of a long series of money-raising matches against foreign teams which have become counter-productive.

Fortunately a few Victorian administrators have already seen the writing on the wall.

At a press conference, only two hours before yesterday's kick-off they combined with a private sponsor to launch a new $500,000 inter-continental soccer tournament to be held in Australia in July.

Organised by a private promoter, "World of Soccer" the competition will bring Arsenal, Celtic and Red Star to Australia to compete with the National team for more than $50,000 prize money.

In the opening rounds Celtic is drawn to play Red Star in Sydney on Wednesday, July 27.

Arsenal meet Australia at Olympic Park the following night with the winning teams meeting in the final, also at Olympic Park on Sunday, July 31.

● West back at the top — Page 57.

Left picture: Victorian State goalkeeper Mike O'Hara makes a magnificent fingertip reflex save from a goal bound Middlesbrough strike.

Right picture: Mike O'Hara hurtles into a Middlesbrough player sending him to the ground and calmly collects the ball!

pictures: Laurie Schwab – *The Age* – 1977

O'HARA, WALKER ARE TOPS IN STALEMATE

Victorian State League
round-up by LES SHORROCK.

Hakoah goalkeeper Mike O'Hara — an anxious moment. Picture by SAM BELFONTE

HAKOAH 0 JUVENTUS 0

HAKOAH: O'Hara 8, Rainey 8, Parkin 6, Jordanou 6, Baker 7, Blair 6, De Placido 6, Edmondson 6, Gadsby 6, McNeil 6, Roberts 5, (sub Ferguson 80).

JUVENTUS: Graham 6, Della Rocca 7, Sabadini 7, Walker 8, Pfisterer 7, Bannon 6, Watkins 6, Lucchesi 5, Armstrong 5 (Sub Sabiduss), Smith 6, Hotson 6.

Stalemate! At Middle Park on Saturday, the irresistable force met the immovable object, with the inevitable conclusion.

In retrospect, the result of this match was a foregone conclusion.

The first League match ended 1-1, when Hakoah gained an equaliser through the unfortunate **Fausto Tarquinio**, and the Dockerty Cup match, after 120 minutes of hard slogging, finished scoreless.

Now these two teams have confronted each other for 300 minutes and have only a goal apiece to show for it.

But how close Juventus came to winning!

The Juve forwards squandered chances like drunken sailors ashore, and some of the misses were quite unbelievable.

In the first half, for instance, **Hotson, Watkins,** and **Bannon** should have put their side three up.

First **Claude Lucchesi** threaded his way past three opponents and shot, and saw **Mike O'Hara** make a brilliant diving save.

However the goalie pushed the ball straight to the feet of **John Hotson**, who fired over the empty goal from only 10 yards out.

Then Hotson himself brilliantly carved out an opening on the left and crossed the ball for **Mick Watkins** to fire yards wide.

Three minutes from half-time, in a sustained Juventus attack, **Jed Bannon** found himself clear in front of a yawning open goal and **Mike O'Hara** sprawling helplessly on the ground, but somehow he managed to miss.

It was the same story straight after the interval, as Watkins missed again, then **Jim Armstrong** brought O'Hara to his knees and **Steve Walker**, up for a corner, headed across the face of goal.

So far this season it has been a case of Juve's brilliant attack carrying a suspect defence, but this week, the defence really came into its own.

Steve Walker played his best game since coming from Hellas, and Pat Della Rocca, Uli Pfisterer and Serge Sabadini gave him great support.

This back four gradually assumed such domination over the threadbare Hakoah attack that **Hugh Graham** in goal was only an interested spectator.

It was this domination by the defence that enabled Juve's forwards to give the Hakoah goal such a heavy pounding in the second half.

I thought the Hakoah defence was superb, as indeed has been the case every time I've watched Hakoah this season.

In Mike Rainey it has the best right back in the State League, and Dave Baker always appears cool, calm and collected.

Bill Jordanou had a good game, and crowned it by heading off the line once when Watkins sneaked the ball past O'Hara.

As for O'Hara, well, 'Mad Mike' was his usual self — brilliant, abusive and abrasive.

He got involved with an old enemy, **Jim Armstrong**, and both were chatted by the ref, **Tudor Jenkins**, after an episode that qualified them both for an 'Emmy' award.

It was a pity that O'Hara was also involved in an incident near the end with Lucchesi.

Lucchesi was lying in the box, and the ball had gone out of play when O'Hara, rushing across impetuously to take a quick goal-kick, jumped over him and caught Claude's head a glancing blow with his boot.

I was only a couple of yards away from the incident and I thought it was an accident, a view shared by the policeman alongside me, but Lucchesi, sensing that a penalty might be the only way that Juventus could break the deadlock, made a meal of it.

In fact, he, like O'Hara in the first half, was lucky that the referee took a lenient view of the abuse he copped.

Some refs would have been waving the red card after the first few mouthfuls.

But, incidents apart, it was an absorbing struggle, despite the unhappiness of some frustrated Juventus supporters who were angry that their team's superiority on the day wasn't rewarded with a goal or two.

Mick Watkins was absolutely brilliant on the ball. How this fellow loves to take on opponents! However he ruined it all by bad finishing and his selfishness.

Jim Armstrong, coming back after injury, will be more match fit next week and the Juve forwards can console themselves with the thought that they don't come up against **Mike O'Hara** every week.

Team of the week

O'HARA
(Hakoah)

RAINEY (Hakoah) | DONALDSON (G. Gully) | WALKER (Juventus) | BARRON (G. Cross)

T. BANAGAN (Sunshine) | BEECH (Preston) | WISNIEWSKI (Polonia)

CUMMING | O'CALLAGHAN | WILLIAMS

SQUAD HAVE STRENGTH . . .

A strong Victorian squad has been named for the coming clash against English first division club Middlesborough, to be played at Olympic Park on Sunday, May 29.

The squad is: P. Laumets, M. O'Hara, K. Adams, S. Kokoska, D. Baker, F. Tarquino, T. Cumming, J. Gardiner, C. Gilder, B. Roberts, J. Tront, P. Ollerton, M. Ristovski, B. Wilkinson, D. Barron, G. Groanwald.

The PSL said today that national clubs will be allowed to make their players available for this international game.

If this is the case, where are the Fitzroy players, such as Branko Buljevic, one of the country's top forwards?

VICTORIAN ROTHMANS MEDAL, OCTOBER 7

KEEPERS HAVE A BIG SHOW

THE SECOND OF A TWO-PART ARTICLE BY LES SHORROCK, ON THE CANDIDATES FOR VICTORIA'S MAJOR BEST PLAYER AWARD.

Hakoah goalkeeper Mike O'Hara — dives onto the ball in a game for Victoria.

GREEN GULLY

Green Gully has called on the services of no less than 25 players this season, but amidst all this coming and going, **Peter Donaldson** has missed only one game, the first, whilst **Lou Denys** has been ever-present after coming from St. Albans for the fourth game of the season.

In the Riversdale travel award, Denys and Donaldson both polled well in a side that has struggled all season.

Frank Campbell

Mike Rainey has had an outstanding season too and headed the Riversdale award with one game to go.

Dave Baker, winner two years ago, is still consistent and I feel that these three are Hakoah's pick.

JUVENTUS

The Juventus side has been a fairly settled one for many weeks and as befits a team sitting in third place, has some good medal prospects.

Jed Gannon was an early leader in the Riversdale Award and is one of Juventus ever-present.

Of course he won't want reminding that his two brothers Vince and Pat are previous medal winners.

Steve Walker and **Pat Della Rocca** have been consistent all season, and would get favorable mention as defenders.

If a forward wins the Rothman's, it could well be the brilliant **Mick Walkins**, who has already won the Bill Fleming Medal.

Speedy **Phil Williamson** too would have been a possibility if he had not had the misfortune of breaking his leg.

Of the others, **John O'Callaghan** would seem to be Ringwood's best chance, with **Keith Adams**.

Jim Train (Slavia)

SLAVIA

Slavia produced the Rothman's winner last year, **Jim Tansey**. Can it repeat the feat this year?

Only three players, **Peter Clarke** the captain, **Jim Train**, whose benefit year it was, and **Frank Thomson**, played all through the upheaval of the players' strike, and if

Les Shorrock's team of year

O'HARA (Hakoah)

RAINEY (Hakoah) — IRVINE (Frankston) — GRAMSBERGEN (Altona) — BARROW (George Cross)

PECOCK (Sunshine) — GANNON (Juventus) — SMITH (Juventus)

WATKINS (Juventus) — REED (George Cross) — DAVIDSON (Lions)

O'HARA'S STYLE LIKE THE GREATS'

Victorian State League round-up by LES SHORROCK.

HAKOAH 0 GEORGE CROSS 0

HAKOAH: O'Hara 7 (sub Amici 8), Rainey 7, Valli 6, Gadsby 6, Baker 7, McNeill 5, [illegible] ... Blair 6, Edmondson 5.

GEORGE CROSS: Kapiner 5, McConville 6, Baxter 6, Webb 6, Lacive 5, Wilkinson 6, Elliott 5, Murphy P. 7, Reed 6, Kelly 5, Walker 5.

Thanks to a brilliant goalkeeping display by O'Hara, sound defence by David Baker and Mike Rainey, and a promising debut by 15 year-old Bert Amici, Hakoah earned a draw from a jaded George Cross on Saturday.

O'Hara's saves in the first half had to be seen to be believed and when he had the misfortune to break a finger early in the second half it seemed that Hakoah must go under.

But an unknown, named Bert Amici, sent in by **Mike Mandelis** to substitute for O'Hara had different ideas, and he held everything that George's forwards threw at him in highly competent fashion.

The Cross had started the game with champion-like swagger and it seemed only a matter of time before Hakoah succumbed.

A sign of things to come came when **Reed** unleashed a fierce shot only to see O'Hara nonchalantly flick the ball over, it seemed, without moving.

The Hakoah goal was under siege then and O'Hara was everywhere.

Once, during a sequence of [illegible] successive corners, he made a save from a flying header from Ken Reed that **Gordon Banks** himself would have been proud of.

When, inevitably, O'Hara was beaten, there was the reliable

Bunce 'not interested'

Hakoah coach Fred Bunce will not be Victoria's new Director of Coaching.

Bunce ruled himself out of contention for the prestigious job before flying to New Zealand for a two-week coaching course.

"I've got no intention of applying for the Director of Coaching position and I don't want the job," said Bunce.

Hakoah, from left, standing: Fred Bunce (coach), Anton Dosen, Steve Gadsby, Richard McClunie, Graham French, Gerry Edmondson, Mike O'Hara, Ged Bannon, Denis Krongold (president). Front: Bill Allison (reserve coach), Stan Webster, Michael Gesos, Colin Allison, Sean Rooney, Bill Jordanou, Chris Kent, Ian McNeil.

Hakoah

By CRAIG MACKENZIE

Hakoah has a proud record of success in cup competitions but the odds are against it in Section A of the inaugural Victoria Cup.

Harry Sutherland played with English clubs Leeds United, Exeter and Bournemouth and joined Hakoah in 1954 and played for four seasons.

Full back Bill Harburn came from Bishop Auckland in England and Tom Jack was capped many times for Australia.

Mike O'Hara's final season with the magnificent Hakoah Melbourne Football Club.

Mike commenced his Australian football career with Hakoah in March 1966 at the age of 19, and played his last game for the 'Sky Blues' in October 1980 at the age of 34.

The picture that follows relates to this article that has been written by Hakoah goalkeeper Mike O'Hara.

The legendary English Charlton Athletic goalkeeper Mr Sam Bartram who signed me as a professional footballer with Luton Town AFC in the English Football League when I was still 15 years old, told me in no uncertain terms that 'When you have decided your going to take a high cross, make sure you shout clearly "My ball Jack" so your defenders will leave it to you.'

That is exactly what I did in October 1980 at Olympic Park against a powerful Makedonia team in a cup match. Problem was my central defender, the burly Anton Dosen either didn't understand English or had real bad hearing, and as I charged out and jumped high at speed for the ball, Anton came from nowhere and smashed into my nose with the back of his head! The picture that follows shows the result.

Had David Baker been the central defender, he would have just left the ball to me, that easy! That's why David Baker won two Victorian State League Best & Fairest medals and Anton Dosen won nothing! Baker, cool as Antarctic block ice under pressure! Dosen, like his house was on fire!

O'Hara hurt, Ajax triumphs

MAKEDONIA 4 (Lucchesi 2, McMillan 2) HAKOAH 2 (Webster, Rainey o.g.), Wednesday night.

MAKEDONIA: Kastner 8 – Rainey 6, Higham 6, Flavelle 7, Beech 8 – Petrovski 7, Faulkner 8, Lucchesi 8 – Cullen 9, Ollerton 7, McMillan 8.

HAKOAH: O'Hara 7 (carried off 45th, Fryzer 7) – Gadsby 6, Dosen 6, Jordanou 6 (Rooney 65th) Edmondson 6 – Bannon 5, McNeil 6, Kent 5 – Webster 6, McClume 6, French 6.

Hakoah stunned Makedonia with a first-minute goal but it stung Brian Edgley's side into action and Makedonia's second half blitzkeies produced three goals and a well deserved 4-2 victory.

Ian McNeil played the ball to Richard McClume who played it inside to Stan Webster and the little Scot steadied, then struked the ball firmly past Lou Kastner who had charged off his line to narrow the angle.

The Makedonians in the crowd were as stunned as the players they support but the goal heralded an onslaught inspired by the dynamic Rob Cullen who time and again charged down on Hakoah defenders, turned them inside out and set up chances for his fellow forwards.

Poor finishing, desperate defence and the bravery of Mike O'Hara robbed Makedonia of the reward its pressure deserved until Claude Lucchesi took off down the left, beat one defender and chipped the ball over O'Hara at the near post and into the far corner of goal to level at 1-1 in the 25th minute.

Hakoah rarely went forward with any penetration and when O'Hara crashed into Anton Dosen and was carried off with severe concussion and a broken nose Hakoah's stocks fell but replacement keeper Mike Fryzer pulled off three fine second half saves to stop what could have been an embarrassing scoreline.

But Hakoah could have stolen the lead had shots from

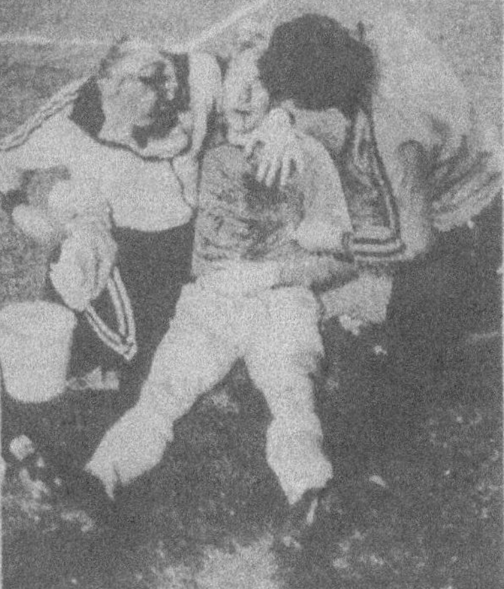

Hakoah goalkeeper Mike O'Hara gets first aid after breaking his nose in a clash with team mate Anton Dosen.

Graham French or Chris Kent found the mark early in the second half.

Kastner parried well from a McClume shot from 15 metres and in the 68th minute Makedonia went 2-1 up.

Cullen went down the right and played the ball inside to George McMillan who pushed it square to goal then slid down and shot low past Fryzer and into the far corner.

In the 83rd minute Cullen lobbed the ball over Gerry Edmondson's head and McMillan burst forward, then poked the ball home from eight metres to put the game out of Hakoah's reach.

Three minutes later McMillan's persistence paid off and he gained possession on a tight angle on Makedonia's right, crossed to the far post and Lucchesi, unmarked, nodded truly from the edge of the six-yard box.

Hakoah gained a consolation goal almost on full time when a low cross intended for French was intercepted by Mike Rainey but sent into his own goal with Kastner stranded.

AJAX 2 (Segi, Bennie) CROATIA 1 (Batinovic), Wednesday night.

AJAX: Danys 8 – Smart 7, Patten 7, Dunne 8, Hogben 7 – Vojtek 7, Bennett 7 (inj. Parkin 77th), Vassallo 7 – Segi 7, Bennie 7, Morrey 8.

CROATIA: Kovac 6 – Short 7, Adams 6 (Andrews 74th), Kokoska 6, Bilaver 7 – Front 7, Gardiner 7, Murphy 6, Ietuk 5 – Klein 5, Batinovic 7 (Mitten 79th).

Ajax ended its run of outs in the State League Cup with a deserved 2-1 victory over the Croatia "reserves."

This game followed the Hakoah-Makedonia match which assured Croatia of its place in last Sunday's final so John Gardiner took this opportunity to try out the lesser lights of his squad while resting Noel Mitten, Cort Gilder, Alan Kerr, Peter Blasby, Tommy Cumming and Howard Andrews.

Andrews and Mitten came on late in the game but Croatia's inability to break down the Ajax defence proved costly.

Mitten went close in the dying stages with a header at the far post from Mick Klarin's cross but the ball hit the base of the near upright and cannoned into safety.

However had Mitten's effort been successful it would have punished Ajax for poor finishing, as Bill Morrey and Steve Bennie should have scored.

Croatia was not a patch on the side which had carried all before it in recent games and the second half, aside from five goalmouth incidents, was a poor spectacle.

In the 47th minute Morrey went down the left and cut the ball back to the unmarked Andy Segi whose first time shot put Ajax 1-0 up.

Four minutes later Ned Batinovic followed in on a Steve Short shot and equalised from close range.

In the 58th minute a long ball by Jimmy Dunne was misjudged by Steve Kokoska and Bennie had the simple task of slipping the ball to one side of Chris Kovac and score what was to be the decisive goal.

Ajax should have gone further ahead in the 78th minute but Morrey was unable to finish well from eight metres.

Had Hakoah knocked off Makedonia, Croatia would have been forced into playing more of its top liners and the paying public may have been deservedly entertained.

The following shows a Christmas picture card sent by the great Mr Kurt Defris, Secretary Manager of Hakoah Melbourne Association Football Club in 1977, to the Mike O'Hara family.

This simple caring gesture by Hakoah's number one Jewish Hero was typical of the humanistic nature and genuine love that this great man had for his players and their families.

Winning is not everything
(it is the only thing)

If you've got two left legs —
try your head

Birthdays are O.K —
but goals are better

What good is a head —
if you don't use it?

You don't have to look pretty —
as long as you deliver the goods

Keep your head in a crisis —
but use it in football

HAKOAH SOCCER CLUB

HAKOAH S.C.

If you can't do it with your feet —
try your head

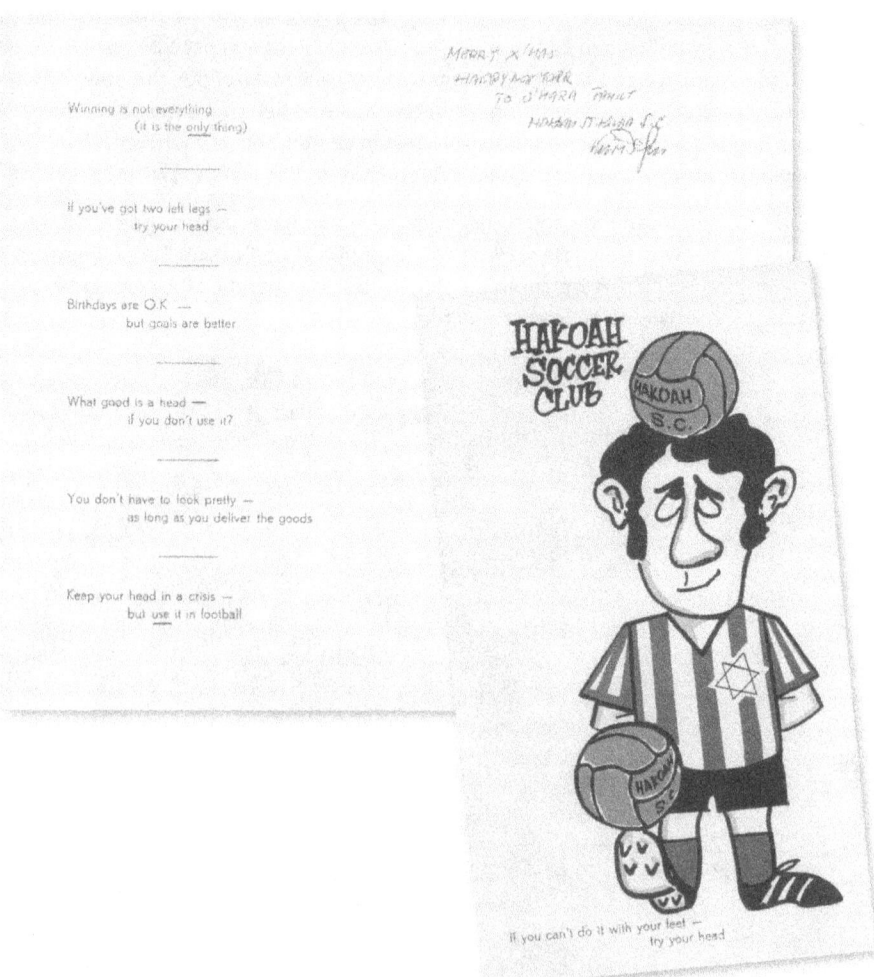

'I fell hopelessly in love with Jewishness and it's people when I walked into Middle Park Football Stadium Melbourne in February 1966. I am as honoured now as I was then, to still carry the beautiful legacy of Jewish humbleness today.'

Mike O'Hara

Hakoah Melbourne Football Club, Statistics, Records, Honours and Awards

1927–1981

Hakoah/Maccabi

Date	Event	Note
1884	Victorian Soccer Federation was formed.	
1909	Earliest State League records available	
1928	First official general meeting took place in January 1928	VSF
	Sam Yaffe appointed first club President	
	Hakoah's 1st game vs. North Carlton at Fawkner Park 1–0 win	
	Affiliated with the Victorian Amateur Soccer Federation	
1929	Hakoah playing in Suburban League	
23 May	Dockerty Cup vs. Wonthaggi Magpies (opening fixture)	
12 Jul	Hakoah vs. Springvale SFC at Princes Park, North Carlton – large crowd – Played (6/7/29)	
29 Aug	Hakoah announce they are playing a game against Sydney Hakoah (13/9/29)	
1930	Hakoah – Played in Grade Three Competition	
1933	Hakoah – As at May 22nd – supreme team in 1st. Division	
	Hakoah vs. Caledonians – 4000 crowd at Exhibition Oval	
	Big rivalry with South Yarra team	
	Problems with injured players towards end of season – losing top spot & knocked out at semi-final stage of Dockerty Cup by Melbourne Thistle	
1934	Hakoah – Champions – Premier/State League – Victoria	
05 May	Hakoah – Olympic Park home ground – Middle Park facilities described as 'very poor'	
	Grand Ball at New Kadimah Hall in North Carlton Cnr. Faraday & Lygon Streets – meeting point to go to away games.	
02 Jun	Hakoah – 8th. win in a row vs. Footscray Thistles – Johnnie Orr fractures collarbone	
	Possibly undefeated all season	
07 Jul	vs. Kingswood Soccer Club (Adelaide) – Australian Championship Won 7–2 in Adelaide	
	Played at Hindmarsh Stadium – 'best soccer ever seen'	
	RC Cleland & JA Karsten – donated medals to players to commemorate above game	
1935	Hakoah – Champions – Premier/State League – Victoria	
	Hakoah – Dockerty Cup Winners	
15 June	Hakoah – defeated Melbourne Thistle at Olympic Park 17–1	

1936	Hakoah – Runners up in the State League – Moreland won championship	
1937	Hakoah team considerably strengthened pre-season Hakoah season starts April 17th. vs. Moreland Olympic Park	
12 Jun	Hakoah vs. Prahran – Como Park – won 3 in a row before that game.	
1938	Hakoah – Champions – Premier/State League – Victoria	
July	Appeal to supporters to take players to Dockerty Cup Final in Yallourn (Amusing) Game arranged for Palestine team to come to Australia Olympic Park home ground First loss for season vs. Heidelberg on July 9th. 1938	
1943	Hakoah – Champions – Premier/State League – Victoria	Won as Moreland–Hakoah
1945	Hakoah – Dockerty Cup Winners	Won as Moreland–Hakoah
1946	Hakoah JRC vs. Sydney Hakoah – 1st. inter Jewish game after the war	
1950	Hakoah – Club finished 5th.	
12 Jun	Played for AN Roth & S. Newton trophy – Sydney won	
1953	Hakoah – Dockerty Cup Winners	
1954	Hakoah – Dockerty Cup Winners	
1955	Hakoah – Runners Up – Premier/State League – Victoria Hakoah – Dockerty Cup Winners Hakoah – Harry Armstrong Cup Winners	Juventus – Champions
1956	Hakoah – Runners Up -Premier/State League – Victoria Hakoah – Dockerty Cup Winners – Defeated Brighton 2–0 Hakoah – Harry Armstrong Cup Winners	Juventus – Champions
1957	Hakoah defeats JUST 4–2 to end 9 game winning run for JUST	
1958	Hakoah – Harry Armstrong Cup Winners	
1961	Hakoah – Club finished 4th.	
1962	Hakoah – Club finished 6th.	

1964	Hakoah – Harry Armstrong Cup Winners
June	Hakoah vs. Juventus – crowd 2000 – 2–3 Loss Hakoah Ajax Juniors given special permission by VSF to play games on Sundays. Hugh 'Shuggy' Murney arrives from Scotland (30/5/64) Middle Park Stadium – Opening of new 9000 Pound Grandstand
1965	Hakoah vs. Hapoel Tel Aviv
May	Hakoah/Hellas combined vs. Hapoel Tel Aviv – South Melbourne Cricket Ground Hakoah vs. Hellas Middle Park – Crowd 8600 – Result 0–0 Michael Weinstein elected Chairman of National League formation committee.
1966	Ampol Cup Night Game vs. South Melbourne Hellas – 9000 spectators (3–1 win Hakoah)
July	40th. Year Anniversary Ball for Hakoah. Year Book written by Aku Roth Hakoah–Ajax formed (all age players – Jewish) – Coached by Jack Roessler Hakoah – Mike O'Hara and Jim Armstrong debuted as 19-year-olds. Hakoah – Manny Poulakakis takes over as Senior coach Hakoah – Highest Victorian State League position in the history of the club (3rd). Hakoah – Dockerty Cup Winners
1967	Hakoah – State League leading goalscorer – Jim Armstrong (19 goals) Football Federation Victoria (FFV) Record. Hakoah record holders – 677 minutes (7½ + games) without conceding a goal from the start of any season. David Baker makes debut for Hakoah.
1969	John O'Neill Bill Fleming Medal Winner – Best & Fairest for the Competition
1970	Hakoah – Harry Armstrong Cup Winners Hakoah – State League leading goalscorer – Mike Clarey (16 goals) Jim Armstrong sold to South Melbourne Hellas
1972	Hakoah – Reserves Champions

1973	Hakoah – Dockerty Cup Winners – defeated Fitzroy-Alexander (Heidelberg) 1–0 scorer: Stewart Blair
1975	Hakoah – Harry Armstrong Cup Winners David Baker – Rothmans Medal Winner (Best & Fairest) Record Vote win in history of the competition at that stage (43 votes)
1977	David Baker – Rothmans Medal Winner (Best & Fairest) Hakoah – Lowest goals against record in the history of the club, 1927–1981. (20 goals conceded in 22 league matches)
1978	David Kraus top goalscorer (16) Maccabi
1979	Victor Rosenberger top goalscorer (15) Maccabi
1980	Harry Armstrong Cup winners def. Polonia 4–0 (McLunie, Webster) Coach: Bill Allison Fred Bunce becomes senior coach Testimonial game for David Baker. Jim Mackay & Jim Armstrong guest appearance Chris Kent transfers from Adelaide City to Hakoah for $11,000 Hakoah Reserves – won championship – huge debts causes financial problems. Maccabi Top Scorer > Danny Fridman (31)
1981	Hakoah – Ampol Cup Night Game knocked out in semi-final by Croatia 0–2 Merger talks commenced between Hellas & Hakoah. Maccabi–Hakoah wins Amateur Cup d. Kooyong Rangers 3–1 Maccabi–Hakoah wins Amateur Club Championship Maccabi–Hakoah wins Victorian Amateur Cup – Triple Championship year. Hakoah (State League) merged with Hellas. Maccabi Top Scorer > Moshe Melek (16)
1982	Hakoah – Harry Armstrong Cup Winners Maccabi Top Scorer > Moshe Melek (16)
1983	Maccabi Top Scorer > Michael Sher
1984	Maccabi Top Scorer > Steven Pugh
1985	Maccabi – Steven Freund – Amateur League Best & Fairest
1989	Maccabi Best & Fairest Winner > Steven Pugh Maccabi Top Scorer > Zvi Kalb (15)

1990	Maccabi Best & Fairest Winner > Steven Pugh Maccabi Top Scorer > Benji Pushett (11)
1990/91	Victoria Maccabi wins Gold Coast carnival – 1st. Carnival Win for Victoria.
1991/92	Victoria Maccabi wins Melbourne carnival for 2nd back to back victory.
1998	Maccabi wins Fairest team award for season 1998 for club with least yellow & red cards. Maccabi – B&F winner: Boris Seroshtan Maccabi – Oran Harel leading club goalscorer – 15 goals
1999	Maccabi – Justin Scrobogna wins B&F VSF award & Top goalscorer (28) Club promoted to Prov. League Div. 2 South East

Past Presidents

- Larry Goldman
- Harvey Silver
- Jonathan Munz

Life Members

- Max Stem
- Jonathan Munz
- Harry Zaitman

League statistics 1931–1981

Note: Hakoah Football Club finished officially third in the Victorian State League in 1966, ahead of Melbourne Hungaria Football Club on goal difference. Accordingly the '4' attributed to Hakoah in the records is incorrect. Hakoah Melbourne Football Club finished third official place holders in 1966 – the highest placing ever recorded by any Hakoah team in the Victorian State League from the leagues inception in 1958 to 1981.

1966 Victorian State League final standings

Hakoah Melbourne [3rd]

P:22 W:10 D:5 L:7 F:30 A:24 GD:+6 PT: 25

Melbourne Hungaria [4th]

P:22 W:10 D:5 L:7 F:31 A29 GD:+2 PT: 25

Hakoah Melbourne finished 3rd with a superior goal difference of + 4.

First Grade Divisional History

Season	League	Pos	P	W	D	L	F	A	Pts
1982	Victorian State League	6	26	10	8	8	32	31	28
1981	Victorian State League	7	22	6	8	8	27	41	20
1980	Victorian State League	4	22	10	6	6	29	24	26
1979	Victorian State League	8	22	6	8	8	23	26	20
1978	Victorian State League	4	22	9	7	6	33	23	25
1977	Victorian State League	9	22	4	11	7	16	20	19
1976	Victorian State League	11	22	4	7	11	16	34	15
1975	Victorian State League	6	22	10	4	8	36	25	24
1974	Victorian State League	6	22	10	6	6	25	28	26
1973	Victorian State League	4	22	11	6	5	37	23	28
1972	Victorian State League	5	22	12	1	9	33	31	25
1971	Victorian State League	9	22	9	2	11	29	30	20
1970	Victorian State League	7	22	7	7	8	33	38	21
1969	Victorian State League	5	22	10	6	6	34	29	26
1968	Victorian State League	4	22	9	6	7	30	27	24
1967	Victorian State League	6	22	11	3	8	41	32	25
1966	Victorian State League	3	22	10	5	7	30	24	25
1965	Victorian State League	7	22	8	7	7	32	27	23
1964	Victorian State League	7	22	7	6	9	44	48	20
1963	Victorian State League	10	22	6	5	11	37	47	17
1962	Victorian State League	6	22	12	4	6	43	29	28
1961	Victorian State League	4	22	12	3	7	53	40	27
1960	Victorian State League	7	22	10	2	10	44	43	22
1959	Victorian State League	4	22	15	2	5	56	30	32
1958	Victorian State League	4	22	12	4	6	59	30	28

1957	Victorian Division 1	4	18	8	3	7	32	31	19
1956	Victorian Division 1	2	18	13	2	3	66	31	28
1955	Victorian Division 1	4	18	9	3	6	59	40	21
1954	Victorian Division 1	2	18	13	2	3	80	36	28
1953	Victorian Division 1	2	18	13	2	3	66	27	28
1952	Victorian Division 2	2	18	16	0	2	92	29	32
1951	*records not available*	–	–	–	–	–	–	–	–
1950	Victorian Division 1	9	18	6	2	10	38	52	14
1949	*records not available*	–	–	–	–	–	–	–	–
1948	*records not available*	–	–	–	–	–	–	–	–
1947	*records not available*	–	–	–	–	–	–	–	–
1946	Victorian Division 1	5	14	7	1	6	32	45	15
1945	*records not available*	–	–	–	–	–	–	–	–
1944	*records not available*	–	–	–	–	–	–	–	–
1943	*records not available*	–	–	–	–	–	–	–	–
1942	*records not available*	–	–	–	–	–	–	–	–
1941	*records not available*	–	–	–	–	–	–	–	–
1940	*records not available*	–	–	–	–	–	–	–	–
1938	Victorian Division 1	2	14	11	2	1	46	19	24
1937	*records not available*	–	–	–	–	–	–	–	–
1396	Victorian Division 1	4	14	7	2	5	40	31	16
1935	*records not available*	–	–	–	–	–	–	–	–
1934	*records not available*	–	–	–	–	–	–	–	–
1933	Victorian Division 1	3	18	13	1	4	53	25	27
1932	*records not available*	–	–	–	–	–	–	–	–
1931	Victorian Division 3	1	14	13	1	0	52	14	27

Player appearances

Season	Gadsby	Stenhouse	Baker	Murney	O'Hara
1963	—	18	—	—	—
1964	—	19	—	14	—
1965	—	21	—	22	—
1966	—	29	NIL	28	29
1967	—	24	3	25	25
1968	—	25	4	25	4
1969	—	—	—	—	—
1970	7	19	8	—	—
1971	12	7	8	23	—
1972 *	13	—	9	1	—
1973 *	17	—	17	—	—
1974 *	13	—	10	—	—
1975 *	9	—	7	—	—
1976	19	—	22	—	9
1977 *	5	—	6	—	5
1978	20	—	22	—	—
1979	28	—	21	—	14
1980	35	—	16	—	31
1981	27	—	—	—	—
Tally	**205**	**162**	**153**	**138**	**117**

All player appearances taken from OzFootball Victoria.

There has been much debate over many years concerning who played the most games for Hakoah Melbourne Football Club, prior to the clubs demise as a sole entity at the end of the 1981 season.

From all Hakoah player appearances obtained from OzFootball Victoria records since WWII, it has been satisfactorily established that the following players have recorded the highest number of appearances in the history of Hakoah Football Club.

1.	Steven Gadsby	(1970–1981)	205+
2.	Alan Stenhouse	(1963–1971)	162
3.	David Baker	(1966–1981)	153
4.	Hugh Murney	(1964–1972)	138
5.	Mike O'Hara	(1966–1968) (1976–1977) (1979–1980)	117

League & Cup Statistics

1931	Division 3 Premiers
1934	1st Division Premiers
1935	1st Division Premiers Dockerty Cup Winners
1938	1st Division Premiers
1945	Dockerty Cup Winners (Moreland / Hakoah)
1953	Dockerty Cup Winners
1954	Dockerty Cup Winners
1955	Dockerty Cup Winners
1956	Dockerty Cup Winners
1966	Dockerty Cup Winners
1973	Dockerty Cup Winners
1927–1957	Hakoah played in the Victorian Amateur Football Association
1958–1981	Hakoah (as a sole entity) played in the Victorian State League Premier Division
1982	Hakoah amalgamated with its Middle Park ground co-occupier, National Football League Club South Melbourne Hellas to become Hellas – Hakoah, playing in the Victorian State League.

Hakoah at this time ceased to exist as a sole entity, and 54 years of great history was lost forever.

Football Federation Victoria official record – current 2017

Hakoah Melbourne Association Football Club are the current record holders for conceding the lowest number of goals from the start of any season since the founding of the Football Federation of Victoria in 1884.

Hakoah Melbourne Football Club, with Michael (Mike) O'Hara as its goalkeeper, conceded zero goals in seven and one half + matches from 26 March 1967 to 13 May 1967, in the Victorian State League.

The Hakoah Melbourne goalkeeper remained unbeaten for a total of 677 minutes of match play.

Details of the current record as at the time and date of this publication (2017) are:

Preston Macedonia	3–0	(home)	90 minutes
Croatia	4–0	(away)	90 minutes
Polonia	1–0	(home)	90 minutes
South Melbourne Hellas	2–0	(away)	90 minutes
Lions	0–0	(home)	90 minutes
Juventus	0–0	(away)	90 minutes
Alexander	3–0	(home)	90 minutes
Port Melbourne Slavia	0–0	(away)	47 minutes

The record breaking team that created this magnificent feat of football history in the Victorian State Premier League in 1967 was: Mike O'Hara (goalkeeper); George 'Dick' Keith, John O'Neill (Captain) (full backs); Alan Stenhouse, Dick Van Alphen, Hugh 'Shug' Murney (half backs); Keith Fry, Ted Smith, Ian Monan, Jim Armstrong and Alex Purdie (forwards).

The greatest Hakoah team in history 1966 – 1967

Mike O'Hara

George 'Dick' Keith   John O'Neill (Captain)

Hugh Murney   Dick Van Alphen   Alan Stenhouse

Keith Fry   Ted Smith   Alex Purdie

Jim Armstrong   Ian Monan

Dockerty Cup winners 1966

Highest league position ever [3rd] 1966 since the formation of the Victorian State League in 1958 to 1981.

Current Football Federation Victoria Premier League record holders for the longest period of time without conceding a goal from the start of a season (1967).

Hall of Fame

The Top 20 all time Hakoah immortal legends

MAGNUM OPUS

(in alphabetical order)

Jim Armstrong
David Baker
Phil Bowman
Alan Forrest
Steve Gadsby
Bill Harburn
Tom Jack
Frank McIver
Frank Moucka
Hugh Murney
Mike O'Hara
John O'Neill
Jackie Ressler
Aku Roth
Moishe Slonim
Alan Stenhouse
Harry Sutherland
Syd Thomas
Dick Van Alphen
Charlie Yaffe

Longest serving top 5 players in the history of Hakoah Football Club

1.	David Baker	16 years
2.	Steven Gadsby	12 years
3.	Alan Stenhouse	9 years
4.	Hugh Murney	9 years
5.	Mike O'Hara	7 years

The Kurt Defris Commendatory Medal

In Recognition of Outstanding Achievement

The Kurt Defris Gold Medal of Honour
Awarded for loyal and dedicated service
Longest serving player

David Baker (16 seasons)

The Kurt Defris Gold Medal of Honour
Awarded for most appearances of any
Hakoah player from 1931–1981

Steven Gadsby (215+ appearances)

Hakoah top goalscorer of all time

Goals in a Season

Golden Boot Award

Harry Sutherland
31 goals
Season 1954

Hakoah top goalkeeper of all time

Lowest number of goals conceded in any season from 1931–1981

Golden Gloves Award

Mike O'Hara
22 Victorian State League matches
20 goals conceded
Season 1977

Photo Gallery

Mr Jack Jacobs and Mike O'Hara before leaving to do some work for the Israeli's.

Jack Jacobs is pictured in his beloved Poland with a member of the Polish national team prior to an international football match. Jack was known in virtually every corner of the football world. Jack is one of the rare few who have received a Brazilian World Cup shirt from the legend 'Pele.' **picture**: Laurie Schwab – *The Age* – 1970

Left: Mr Jack Jacobs

Below: This press box ticket was given to Mike O'Hara as a souvenir by the great Jack Jacobs following their first meeting at White Hart Lane, London, England, the home of Tottenham Hotspur Football Club. At this meeting Mike O'Hara's future in Australia was determined. Mike O'Hara's never ending love affair with Hakoah Melbourne Association Football Club and the worlds Jewish people was about to begin!

article by: Laurie Schwab – *The Age* – 1978

Tottenham Hotspur Football and Athletic Company, Limited

Admit Bearer to

PRESS BOX

ON 1st January, 1966

NAME Mr. Jacobs (Australian Soccer News)

R. J. Jarvis.
Secretary

Mr Robert Levin

Pictured is Mr Robert Levin, who served Hakoah Melbourne Football Club from 1966 to 1981, as a member of the Hakoah Club administration. Mr Levin, a Melbourne business man, continues to this day, to hold nostalgic re-unions at his Melbourne home for all past Hakoah players and friends of Hakoah Football Club. All functions are well attended such is the players respect for this noble of men. Bob Levin's enduring legacy and dedicated passion to Hakoah Melbourne Football Club for over half-a-century is legendary within the players ranks, and reflects comprehensively Bob Levin as a truly magnificent ambassador of his beloved Hakoah Melbourne Football Club.

Laurie Schwab

Lawrie Schwab was a veritable legend of Australian journalistic 'soccer' writing.

Lawrie Schwab was a senior journalist for the Melbourne Age newspaper and editor-in-chief of the Melbourne 'Soccer Action'.

Lawrie Schwab was a protagonist for the Hakoah cause, not only because of his rich Jewish heritage, but because as a professional journalist he was acutely aware that Hakoah AFC had a significant role to play in establishing a solid foundation for all Jewish youth who would want to be involved with the greatest game in the world.

Laurie Schwab was a man of extraordinary vision and nurtured his belief that the day would come when Australia would make a positive impact on world football. Australia's recent international results over the past 5 years have proved Laurie Schwab's predictions very true.

Laurie Schwab was a valued friend and confidant of Hakoah goalkeeper Mike O'Hara, and their friendship endured from February 1966 when O'Hara first arrived in Australia until Laurie's tragic and sudden death on Wednesday 11th June 1997. Laurie was just 50 years of age.

Laurie will be best remembered for pushing 'soccer' to the front pages in a biased press, at a time when 'soccer' was denigrated and openly called 'wogball' by red neck AFL fans!

Hakoah Football Club
Victorian Football League Division 3 Premiers – 1931

Hakoah Football Club (Vic)
Interstate Team, Adelaide 1937

Hakoah Soccer Club
Under 17 Team – 1944

Hakoah Football Club
Dockerty Cup Winning Team 1966

Back row, *left to right*: Hugh Murney, Mike O'Hara, Keith Fry, Dick Keith, Ian Monan, Jim Armstrong, Dick Van Alphen, Bench: Jim O'Neil, David Baker
Front row, *left to right*: Bench: John Walker, Ted Smith, Alan Stenhouse, John O'Neill (captain), Alex Purdie, Bench: Ian Gow, Wim Van Werkhoeven (trainer)

Result: Hakoah Melbourne 4, Slavia Port Melbourne 2

Hakoah Football Club
Dockerty Cup Winners 1966

Third [3rd] in the Victorian State Premier League (the 1966 Hakoah team finished the 1966 season in its highest league position ever attained by any Hakoah team since the formation of the Victorian State Premier League in 1958). Coach: Mr Manny Poulakakis. Extreme right of the picture is Mr Fred Hutchison, Hakoah's magnificent legendary Team Manager.

The picture shows a jubilant Hakoah captain John O'Neill holding aloft the coveted Dockerty Cup. Also carried and sharing the golden moment is Hakoah super coach Mr Manny Poulakakis.

The Hakoah team – Back row (*left to right*): H. Murney, M. O'Hara, K. Fry, G. Keith, I. Monan, J. Armstrong, D. Van Alphen, J. O'Neil (Reserve), D. Baker (Reserve). Front row (*left to right*): J. Walker (Reserve), E. Smith, A. Stenhouse, J. O'Neill (Captain), A. Purdie, I Gow (Reserve), W. Van Werkhoeven (Trainer).

The Slavia team – Back row (*left to right*): J. Goodwin, R. Barotajs, N. Shepherd, T. Randles, P. Laraman, W. Cook, D. High
Front row (*left to right*): I. Reid, G. McGregor, W. Savage, C. McCorquodale, A.N Other, J. Young.

Victoria State Cup Final, Australia 1966
Hakoah Melbourne 4, Slavia Melbourne 2.

The picture shows Hakoah goalkeeper Mike O'Hara punching clear following a Slavia attack. Former Republic of Ireland full back and Hakoah captain John O'Neill watches the outcome at far left of picture.

Above left: The two giants of Soccer – Ray Barotajs (Slavia's 6'1" goalie) and Ian Monan (6'3" forward) battle for the ball in the Dockerty Cup final at Olympic Park on Sunday.

Above centre: Hakoah player Dick Keith falls in a sliding tackle and drags Slavia's McGregor down with him.

Above right: Hakoah players celebrate their fourth goal. It's the end for Slavia!

Hakoah goalie Mike O'Hara charged into a pack of players after a corner kick. He sent team mate Hugh Murney flying. Hakoah's Keith Fry, number 7, watches the outcome.

After the incident the referee had words with Hakoah keeper O'Hara.

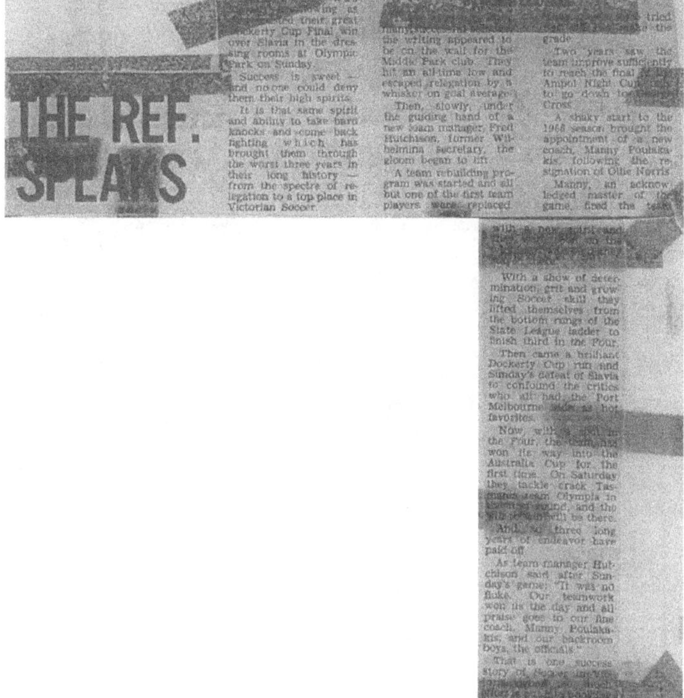

THE REF. SPEAKS

[illegible] was [illegible] ing as [illegible] their great [illegible] Dockerty Cup Final win over Slavia in the dressing rooms at Olympic Park on Sunday.

Success is sweet — and no-one could deny them their high spirits.

It is that same spirit and ability to take hard knocks and come back fighting which has brought them through the worst three years in their long history — from the spectre of relegation to a top place in Victorian Soccer.

[illegible] the writing appeared to be on the wall for the Middle Park club. They hit an all-time low and escaped relegation by a whisker on goal average.

Then, slowly, under the guiding hand of a new team manager, Fred Hutchison, former Wilhelmina secretary, the gloom began to lift.

A team rebuilding program was started and all but one of the first team players were replaced.

[illegible] tried [illegible] the grade.

Two years saw the team improve sufficiently to reach the final [illegible] Ampol Night Cup [illegible] to go down to [illegible] Cross.

A shaky start to the 1968 season brought the appointment of a new coach, Manny Poulakakis, following the resignation of Ollie Norris.

Manny, an acknowledged master of the game, fired the team with a new spirit and [illegible]

With a show of determination, grit and growing Soccer skill they lifted themselves from the bottom rungs of the State League ladder to finish third in the Four.

Then came a brilliant Dockerty Cup run and Sunday's defeat of Slavia to confound the critics who all had the Port Melbourne side as hot favorites.

Now, with a spot in the Four, the team has won its way into the Australia Cup for the first time. On Saturday they tackle crack Tasmanian team Olympia in [illegible] round, and the [illegible] will be there.

And so three long years of endeavor have paid off.

As team manager Hutchison said after Sunday's game: "It was no fluke. Our teamwork won us the day and all praise goes to our fine coach, Manny Poulakakis, and our backroom boys, the officials."

That is one success story of Soccer [illegible]

[illegible] experts saw Cup final

JIM COOK

Sorry, Hakoah! I didn't tip you to win the 1966 Dockerty Cup, but I did say you would provide formidable opposition. And that you did.

IT was a splendidly fought out game in the true tradition of the competition. Hakoah's direct and orthodox type Soccer gave it the win despite being twice in arrears.

Highlights of the day were:

Nigel Shepherd, the Slavia full back and captain, and Australian international, turned out for his [illegible] game for Slavia.

★

[illegible]

★

[illegible] years ago, in 1962, [illegible] crushed Slavia 6-1 [illegible] the Dockerty Cup semi-final. The man who scored [illegible] trick for Hakoah that [illegible] — Eric Haynes, the [illegible] Sheffield Wednesday [illegible] is now with Slavia [illegible] manager of their Under [illegible]. George Cross beat [illegible] in the final that [illegible] the semi-final of the Dockerty Cup. So last week's win by Hakoah was sweet revenge indeed.

★

A lot of credit for the Hakoah win goes to coach Manny Poulakakos, who has gone quietly about his task in moulding them into a top class side. And the Hakoah players after the game last week were not slow in showering their appreciation [illegible] the valuable [illegible] has imparted [illegible].

★

Abe Speigal [illegible] before the match that Hakoah would win 3-1. After the game he couldn't be blamed for thinking that the needless penalty given away by George Keith and the own goal scored by Tom Randles prevented him from guessing correctly.

★

The six feet plus Hakoah centre forward Jan Moran, who scored a brilliant third goal for [illegible] team with a great header, now has two cup medals, one he got last Sunday and the other he won in [illegible] Australia when he [illegible] member of the Lions [illegible] cup-winning side in [illegible].

★

[illegible] Murray, the Hakoah [illegible] half, and Charlie [McCorq]uodale, the Slavia [illegible] forward, played together with Dumbarton in [illegible] second division.

[illegible]

GEORGE YELLAND

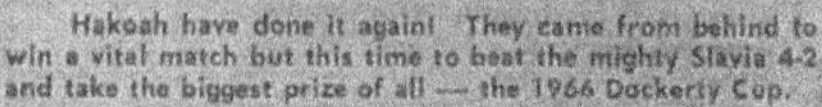

Hakoah have done it again! They came from behind to win a vital match but this time to beat the mighty Slavia 4-2 and take the biggest prize of all — the 1966 Dockerty Cup.

'I was there'

By George Yelland

A disappointing crowd of 4,475 saw a titanic struggle at Olympic Park on Sunday which ended with Hakoah indisputably the better side. It was the Middle Park club's 10th Dockerty Cup win.

On a bitterly cold day, with rain threatening, Mr Armstrong and his linesmen led the Slavia and Hakoah players on to the arena to be presented to Mr F. Beaurepaire, Lord Mayor of Melbourne, before the start of Victoria's top game of the season.

In the first minute, after Hakoah won the toss and played towards the river end, Randles put a ball down the right wing for [illegible] to dash forward, dispossess O'Neill who had [illegible] too far [illegible] and cut in at high speed to deliver a crashing drive which O'Hara never saw, into the top of the net.

Momentarily stunned by this set back, Hakoah [illegible] back and Moran [illegible] [illegible]

[illegible] drive against the crossbar and a minute later flashed another narrowly over, from 30 yards. Hakoah were using their wingers more which kept the Slavia rearguard at full stretch.

Neither side pulled back in the tackle and some of the physical clashes would have delighted Aussie Rules fans. It was real Cup-tie football.

In the second half, Savage moved to the left flank and Jurecki came in on the right, but Slavia's wingers had a poor game. McCorquodale and Reid [illegible]

[illegible]

Six minutes from time the issue was settled when Randles, attempting to turn a centre from Fry for a corner, only succeeded in flicking the ball into his net. It was the end of the road for Slavia, and Hakoah ran out worthy winners.

Murney stood out as the best player on the ground, but Van Alphen, Keith (apart from that one unfortunate lapse), Smith and in the second half Moran, Armstrong, Fry and Purdie gave fine performances. Shepherd, High, Randles and particularly in the first half Goodwin, turned in first-class efforts for Slavia.

The game never quite rose to the standard expected. Too much tension was obvious in the first half, which probably was responsible for the frequent errors. Hakoah's great second half effort turned the tide and provided a thrilling climax.

Black mark to all those one-eyed so-called Soccer lovers who did not support their own "grand" final just because their team was not involved.

[illegible]

Hakoah players 'take to the field' before a pre-season Adelaide friendly with Adelaide Juventus in early 1967. As usual 'The Clown Prince' is up to his old tricks again encroaching on George 'Dick' Keith's private parts! Dick does not seem to mind the attention he is receiving! But who is the young fresh faced 'schoolboy' at the far left of the picture. Well, well, well, it's none other than a very young looking 'schoolboy' called David Baker among full grown men. The young looking 'schoolboy' is club legend David Baker, Hakoah's longest serving player! David had not played in the Hakoah all star team of 1966 when this picture was taken. Players are (*left to right*): David Baker, Johnny Walker, Mike O'Hara, Dick Keith, Ted Smith, Jim O'Neil, John O'Neill (club captain), and Dick Van Alphen.

Hakoah 'Kingpins' stand united in 1966 after another victory at Middle Park. Left to right: Alex Purdie, Hugh Murney, Dick Keith, Mike O'Hara

Hakoah Football Club 1968

Players and Hakoah Secretary/Manager Mr Kurt Defris (in foreground) enjoy the moment prior to a home game at Middle Park stadium.

Hakoah committee members, players and supporters in happy mood at Olympic Park, Melbourne, before the 1968 Australia Cup two leg cup final.

Hakoah Football Club 1971

Hakoah club captain Jack Reilly receives the 1973 Dockerty Cup at Olympic Park, Melbourne, after Hakoah win the cup final. Hakoah team mates are enjoying the moment.

(Left to right, standing): Z. Poznanski, D. Barbour, J. Reilly (Capt.), M. Clarey, A. Waaldyk A. Dosen, I. McLeod, S. Gadsby, S. Meyer (Coach). (Left to right, front row): D. Baker (Vice-Capt.), M. Mandalis, J. Katz, J. Lapish, B. Saunders, A. Seremitis, J. Durand.

Hakoah Football Club 1973
The 1973 Dockerty Cup Winning Squad

Hakoah Football Club 1977

Above is the 1977 Hakoah squad that created an all time record. Current Football Federation Victoria statistics bear testimony to the fact that in the 1977 season of the Victorian State Premier League, Hakoah created an all time Hakoah record by conceding only 20 goals in the 22 rounds played. The record breaking team is, back row (*left to right*): Mike Mandalis (coach), David Baker (captain), A.N. Other, Mike Rainey, Bruce Roberts, Mike O'Hara, Steve Gadsby, Les Nagy. Front row (*left to right*): Chris Valli, Bill Jordanou, Gerry Edmondson, Stewart Blair, De Placido, Ian McNeil. Coach Mike Mandalis (at top left) is to be congratulated for cleverly introducing talented young players with highly capable and experienced mature team members. Captain David Baker led by example and in doing so, nurtured the younger players to believe in themselves and excel.

Hakoah Football Club 1978 Squad

Hakoah – making a bid for the State League Cup. Standing (*left to right*): Bill Jordanou, Anton Dosen, Bill Whiteside, Steve Gadsby, Les Nagi, Graham French, George Craig, Mike Clarey. Front (*left to right*): Chris Valli, Ian Gibson, David Baker, Les Owens, Stewart Blair, Sean Rooney.

The End of Hakoah Melbourne Association Football Club

In November 1981 Mr Kurt Defris the Secretary/Manager of Hakoah Melbourne Association Football Club committed the club into amalgamation with its Middle Park ground share neighbour South Melbourne Hellas AFC.

The decision of Mr Defris, was a last ditch attempt to maintain the Hakoah Football Club in the Victorian State League competition.

This decision meant that Hakoah Football Club as a sole Jewish entity failed to exist, with the 1981 season in the Victorian State Premier League its last!

The 1982 season saw Hellas–Hakoah combine as a loose knit joint entity with loyalty, pride and honour split between two sets of players under one dubious banner.

Interestingly, virtually all of the 1981 sole Jewish entity Hakoah team did not continue their playing careers with this combined Hellas–Hakoah entity.

In any event and for whatever reason, the joint team entity failed and after only one season (1982) the joint team enterprise ended.

At the end of the first and last Hellas–Hakoah joint team season of 1982, the name Hakoah disappeared forever!

The Hellas–Hakoah combined team had 2 coaches in the one season, namely Jim Adam and later that season Joe Szabo.

South Melbourne Hellas itself did not last much longer than

Hakoah, when in the 1983 Victorian State League season, S.M. Hellas, coached by former Hakoah legend Jim Armstrong finished last on the ladder and were relegated. And like Hakoah disappeared forever!

The last sole entity Hakoah Melbourne Association Football team ever to play under that famous name lost its last ever game in final round 22 of the 1981 Victorian State League season, to Sunshine City 0–1 at Chaplin Reserve, Sunshine on 6th September 1981.

The following players represented Hakoah Football Club in its last ever match. They were: C. Allison, D. Davidson, S. Gadsby, G. French, B. Jordanou, G. Hannah, C. Kent, L. Nagy, S. Rooney, D. Slack, L. Thomson, S. Webster, J. Wilson. Coach: Bill Allison.

In its final season, Hakoah Football Club in 1981 as a sole entity in the Victorian State League Premier Division, recorded the following league results:

P 22 W6 D8 L8 F27 A41 Pts 20 (final position 7th of 12)

North Caulfield Maccabi Association Football Club 2016

'The king is dead, long live the king'

From the ashes of the self destructing phoenix golden eagle that had lived for over half a century, arose a supremely beautiful and unique entity that revealed itself to be an integral part of Jewish sporting life for thousands of Jewish men, women and children in a myriad of different sporting codes.

Through this entity, Hakoah's ghost remains alive and well!

Maccabi Australia Football Carnival 1990

The picture shows the Maccabi Victoria squad winners of the carnival.

The Victorian Jewish News of 8 September 2006:

> Hakoah Melbourne Football Club lives vibrantly on through its reborn phoenix, North Caulfield Maccabi Football Club.

Hakoah Melbourne Association Football Club, through the magnificent untiring work of Mr Kurt Defris and many others, forged the future for all Jewish sport in Victoria state, and all who contributed to the great Hakoah Melbourne Association Football Club, both Jewish men and women and non Jewish people alike, will be remembered through this book forever.

'Hakoah' the word itself is our strength!

Neil Wallace (right) attacks the ball during Maccabi's 2-0 victory over Mooroolbark.
Photo: Peter Haskin

North Caulfield Maccabi secures history-making promotion

SOCCER

HARVEY SILVER

NORTH Caulfield Maccabi has secured its third promotion in five seasons after defeating Mooroolbark on Sunday.

The latest promotion means the team, which finished second for the season, will play in the second division of the Football Federation of

knocked us from the very start of the season but for this group of players to keep working, keep believing in themselves and to get themselves promoted to division two ... well I have never felt prouder of anything I have managed in football."

A veteran of the club, Maclean has overseen all three promotions, taking the club from the second division of the Provisional League in 2002 to Division Two of the FFV.

be scoreless at the break until a late corner from Ryan Abrahams was neatly deflected by Dion Esterman through the goalkeeper's legs.

In the second half the ball rarely left Mooroolbark's half. After three missed chances from long range by substitute Adam Rischin, Oran Harel ran on to a lovely through pass and was brought down by the Mooroolbark keeper. The keeper's challenge

North Caulfield Maccabi Association Football Club
2007

North Caulfield Maccabi Association Football Club
2016

Acknowledgements

The author wishes to acknowledge the valuable assistance of the following people who contributed to the successful completion of this book.

Mr Jim Armstrong
Mr David Baker
Mr Steven Gadsby
Mr Roy Hay
Mr Fred Hutchison
Ms Jacquie Lerner
Mr Robert Levin
Mr Hugh Murney
Mr John Punshon
Mr Ted Smith
Mr Syd Thomas
Mr Neil Wallace
Mr Harry Zaitman

All of the world will now know by verse and line from *Hakoah Heroes* the incredible contribution of one man, who, almost single-handedly brought forth from the four corners of the earth, men of all nationalities to represent through the medium of sport a great Jewish symbol of self worth, namely Hakoah Melbourne Association Football Club.

This book and all the men named in it, say as one, with reverent respect, 'Thank You' to Mr Kurt Defris A.M., a truly magnificent human being and Hakoah Association Football Club's number one Hakoah Hero!

Rest in peace our beautiful brother and friend, you are with us always.

www.ingramcontent.com/pod-product-compliance
Lightning Source LLC
Chambersburg PA
CBHW050550160426
43199CB00015B/2601

* 9 7 8 0 6 4 8 1 3 6 3 6 1 *